# The Journey of our Warrior Princess Jerodene Bailey

## Rasheda Thomas-Bailey

**Marion The Scribe**

*Marion the Scribe*
From My Heart to Yours

Copyright © 2022 Rasheda Thomas-Bailey

All rights reserved

No part of this book may be reproduced, or stored in a retrieval system, or transmitted in any form or by any means, electronic, mechanical, photocopying, recording, or otherwise, without express written permission of the publisher.

ISBN-13: 9798846556096
ISBN-10: 1477123456

Cover design by: AllyCreates
Library of Congress Control Number: 2018675309
Printed in the United States of America

*This our first book entitled "The Journey of our Warrior Princess Jerodene Bailey" is solely dedicated to our late daughter Jerodene Bailey, who was diagnosed with stage 4 Rhabdomyosarcoma at the age of 4 and transitioned at the age of 7. Jerodene we loved you in life and we still love you in death. Continue to rest in peace our Warrior Princess. You were loved.*

# Contents

Title Page
Copyright
Dedication
Introduction
Background — 2
The Addition to Our Union # 1 — 4
Jerodene's Formal Education — 9
Rasheed's Conception — 12
Rasheed's Entrance — 13
Jerodene's Medical Journey — 16
Saying Goodbye — 166
Jerodene's Homegoing Celebration — 171
After The Dust Settles — 175
It Started With A Thought — 180
Jerodene's First Birthday After She Transitioned — 181
Our New Blessing — 184
For People Going Through A Similar Situation, Be Encouraged — 186
Reflections of The Heart — 187
Paying Homage To A Lifechanger — 192
Afterword — 228
Acknowledgement — 230
About The Author — 232

# Introduction

This book is a true story of a Jamaican Christian family whose lives were changed forever when we were hit with the most devastating news that our first-born child, our daughter, Jerodene Jaiyana Bailey, was diagnosed with stage 4 Rhabdomyosarcoma (muscle cancer) at the tender age of 4 years old. Unfortunately, she passed at the age of 7, but throughout her few years on earth she taught us to have faith in God, and that we should always listen to the voice of God. She touched and changed many lives, which include that of the gunman, the prostitute, the sexually abused and she helped to heal broken marriages, and the list goes on.

Her favourite scriptures were taken from Philippians 4:13 *"I can do all things through Christ which strengtheneth me"* and Psalm 118:17 *"I shall not die but live and declare the works of the Lord."* Jerodene was a strong believer: she believed in God and the Word of God. Not only that, but she put the Word of God into practice on a daily basis. She was a real warrior for Jesus Christ. She had extraordinary faith like the prophet Job. Despite the pain and agony that she was going through, Jerodene never gave up on God. We always encouraged her to continue to hold onto God's unchanging hands. As a family we have gone through so much but nonetheless we believed God together, we cried together, and we prayed together. Jerodene Jaiyana Bailey was a warrior for God, hence the title: THE JOURNEY OF OUR WARRIOR PRINCESS JERODENE BAILEY.

Included are Jerodene's own words in bold italics and photographs relating some of the events and activities described therein. Join us on this amazing journey.

Prayer is the key to all our situations.

Just pray, believe and have faith that God is listening.

R. Thomas-Bailey.

# Background

Since childhood, my siblings and I always admired our parents being happily married. In the year 2007, I met Jermaine Bailey. A few months into our courtship, he proposed to me and we got married the following year, 2008, a few days before my 24th birthday. I met Jermaine through a friend of mine. What most people do not know is that Jermaine and I had our wedding date set without ever seeing each other face-to-face. Our friendship developed via the telephone. Many people ask me, "Why would you take such a risk in dating someone over the phone?" My answer was and still is "Because we both knew that we were meant for each other."

I had always written down the qualities that I needed in a husband and each time that I would pray, I would lay them before the Lord. Jermaine, on the other hand, told me that when he was seeking a wife he too would pray and ask God to bless him with a wife who loved the Lord and would love him the same. Being a true child of God, I wanted a true man of God. God blessed me with Jermaine - he is trustworthy, caring, ambitious, a Godly man, et cetera. I can recall a week before the wedding when we had our final counselling session, my parents and two representatives from Jermaine's family had to be present. My father raised his hand indicating to the Pastor that he had something to say. He told the Pastor that when his daughter told him that they were going to get married, he reached out to a few persons in the church Jermaine attended to conduct his own investigation of this young man. He said it took him a year to gather all the information he sought. He then uttered that if he had learnt any negative information about this young man, he would have nipped the relationship in the bud. It would not have gotten this far. From that day I had even more respect for my parents. What my dad did made me gain more respect and love for him.

A year after we got married, I got pregnant, but within a few months I suffered a miscarriage. I cried day and night because God knew the desire of our hearts that we wanted a child. We did not know the gender of the child because the miscarriage occurred early in the pregnancy. Some months passed when Jermaine and I went to a healing deliverance meeting, which was planned by our then pastor. That was approximately eight (8) months after the miscarriage. During the service, the microphone was handed over to our then Island Overseer, Bishop W.A. Blair. He greeted the congregation and went on to say *"There's a married couple here tonight; you've had a miscarriage in previous months and you are wondering if you are able to get pregnant again."*

Jermaine and I immediately looked at each other because we knew he was referring to us. Tears rolled down my cheeks and I wrote my prayer request and dropped it in the box. As Jermaine and I agreed in prayer, we both knew it was done in Jesus' name. We both knew that whatever we asked God for believing in His name, He would grant it onto us. We asked for a baby.

# The Addition to Our Union # 1

A few months went by then I found out I was pregnant again. Believe me when I tell you that it was one of the happiest days for us. Words could not express or explain the happiness Jermaine and I experienced. We thanked God for answering our prayer and more so that the prophecy of the Island Overseer came to pass. Jermaine and I secretly prayed and asked God for a girl child. From the moment we learnt of the pregnancy we took every precaution for the pregnancy to go the full term. The pregnancy was very smooth and I gave God thanks for that because not many mothers had that privilege. The months went by so quickly and we went to have an ultrasound done. Lo and behold, our prayer was answered, it was a girl.

I gave my mom the privilege to name the baby. She told me to give her some time to think about it. Within a few days she called with the name - 'Jerodene'. *"J e r o d e n e?"* I thought to myself, how did she come by that name? I asked her. That was when she revealed that it was a combination of Jermaine's and my middle name – 'Jer' from Jermaine and 'Odene', my middle name. Even though she told me, I was not comfortable with her response. I knew that mom was very creative, but we decided to do some research on the name to satisfy our curiosity. I asked a friend of mine to do the research. She told us that the name means *"holy name"*. That immediately sealed the deal. I shared it with Jermaine and we both agreed with the choice of name and felt happy that it was a perfect name for our little princess.

Most nights we read bible stories to the unborn child and spoke to her as if she was already born. I recall vividly her first movement. It was amazing and unexplainable. It was as if she was saying, 'Mommy, here I am'. Jermaine was at his Aunt Charmaine's and I was so excited I could not wait until he got home. I called him and blurted out the good news of the movement. You can imagine how elated he was. Happily, he was present at the second movement, he experienced it firsthand. He smiled from ear to ear. He was just overwhelmed and ecstatic. In a moment like that, one does not know if one should laugh or cry. If you choose to cry, it would be tears of joy. We looked and saw how amazing our God was. Nobody could be God but Him. He's irreplaceable. He is just God all by Himself.

We made all the necessary preparations for the newborn. Her crib was in place, full white and most of the outfits were pink. Oh how she would look extremely beautiful in pink. We anticipated our little girl and wondered who she would resemble, or whether she would look like both of us.

During the pregnancy, quite a few times I had some terrible headaches, those headaches felt as if my head would explode. There were not many painkillers I could take since I was pregnant. A friend of my mom called me one day and told me she had a vision of me having those headaches. She immediately called and prayed for me. I lifted my faith and believed God that they would go away.

A few months before giving birth, I started to have some terrifying dreams. For persons who can relate to dreams like those, they were dreams that you wish you could jump out of your sleep. Well, that was the situation with me, when one night I dreamt that a man was chasing me. It appeared as if I was in a wilderness. The man in the dream had a very sharp machete in his hand as I stood below and was looking up. He pointed the machete at my head. As he let go of it, I had to rest my hand over my head for protection. As I ran off, he continued to chase me. I was awakened from the dream with the sound of my husband's phone ringing. On the other end of the telephone was Jermaine's aunt, Charmaine's husband. He asked, *"Jermaine, are you going to work?" "Yes,"* Jermaine replied. *"Okay then, but don't leave just yet, I am on my way to your house, to pray for your wife."*

Within 15 minutes or less he arrived at the house. He poured some olive oil on Jermaine's hand then instructed him to rest his hand on my belly and anoint it while he, Evangelist Jackson, prayed earnestly and interceded on our behalf. When he was through praying he told us that God had awakened him in the wee hours of the morning and instructed him to come to our house to pray. He said that he had to be obedient to the voice of God and that was when he called Jermaine's phone. When he called, I told him about the dream I was having when the ringing of the phone woke me. After he heard the dream, he was even happier that he obeyed the voice of God. He said if he had not been obedient, we have no idea what the outcome would have been. To God be the glory, great things He hath done! We gave God thanks for all the spiritual persons He placed in our lives.

Throughout the entire nine months of pregnancy I made sure that I met all doctors' appointments at the designated clinic. I was, however, referred to a high-risk clinic at the Mandeville Regional Hospital. I had no idea why I was referred there but when I inquired at the local clinic that was when they told me I had a rare blood type; therefore, that clinic was the ideal place to deal with the situation.

I give God thanks for Jermaine; he is a wonderful man. He gives me the best treatment that any wife could desire. He was always a hard worker, but worked even harder during the pregnancy to ensure that I had all I needed. As a result of the smooth pregnancy, I was able to work up to two weeks before delivery. On August 14, 2010, while I was at home, Jermaine went to work. I told him I felt for a piece of KFC. He brought the chicken home. However, as soon as he came home, I started having some abdominal pains. I thought to myself: that could not be a contraction because I believed that the signal that I needed to go to the hospital was when my water broke. I ignored the warning and was about to indulge in my meal, but I felt another sharp pain that began getting worse. My husband then decided that he must get me to the hospital. He called a taxi and before long we were on our way, prepared for any emergencies. On the way, the pain became unbearable. I then called my mother and a few other relatives and told them what was going on and solicited their prayers.

Upon arriving at the hospital, we were sent directly to the maternity ward. Nurses and doctors were on hand. To my surprise, upon examination, the nurse told me I was 8cm dilated. My heart began pounding even harder when I realised that the baby was nearer than we thought. I began talking to God in my mind asking Him for a safe delivery. Jermaine and I then packed stuff as instructed in the basin since they were sending me straight to the delivery room. Since it was a public hospital, my husband was not allowed in the delivery room. I could see the concern and worry etched on his face since he did not know what to expect in the delivery room. I knew that he would be seated on a bench outside the delivery room, on edge. Due to the hospital's restrictions Jermaine had to leave. However, before he left, he sent a message with a nurse to tell me how much he loved me and was wishing for me a safe delivery. My silent prayer was for God to send an 'angel nurse', one who was kind and gentle, to help me through the ordeal. As I was lying on the bed in the delivery room with increasing pains, Nurse Morgan, a church sister of mine, walked in. Can you imagine the smile, amidst the pain, on my face? I knew God answered my prayer immediately. Oh, how happy and overjoyed I was!

The labour experience was better than I imagined. I was surrounded by heavenly angels and Nurse Morgan. She was as gentle as an angel and within a few hours, our princess, Jerodene was born on Sunday, August 15, 2010 at 12:04 a.m. The nurse told me the umbilical cord was wrapped around her neck so she had to unwrap it. Honestly, I was the happiest mother alive. I could not wait to hold her and when I did, I did not want to let her go. She weighed 7 lbs 4 oz. She was tiny and just as I thought she resembled her dad. I was so eager to call my husband and give him the good news. He was elated to hear the good news, he could not contain himself. He wished he could get back to the hospital but he had to wait for the appropriate time. I was so excited that I could not go to sleep. I just had to call my family to share the joy.

The following day we were sent home. Mother and baby were doing well except that the baby had eczema. The doctor told us what to do to take care of that condition. We were very excited to take her to her own home. My mother came to spend a few days to assist us. After she left, my aunt came to take up where her sister left off. I realised that the moment you are getting some sleep was when the baby would wake and begin crying either for food or to be changed. That was not such a good feeling but when you realise it is for your child's benefit, you had no choice but to get up and attend to her. Such was our experience with Jerodene. Every step of the way we had to give thanks for a smooth pregnancy and a safe delivery. Had it not been for God's grace and mercy we do not know what would have happened to us. Giving birth is going to death's road so to Him be all the glory, honour and praise.

Days went by and Jermaine did not hold Jerodene. He told me she was too little and that his hands were too rough. One day when he came home early from work my dear Aunt Sandra, my mom's sister, held the baby, singing, humming and playing with her. She then went and stood in front of the chair Jermaine was sitting on and handed him Jerodene. He trembled with fright but that was the beginning of their bond. I thank my aunt for what she did because after a while, Jermaine got used to holding her. She stayed for a few days to ensure everything was going well. For that gesture of thoughtfulness we gave thanks.

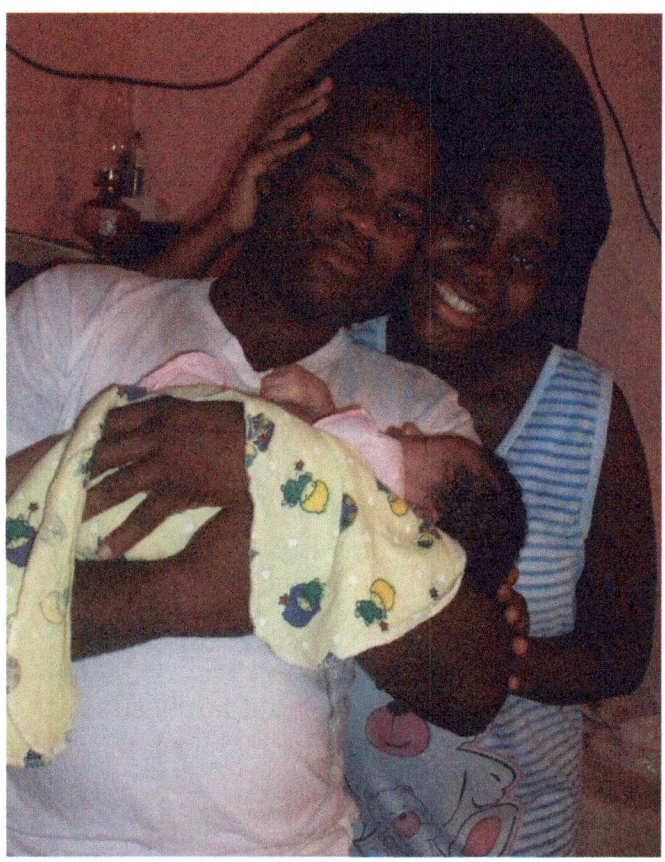

Jerodene was so beautiful and energetic. She was her dad's pride and joy. He enjoyed kissing her on her chin and every time he did it, she smiled as if she understood the gesture. We were so happy; everyone could tell we were the happiest couple, as we bubbled with joy both inside and out.

A few weeks after Jerodene got home, Jermaine was on his way home from work when a young woman saw him and said *"unu a gwaan like a sky shi drap fram an drap in a unu lap"* (*You are both behaving as if she fell from the sky into your laps*). Knowing my husband, he seemingly did not say much. When he told me of the encounter, I was shocked and angry at the same time and thought to myself why someone would pass such a remark. I wanted to confront her, but my husband said *"no"* so I obeyed. It left me puzzled but I said I would leave everything to God. Months went by and our little angel was just thriving. She enjoyed her breast milk like any other baby would. She always had a smile. One of her pleasures was her sucking her right thumb. She was just precious and everything we could have ever asked God for. Jerodene would smile and laugh when we sang her lullabies and read her stories. She enjoyed every moment of it.

Jerodene was three months old when it was time for her christening. The service was scheduled for November 7, 2010. Relatives and friends from near and far were invited to this special celebration. The day was well spent in the house of the Lord. After the service, we all gathered at our house for refreshment and prayer. The act of giving thanks to God for his blessings and for all that He had done. After a while everyone made their way home.

As the months went by, Jerodene had almost everything to her comfort - books, educational stuff, toys, et cetera. She enjoyed her own company. Jermaine and I had taught Jerodene how to pray from an early age and she knew right from wrong. We would take her to church most Sundays and most of all she loved her little tambourine. She would play it every time a song was being sung and sometimes even when the pastor was preaching, which we found to be very funny.

Growing up as a child, my siblings and I were raised in a Godly home. My mom at the time was the clerk of our home church, is now a pastor and our dad was a deacon and musician for the church. My parents would wake us up at 5:30 every Sunday morning for family devotions. With them being active members of the church, we had to adhere to the rules and regulations that were laid down. We truly gave God thanks for them and the values that were inculcated in us through God. As young parents we decided that these values would be instilled in our children, by the help of God.

Our little princess, Jerodene, loved dressing up and going out. She loved the idea of meeting new people. She was not a sickly child, so we did not have to worry about hospital visits. She was a jovial and active child.

'Time waits for no man' and the time came for me to return to work. We took her to a well recommended day care centre. It took a while for her to be adjusted to that change but I was happy because I knew she was in good hands. She was a fast learner. She was already hands-on with nursery rhymes and songs that were taught at the daycare by Aunt Monica and Aunt Deon.
Jerodene got so attached to her new aunts that even when she got home she would be calling their names smiling. She always anticipated going to the daycare on a daily basis. Jerodene was loved by all. She was just lovable. We always looked forward to picking her up at the end of the day. I was a store clerk at the time and her father was a farmer and plumber.

# Jerodene's Formal Education

    Oh how time flew by quickly. Three years had passed and she was due to begin basic school September 2013. Jermaine and I had made the necessary preparations for Jerodene to begin on the right path. We always thought about this moment but time went by so quickly we hardly realised how fast it was approaching. We had selected her basic school and got all her school supplies ahead of September. All students were required to do a medical. She did hers and was assured by the doctor that all was well and she was fit for school. Honestly, we expected nothing less. Her uniform and just about everything for school was on point.

    Orientation was scheduled a few days prior to the opening of school. All Kindergarten 1 students were present with their parents. So, there we were seated beside a lady and her son. Knowing how friendly Jerodene was she started talking to the little boy. The little boy started to eat his snack and offered some to Jerodene. Only to hear Jerodene say to the little boy, **"My daddy said that I am not supposed to beg"**. His mother then looked at Jerodene and said, *"But he is just offering you some"* Jerodene replied, **"I said, no, thank you because my daddy said I should not beg."** Jerodene was not paying any attention to the little boy's mother. She was not letting go of her father's instructions. Silently I was happy with her because we taught her to be satisfied and contented with what she had.

    After the orientation we introduced ourselves. I then learnt that the little boy's mother was Simone Mason-Mitchell and her son was Raheem Mitchell. Both children grew to become best friends. They even started calling each other cousins. Oh how they loved each other. September 7, 2013 finally arrived. It was just as most parents felt about sending their child off to school for the first day - nervous. Jermaine and I did not know what to expect. As I took her to school, I thought to myself that she might cry, but to my amazement she was so happy. I could not wait to share the news with her dad. Instead of her crying, she was consoling the other children who were crying and telling them that their parents would come for them after school. I smiled when I saw how mature my little princess was.

As time went by she was loved by all the staff of the Hope Demonstration Basic School. Jerodene became the 'mother' for the class, by giving out instructions to the class. I remembered her then teacher, Mrs. Allison, asked me if Jerodene was attending another school before due to the fact that she behaved so mature and responsible. I told her *"no"* and my answer puzzled her. She said Jerodene would ask a lot of questions and was always ready to carry out tasks that were given to her.

I gave thanks to Almighty God for the husband He blessed me with. I could not have asked for another. He was so helpful, considerate and most of all a wonderful father. Due to the fact that he is self-employed it was easier for him to take Jerodene to the clinic for her scheduled check-ups. However, on a particular day, I was off from work for the day, so I decided to take her to her appointment. Unlike other children, Jerodene was looking forward to the appointment. For most children, once they see the needle they would begin to cry but for our baby girl, it was the opposite. When we were in the waiting area, and children went in and began to cry, Jerodene would laugh at them because she knew she would not be crying when she got her shot. I recalled on one occasion the nurse asked me *"where in the world did you get this child? She is so brave and bubbly. I wish I had children like her to deal with every day"*. For the nurse attending to Jerodene, it was easy like a 'piece of cake'.

Jerodene was very light skinned. On the third day of school she came home and told me that a little boy kissed her on her cheek. Out of curiosity, I asked her which of the cheeks was red when I saw that the cheek was indeed red. She actually had a 'hickey' there. I was livid because this should not have happened. When I asked her how it happened she said **"Mommy I was in the taxi with the other children and the little boy kissed me and cover my mouth that I don't make any noise."** O my God, I thought to myself, what am I hearing?

Jerodene aided the investigative process because she was very smart. She was able to give us a full description of the house where the boy lived. I immediately called her father, told him what had transpired. He left work instantly and came home. All three of us went searching for the house as described by Jerodene. Jermaine was extremely angry as I was. We thought to ourselves, *"what does that little boy know about covering someone's mouth in order for her not to make any noise?"* We found the house and Jerodene was able to point him out. We had a lengthy discussion with the boy's guardian. The little boy vowed not to do anything like that again. Jerodene was so concerned she kept asking us if the mark was going to go away. We assured her yes, but it would take some time. It actually disappeared fully within a two-week period and we were relieved, especially Jerodene.

Jerodene was Daddy's little princess. She enjoyed going to the shop with him and each time she accompanied him she would return with a lollipop, ice-cream or something of the sort. She loved the idea of going out and having fun. If we were going out as a family, she would have to be the last to get dressed because she did not like the idea of waiting on others. Jerodene loved to sing, and most times she would be singing in the shower. It did not matter if she was singing off key because she was just a happy singer. She was also a spiritual individual, whenever it was prayer time she was the first to pray. She was very brave. If one was to ask Jerodene what her favourite bible verse was, she would boldly say Philippians 4:13. Her favourite song was "Jesus on the telephone". One Easter holiday, my Aunt Rose came to spend a few days with us. While she was seated on the verandah, Jerodene was singing 'Jesus on the telephone'. Aunt Rose began humming the tune. Jerodene stopped at the chorus and directed a question to Aunt Rose, **"Aunt Rose, what is that you want Jesus to do for you?"** Aunt Rose was so shocked she could not answer. Jerodene then said to her **"do you want Him to draw you closer to Him?"** Aunt Rose answered her in surprise, "*Oh yes!*" Aunt Rose then told Jerodene how special a child she was.

In 2012 while working as a store clerk, I suffered a spinal injury, which caused my lower back to curve. This caused unbearable pain on a daily basis. Only God knows the sleepless nights I experienced, but through it all my husband Jermaine stood with me. He was true to our vow: "…in sickness and in health" As a result of the injury I was unable to stand or sit for long periods of time. I had no idea when I would be able to return to work. I, unfortunately, had to quit my job.

# Rasheed's Conception

In 2013, when Jerodene was three years old, we found out that I was pregnant. Oh how happy we were. We prayed and hoped it would be a boy. We were overjoyed that Jerodene was about to have a sibling. Our prayers were centred on me having a smooth pregnancy as I had with Jerodene but within a few months we began experiencing the opposite. I began experiencing severe abdominal pain. We ensured that we kept all clinic appointments. Just as with the pregnancy with Jerodene I was referred to a high-risk clinic. Experiencing these abdominal pains, Jermaine and I thought that 'it must be a boy'. We would have to wait until the ultrasound was done to determine the sex. When Jerodene found out that I was pregnant words could not explain how overwhelmed she was that she was going to be a big sister. Jerodene and I would have a warm bath each evening and spend bonding time. The most exciting time for Jerodene was when she felt the first movement. She laughed so hard and was very eager to tell her friends at school, especially her friend, Raheem.

I had to say 'hats off to my husband', because throughout the entire nine months of pregnancy he had to prepare Jerodene's clothes for school and got her ready each day. He did not once object. He was just as helpful as he had always been.

Jermaine and I waited anxiously to get the ultrasound done. When we received the results, oh how our hearts leapt for joy because to God be the glory, our prayers were answered. It was indeed a boy. We were so elated that we would have the pair. Within a few days, Jermaine and I began the process of seeking a suitable name. We came to one conclusion that since Jerodene's name was close to her father's then it would be nice for the boy's name to be close to mine. Fortunately, we came across the name 'Rasheed', which in Arabic means 'thinker and counsellor'. We also found out that the name translated to 'wise thinker' in the African language. On hearing those definitions our search was over. It was official that his name would be Rasheed Carlington Bailey. He shares his fathers' middle name, which made it even better.

The projected birth date that we had got from our doctor was mid-June. I honestly prayed that the delivery would not go over a day. That's how anxious we were. Most Sundays, Jermaine and Jerodene went to church because I was unable to attend. I longed to attend church so badly but knew that everything would eventually fall in place after the birth of the baby. A few weeks after the ultrasound was done we went ahead and did our shopping for our prince. We already knew that there was no need to purchase a cot since he would use the one that was prepared for Jerodene.

# Rasheed's Entrance

June 20, 2013 was just a normal day, Jerodene was off to school and Jermaine to work. In the early afternoon I felt a sharp abdominal pain. It came to our minds that Rasheed was ready to enter the world. I told Jermaine that I would not leave for the hospital until the pain became more severe. Just as with the pregnancy with Jerodene my water never broke so we were not quite sure it was time. Within a short time the pain got worse. So a taxi was arranged for the trip to the hospital. Jerodene had to be left in the care of Mervalyn, my hairdresser, since it was clear that Jermaine would not be home in short order.

By the time we got to the hospital the doctors and nurses did their examination and approximately 9:50 p.m. our bundle of joy made his entrance into this world and into our family. He weighed 8 lbs 6 oz. He was such a handsome and most energetic little human being I had ever seen. Jermaine could not stay because he had to go to attend to Jerodene. However, upon hearing the news of the safe delivery they were both elated, they thanked God for the safe delivery. Jerodene was eager to visit the hospital to see the Rasheed just as I was eager to take him home. There was a little problem, however, as he did not defecate. He urinated frequently but did not defecate. The stay in the hospital extended to at least 4-5 days. My mom had come to stay a few days to help out but upon hearing the news of the delay, she visited the hospital. She took a bottle of consecrated olive oil. She interceded on Rasheed's behalf for the issue. She anointed the Rasheed's anus with the olive oil. Within about three minutes of the prayer, Rasheed's stool loosed. When he started to pass stool, it was as if he could not stop. So, if anyone asks you if prayer works? Well, yes it does, and God came through for us just as He always does. We were discharged from the hospital the following day in good health. We were happy to introduce Rasheed to his sister and his new home. Looking at both children, they resembled their father in so many ways. That made me even happier because that was what I really wanted and again we saw how God answered our prayers.

My mom stayed with us for almost a month to help us as she did when Jerodene was born. We were so grateful because Jermaine had to go to work so it would have been much on his hands. We gave God thanks that I carried the pregnancy to full term. During those days, Jerodene had two emotions. She was very sad when leaving for school because she wished she could carry Rasheed to school with her, and in the evenings when she returned home she was so happy to be able to see and play with him. The same way Jerodene bonded with the unborn baby was the same way she bonded with him after he was born. They grew to love each other and became each other's company. Shortly after my mom left, my Aunt Sandra stood in the gap left by her. For this we were overly grateful.

We always told Jerodene that she should always be a good girl and eat up her vegetables. We told her the importance of eating her fruits and vegetables. She, however, hated carrots. We always told her that carrots would give her 'proper eyesight'. One morning, I was packing her lunch bag for school but I could not find her lunch dish. I called her and asked her if she saw the dish. Her response was, *"No Mommy"*. By this time she was on her way to the kitchen. When she got there, I heard her laugh and loudly declared, *"Mommy, see it there, yu naa eat up plenty carrot eno, because if you were eating up your carrots, you would have been able to see the dish right in front of you!"* I was so frightened by her response, all I did was look at her and smile.

A few months went by and we continued to thank God for 'The Fantastic 4 Bailey Family', as Jerodene called us. We were so happy and as the days went by Rasheed was more and more the exact image of Jerodene and people always asked jokingly, *"wow, are they twins?"* Rasheed was christened when he was three months old and we invited friends and family to the service just as we did for Jerodene. It was a successful day in the Lord. All were happy that we gave birth to a baby boy and now had a pair of children. We told them that all praise goes to the Almighty God for favouring us.

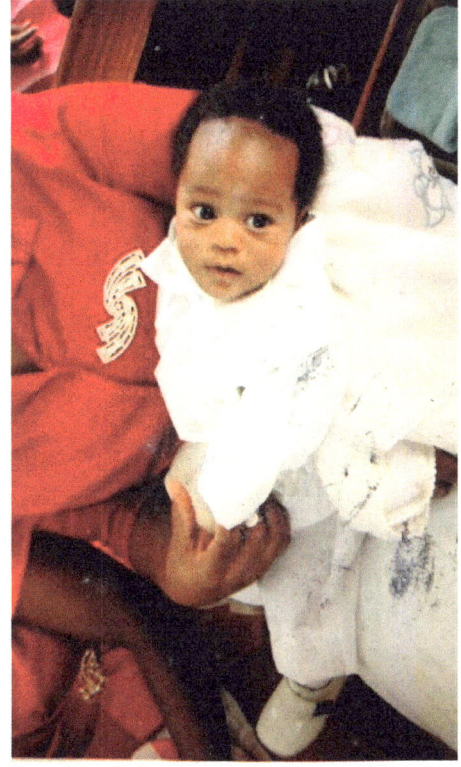

Breastfeeding was very difficult with Rasheed. He did not get the chance to fully enjoy a few months of being breastfed because I became ill. We noticed that every time he was breastfeed, he would begin to cough and vomit. I went to the doctor and that was when I was told I had chikungunya in my system (a virus transmitted by the Aedes aegypti mosquitoes). We were told to desist from giving the baby breast milk. Hence, Rasheed was introduced to formula. We learned more about the chikungunya, otherwise called 'ChickV' by way of the media, especially our local news cast here in Jamaica. The ChickV was a severe sickness which causes excruciating pain over the entire body, some persons had it coupled with body rash and lack of mobility. Some people had to walk with a cane. Almost every household suffered from the virus. Without a doubt, it had rocked the entire nation. Unfortunately for me, I had it full blown and it was very terrible. This virus was treated with only Panadol and a lot of liquids. For me, even months after, the pain lingered but not as severe as it was at the get go.

Jerodene and Rasheed loved each other and all that love started in the womb. God allowed us to pass on such love to our children and we give all thanks to Him. Jerodene would do anything and everything to make Rasheed comfortable. At times when she got home from school she would be seated on the floor and would have Rasheed in her arms cuddling and talking to him. Even though Rasheed could not talk he would smile with Jerodene as if he understood what she was saying. Jerodene always spoke highly of becoming a nurse in the future. So on career day occasions at her school, she would step out in her nursing uniform with her head held high. By the time Rasheed was mumbling his little baby language Jerodene would teach him additional words. She did well in teaching him so that we wondered if she would have changed her profession choice from a nurse to a teacher. We would not have had an issue with the choice since their father always told them to be a leader and not merely a follower.

We hoped for the day when Jerodene would have stopped sucking her thumb. So for her birthday, her aunt, Antoinette, whom she affectionately referred to as Aunty 'Yanto' called and asked her what she wanted for her birthday. She told her that she wanted a Dora cake. I used that to my advantage, I bet you all know the outcome. Yes, she stopped sucking her thumb. Therefore, happily she was able to get her Dora cake.

I recalled when Jerodene was two years old we got invitations from my two brothers, Ryan and Randal, to attend their weddings, two months apart. They requested Jerodene to be the flower girl. We gladly accepted the invitation. Jermaine and I knew we had to give her a lot of practice in order for her to carry out such a task when the time came. In preparation, we rolled out a red carpet, gave her a little basket with petals and instructed her how to proceed. She took a lot less practice than we thought since it was obvious that she was a fast learner. On both wedding days, Jerodene actually stole the show, knowing that she was just two years old. She made us proud. Everyone congratulated her on a job well done. We were all so proud of her. Jerodene seemed more proud of herself than we were of her. Our adopted brother, Neville, was the only one left as a sibling to get married. We knew that when that time came Jerodene would have already been a professional flower girl. This made us wonder whose wedding our son, Rasheed would be able to take part in. Whenever that time comes, we know he would do as well as his sister.

# Jerodene's Medical Journey

## Chikungunya (ChikV)

In January 2015, Jerodene started feeling sick. She started having some minor pains. We realised the pain was getting more severe so we took her to a regular doctor. We were told she had contracted chikungunya. That was the last thing we wanted to hear, since from my own experience, it was a terrible pain-causing virus. She was given Panadol and told to drink lots of fluid. Within a few days Jerodene was okay. She was able to resume school. Going back to school was the happiest moment for her, since she would see her friends again. Jerodene was a fast learner so catching up in class was not hard.

A few weeks later, Jerodene came home from school and did her regular routine. A few minutes before bedtime, she started complaining about a pain in her neck. That was the last thing we wanted to hear. Anyway we gave her some pain medicine. The medicine caused drowsiness so she went to her bed shortly after. The night was not as smooth as others but she made it. Quite a few persons we knew who had the ChikV never complained of neck pain. By the following morning we noticed that her head was tilted to one side. If she was called from behind, unfortunately, she had to turn her entire body since she found it difficult to turn her head. We did not delay, we took her to the Mandeville Regional Hospital in Manchester for an assessment. When we explained to the doctor what had transpired, she diagnosed muscle spasm or "crick neck" as we would say in Jamaica. We got a prescription for Voltaren to apply to the affected area. We went directly to the pharmacy and filled the prescription. The ointment was applied as soon as we got home. Her neck started feeling better within a few days. We prayed and thanked God that it was not worse. At least this time her absence from school was not as extended as when she got the ChikV virus. When she returned to school she was greeted by her principal, Ms. Anderson, of whom she spoke very highly and her best friend Raheem Mitchell.

After a while, Jerodene's neck began acting up again. We still used the Voltaren that was prescribed and was not alarmed as the first time since we were told it was a muscle spasm. Very often, we had to remind her to straighten her head which was hard for her. Being a determined little girl, she was back in school. One day, the principal called and asked us to come get her because she was not feeling well. She was complaining of pain and was running a slight fever. When we took her home we gave her Panadol, which always helped the pain. My husband and I recalled a few days before she was crying about pain and was unable to use her hands or walk. She described the pain as crawling up her legs to her buttocks.

By the following morning, while we were getting her ready for school, we discovered a lump on her left calf. Strangely, it was moving all over the area. We became very concerned knowing that we never saw it before. That was when we began asking ourselves many questions. We decided that we would have to take her to a paediatrician. Jermaine went to work that same day, so I was the one who took her to the doctor. We inquired of a good paediatrician and was recommended to the best one around town. In order to see this doctor, an appointment had to be scheduled. So we just decided to walk-in. We got there and registered to see her. When we actually went in to the doctor, I told her all the concerns from the beginning. I answered all her questions because the aim was to find out what was wrong, bearing in mind that the lump was not hurting or feeling warm in any way, it was simply moving all around. After I answered all her questions and asked ours, she examined Jerodene thoroughly and even measured the size of the lump. She told me that Jerodene might have an infection or inflammation in her body seeing that she was running a temperature prior to that. She also confessed that she had never come across anything like this before during her many years of practice. She said for her to have a better understanding she had to do a blood test. She commented on how pleasant and friendly Jerodene was. During the visit, Jerodene asked a lot of questions and patiently awaited the answers.

After the blood test was ordered, we rushed to have it done even though we knew the results would not be available the same day. One of the tests ordered was the ESR among others, which was in an attempt to conduct an in depth investigation to put our minds at ease. We were told that the normal reading of such a test is normally between 10 and 20. When the results were taken back to the doctor she was alarmed to see the reading. She confirmed that the normal reading should be between 10 and 20, the other test results were not normal in her estimation. This was when our real questioning began. The doctor again mentioned that she had never experienced anything like this before. So she told us she would have to refer her to the University Hospital of the West Indies (UHWI) in Kingston, Jamaica for further investigation. I was not familiar with Kingston, therefore I had to get specific directions to get to the hospital. My brother, Randal, lives in St. Catherine and that would have been much closer to the hospital considering that he knew his way around Kingston. It would have been more accessible. We stayed overnight Wednesday night with Randal because we wanted to be early for the appointment. Jerodene had a lot of fun with her cousin, Xariah because they did not see each other very often. They made up for lost times. On Thursday morning, we were up very early for the 8:30 a.m. appointment. My sister-in-law, Veneica, prepared breakfast for us. Before Jerodene began eating she began complaining that her hand was hurting. I told her to eat up so we could be on our way. I thought it was a prank because she did not want to eat. However, on the way to the hospital Jerodene began crying that her hand was hurting her badly. Upon reaching the hospital, her hand was untouchable because of the pain she was in. Even her inseparable Dora handbag I had to carry. She cried all the way to the hospital, which was when I realised that it was not because she did not want to eat the breakfast but she was truly in severe pain. At the hospital, we got directions from the security officer since we were not familiar with the place. When we arrived at the Paediatric Clinic, we had to wait a while before we were attended to since it was on a first come, first served basis and that we did not know.

After waiting a while, a doctor came to me and asked if I had a referral. I gave him the letter, he said the team would have to examine Jerodene. During the examination, Jerodene cried throughout the entire process. They measured the size of the lump on her left calf and took some medical history from me. Just as I was about to ask about leaving for home, I was told that unfortunately she would have to be admitted for a few days for further investigation to be carried out. She was admitted to Ward 16. When we were escorted to the ward Jerodene cried so much after realising she was surrounded by all new faces in an environment she did not know. At that time I called my brother to get us some clothing, since we had no idea how long the stay would be.

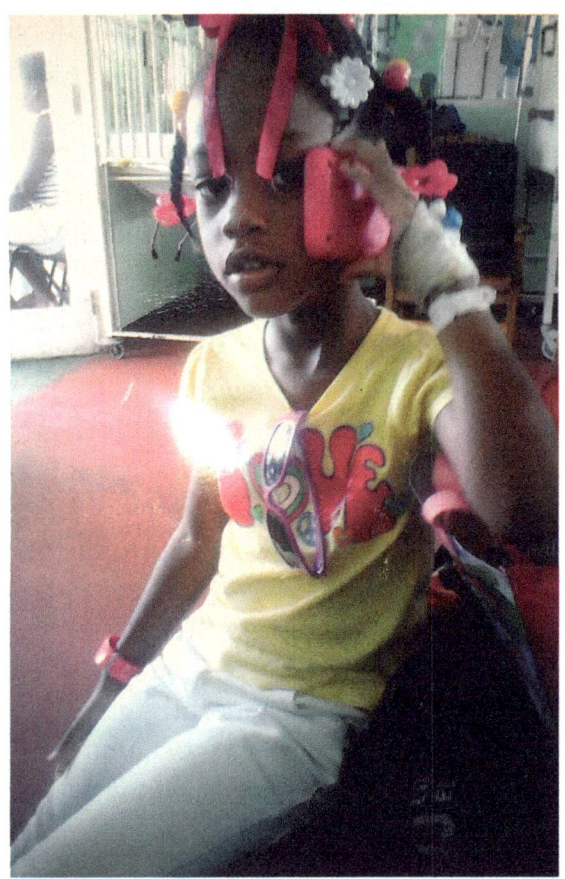

The first nurse we met was Nurse Martin who introduced herself and said in a few minutes she would conduct the orientation. I noticed that even though it was a Paediatrics Ward, accommodation like a bathroom facility was catering to the parents. That was totally new to me because I was not expecting anything like this. They also had a playground for the children, because I guessed that some of the patients were long stayers. The playground was secured and was under lock and key. The nurse told us that children have to be supervised while they are in the play area. Right next to the play area was a wash area with clothes lines. I told myself that would not be necessary because we would not be staying there long. I observed a few doctors' offices and some young doctors, which was when I was told that the institution was a training facility. When the orientation was complete, we were taken back to the ward and Jerodene's vitals were done and recorded.

All this was pretty new to me, so I tried to adjust to the situation. When the night approached, I wondered where I would be sleeping. I then noticed other parents sleeping in wooden chairs. I figured that a chair would be my bed for the period of time we were going to be there. I was accustomed to my comfortable bed and could not imagine how the parents could sleep in chairs. Shortly afterwards Jerodene fell asleep in a new bed. And the fact that she was crying so hard she fell asleep quickly. In my new chair-bed, I was dozing off, then a doctor came and told me to take Jerodene to the treatment room because they would have to do a blood test. Knowing that she just fell asleep it was the hardest thing to wake her for them to take some blood. They insisted so I did as I was told. She cried for a while but before long, the process was over. Not only did they take blood, they attached an intravenous (IV) drip to her hand. They indicated that all the medication that she might need would be given through the IV. She then went back to bed. That was when the doctors chose to collect the data for her medical history. The history took a long time since I had to cross all the 't's and dot all the 'i's. When they left, I fell asleep shortly after. That was the most uncomfortable rest I have ever had. By morning, I felt as if I was beaten all over my body with a log.

By 5:00 a.m., the nurses were ready to administer medication to all the children and do their vitals. As soon as Jerodene woke up for the medication, et cetera, she began crying again. I had to try to calm her down the best way I knew how. As the morning progressed, I was told that the doctors that took the history when I just got there will not be the ones who will be seeing Jerodene during the day, so I had to prepare to give the history all over again. I had to brace myself for the interview again. A few hours later, the doctors came and requested the history. Shortly afterwards, a team of doctors was gathered at Jerodene's bedside. They got a few screens to make sure that she had her own privacy. They stayed a while since they had to examine her thoroughly. I barely understood all that they were saying because they were using medical terminologies that I did not understand. I was so nervous but prayed that all would go well.

## *Cancer Suspected*

The doctors came to the conclusion that they should do a biopsy, where they would take a piece of the lump for further testing, since the lump was of major concern. When they returned, they said it would be better to remove the entire mass because if they took a small portion of it, things might get worse. They told me that a number of procedures were required too, including a CT scan, MRI, ultrasound, X-ray, etc. One of the tests could not be done at the hospital since the machine was malfunctioning so it had to be done at a private facility. The biopsy was done along with the required test. When the results were returned, they told me that they only received a preliminary report, which indicated that the mass that they removed from her left calf was spread over her entire body and that they suspected that it was cancer. I nearly fainted when I was told the diagnosis. It felt as if my heart stopped pumping for a while. I bawled openly in the room. A few minutes later, after receiving the diagnosis, my childhood best friend, Stacy Ann McLeod, whom I had met at a church function, paid us a visit since she worked in Kingston and learned that we were at the hospital. The doctors had to send us to another room for some privacy so that Jerodene did not know we were crying. My emotions burst at the seams and I cried on Stacy's shoulder. We could not scarcely console each other. I kept asking myself *"how can Jerodene have cancer?"* After a while, a nurse came in and consoled us. I then began to think that the doctor said they "suspected" it was cancer so the possibility is it might not be cancer. I used that thought to build my confidence and told myself that was not the situation. I called Jermaine and told him and he said *"no, that can't be true"*. We were both in denial.

A few days after the biopsy was done, we were able to return home and were told that the result would be ready in about two weeks. Jerodene was unable to walk for a long time due to the soreness of the area. She cried constantly because of the excruciating pain that she was undergoing. It was not easy for her to go anywhere because we had to lift her. She would often ask when she would be able to walk again. That was a question neither of us could answer. That was the hardest two weeks for us. We encountered sleepless nights wondering what the result would be. We were simply on edge waiting but in the meantime, we were also praying for God to intercede on our behalf. We were told by the doctors that we could attend the nearest clinic to have the wound dressed. That was when Jerodene asked me *"Mommy when will I be able to run again? Because remember I have to run at Sports Day."* When she uttered that question I just felt tears rolling down my cheeks and that was when I began praying harder. I started telling God that I know He loves my husband and I, the fact that we waited until we were married to multiply our family, the fact that we are Christians, we knew He would not put us through a situation like this. I told God that there's no way our little princess could have cancer as the doctors had said. I thought of the bright future that was ahead of her, how she spoke of going to Disneyland to see her favourite cartoon characters: Elsa and Anna, Mickey and Minnie Mouse. We knew that one day her wish would come through although she had no passport or visa, but the faith that we had, we believed that one day we would be able to travel on a plane.

At that time, Rasheed was not yet one year old and Jerodene was ready to spend as much time with him as possible. She loved him so much and was anxiously awaiting him to start making his first steps. I told her that it was a process. Jermaine and I were so happy because we knew that our family was balanced knowing that we had a daughter and a son.

The two long weeks ended, the doctors called to tell us to bring Jerodene in for the results. My heart pounded so hard because we did not know what to expect. That night was another sleepless night for us. Jerodene did not have any idea what was going on. We decided against telling her until what we deemed was the right time. I combed her hair overnight as I normally do for school most times. When I was combing her hair she said *"Mommy put my favourite bubbles and clips in my hair"* - pink and purple were her favourite colours. She then picked out her favourite outfit. That was when she asked where we were going. I told her that we will be going back to the hospital for a short visit and would get back before her brother falls asleep. The following morning, we arrived at the hospital at approximately 8:45 a.m. for the 9:00 a.m. appointment. When we got to the room we were told that we had to wait for a short while because the doctor was not yet there. By that time, all our relatives in Jamaica and abroad were anxiously awaiting the update, since everybody told themselves that Jerodene did not have cancer. We all did a lot of praying and even told ourselves that even if it is cancer due to the amount of prayers that had been going up for Jerodene it would vanish in the name of Jesus.

## *Cancer Confirmed (Rhabdomyosarcoma)*

Shortly after, the doctor came and apologised for being late. He then offered us a seat. With the expression on his face, we knew that something was not right. He then took us stage by stage through all the symptoms that Jerodene was experiencing and reminded us about all the tests that were done. He then said to us *"it is with regret that I have to inform you that what was suspected was actually true. And that the cancer was at stage 4, which was the most advanced stage"*. Our jaws dropped immediately! Tears began rolling down our eyes as my husband and I tried to comfort each other. My heart stopped for a while, my head began hurting and I knew that my blood pressure had skyrocketed because of disbelief. It felt like a dream that we wished that someone would wake us from. We waited but no one shook us awake so we knew it was not a dream. Our bodies went numb. We were so naive to all of this. I thought that all cancers were the same. I had no idea that there were different types. The doctor was unable to tell us at the time the exact one that they diagnosed. He further said we would have to pay J$10,000.00 for further testing to detect the exact type and to see the way forward. The news spread rapidly and my cousins in England called me because they wanted to talk with the doctor and ask a few questions. Unfortunately, we were told it was against medical protocol. This left Jermaine and I to ask all the questions. We then asked the way forward, although still in shock and feeling dumbstruck.

## *The Way Forward*

The doctor realised that we were speechless, therefore, he began telling us the possible way forward. He told us that when the final result became available that was when we would start treatment. We asked him what treatment that would be. He said chemotherapy. Having never heard the term before, we inquired what it was. We did in fact hear it before but for some reason it sounded so new. We were told that chemotherapy is a cancer treatment that uses one or more anti-cancer drugs as part of a standardised chemotherapy regimen. With that said we still did not get the full understanding because I always thought that chemotherapy was an oral medication. However that was when we learnt that the oral medication is a part of the treatment while some patients normally get it through an IV. We were not processing all of what he was saying. It was as if what was being said was going through one ear and out the other. Quite frankly, he could not be talking about our princess, Jerodene. No, not at all! Not our daughter who was born perfect with all her organs and body parts intact. Our only daughter that God had blessed us with, and with all the prayers that were prayed, this could not be real. We knew that we served a Mighty God and we knew that He was the God that could turn the impossible into the possible. Right there and then we needed a miracle, instantly!

Questions started to boggle my mind again. *"Seriously? Why did this have to happen to Jerodene? Why us? Is this for real? How could this be? Am I dreaming? I really need to wake up because this must be a dream."* We asked ourselves these questions upon hearing the devastating news and the fact that we had to deal with such a harsh reality.

The doctor then told us that they needed to start the treatment right away. He gave us a date to return for admission. He noticed that my husband and I were still speechless so he told us that any questions we had he would be happy to answer when we returned for admission. Jerodene had no idea what was being said; she just stood there watching her dad and I as the tears trickled down our faces. We were helpless and so was Jerodene.

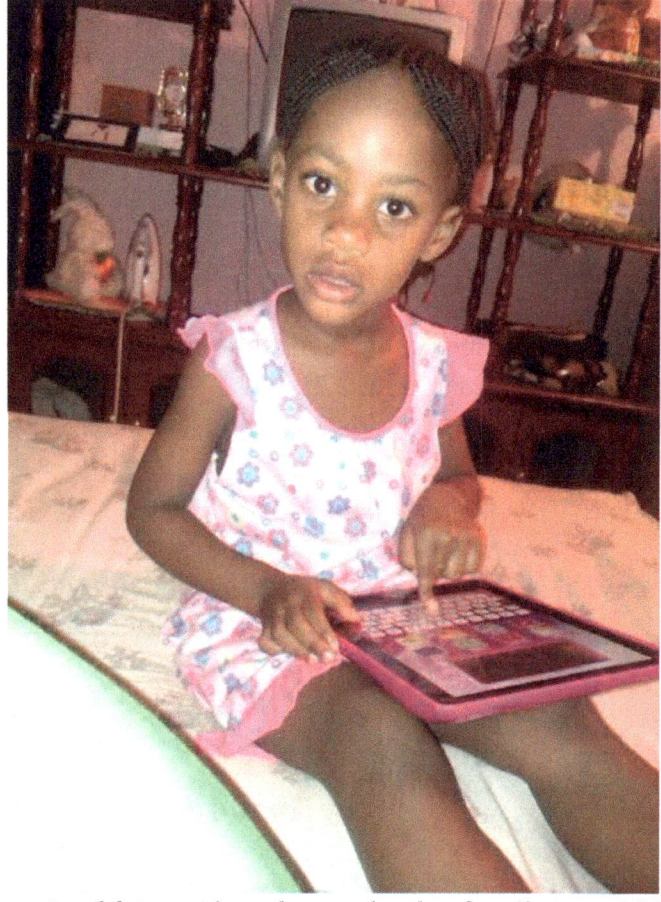

Upon reaching home, I told Jermaine that only the family would know of Jerodene's true situation. We would not say it to anybody else and that she would go through with the treatment and we would keep it confidential. After a few days of being at home trying to get ourselves together, I said to Jermaine again *"you know what, it's not that we went searching for an illness. Even if it was being given away for free, nobody would have chosen it. It does not matter who finds out that Jerodene was diagnosed with cancer. It is nothing to be ashamed of and we would not be the first family to have a member diagnosed with cancer."*

A few days later, our church had a prayer breakfast that was planned prior to the news. It was an event where members from other congregations came together to have a wonderful time in the Lord. There we decided to tell our pastor for him to share with the congregation and ask for prayer on Jerodene's behalf and also pray for our strength to go through the ordeal. After we told our Pastor he called both of us into his office and asked us if we were sure that was what we wanted him to do. We both agreed because eventually people would find out. He greeted the church and after the sermon he called the four of us to the altar and told the church the devastating news. Everyone was stunned, shocked and in awe. It was unbelievable and that was when the Holy Spirit took over. Everyone started praying and calling on God for deliverance. While the prayers were being prayed, others were seated in silence because they did not know what to think (I could not blame them at all). Maybe I would have done the same thing if it was someone else's child. After all that was done our pastor encouraged us and told us that God can make the impossible possible. I could not hold back the tears. Men sometimes hide their emotions but I did not care who was watching. I bawled as if I was being whipped with a belt. I then remembered the thought that "tears are a language that only God understands".

## *Seeking Assistance*

Some days later, we were told of a lady in Mandeville, Jamaica by the name of Mrs. Hanson who normally helped children diagnosed with cancer. I inquired of her whereabouts and was told exactly where I could find her. When I met her and saw her for the first time, her personality made me want to forget our troubles. Her personality was very warm and welcoming. I told her about our situation, and she said when I gather all the information we should let her know. She told us about a group of people that formed a club, the Optimist Club that was based in Mandeville, Jamaica. They try to help children who are critically ill with cancer. I told her that whatever help we could get we would appreciate it because we needed to save the life of our child. I went home and shared the information with Jermaine who was home with both children. He was overjoyed at hearing such news because he knew how expensive it would be to finance everything. The time was fast approaching for Jerodene to be admitted to the hospital. By then, we were putting plans in place since we had no idea the time frame she would be hospitalised for. Jermaine had to go to work, even though he had an occasion to put work on hold until things were stabilised.

## *Admission*

The day came when we had to go to the hospital. Our bags were packed with all the necessities since we knew that we would not be home for a while. We did not know what to expect so we went open-minded. On the other hand, Rasheed was not yet one year old and in order for us to focus on Jerodene's situation, my brother, Randal and his wife, Veneica volunteered to keep Rasheed who was two months younger than their own daughter, Xariah. After settling on where Rasheed would stay, we went straight to the hospital where Jerodene was admitted and was placed on Ward 16, bed 18. The doctors came to advise us that the final result was ready. After a period of information-sharing, they told us that the cancer that Jerodene was diagnosed with was **RHABDOMYOSARCOMA** and that it was fully confirmed to be at stage 4. With Jerodene being age 4 and diagnosed with stage 4 cancer, we were puzzled. The doctors further advised us that about 30% of children with cancer lived beyond age 5. We then encouraged ourselves that Jerodene would be among the 30%. We then asked what **Rhabdomyosarcoma** (**RMS**) was. We were told that it was cancer of the muscles and it affected muscles everywhere in the body. We then asked what the next step was now that she was admitted.

We were introduced to three (3) different chemotherapy drugs namely: Vincristine,

Cyclophosphamide and Dactinomycin. I asked the doctors to write them down because I would like to do some research. Immediately after our meeting, I called my cousins, Natasha Thomas-Francis and Lorraine Colphon who were in England and gave them the update. The following day they called me back with quite a few questions that they would love for me to ask the doctors. I was so happy for the help of my cousins. It seemed as if a heavy load was lifted off my shoulders because they knew that I was not knowledgeable to ask all these questions. That night was a very rough one because there was a baby beside us crying all night. Gosh, I just wished the nightmare would come to an end. During the first stay at the hospital, Mrs. Hanson came to visit us. I remember her carrying the most beautiful red dress and white shoes for Jerodene as a gift. Jerodene really loved her gift. She then told us that she and her team would pay us a visit at home whenever Jerodene was discharged and they did.

The doctors started her off on Vincristine so they gave us a prescription to fill then they told us we could purchase it at the hospital's pharmacy, which we did. After a few days, Jerodene got adjusted and the doctors and nurses really loved her when they found out that she was a very outspoken and intelligent little lady, very vibrant and full of life. She was even telling one of the nurses that she has a baby brother and he is not yet walking. Those sleepless nights on those wooden chairs were no joke. I remember one night, when Jerodene was still on bed 18, we had a long day. I leaned back on the wooden chair trying to doze off, but the chair was so hard and uncomfortable. I remember taking thin cushions from the chair and placing them on the floor and covering myself from head to toe so that no insect could crawl on me. I did that to see if I could have gotten a better night's sleep. When the new day dawned, I got up from off the floor but it took me a while before I could move off because of the severe pain I was in due to sleeping on the hard floor.

After a few weeks of treatment, they told us that in a few days they might be able to discharge her. Within those few weeks my brother's wife, Veneica, called with the good news that Rasheed took his first step. Tears rolled down my cheeks because of circumstances beyond our control, we were not there to see it for ourselves. Jermaine had to be working because there were bills to pay and he was the only breadwinner in the family. We had decided that no matter how long Jerodene was hospitalised I would stay with her because I had to see and know everything that was going on. When she got discharged, we were told to visit the hospital every Friday for a dose of Vincristine and that we did. However, after visiting the hospital for a few weeks and learning about the side effects of the chemotherapy we decided that we would not be taking her back to the hospital and that we would be seeking more of God in the situation.

Quite a few weeks had passed and our life was back to normal of sorts. All four of us were back at home and happy, as happy as we could be. In August 2015, we went to purchase her back to school supplies and we were looking forward to sending her to school for the new school year, which would have been the following month. About mid-August, Jerodene started complaining of headaches. We said to ourselves that we would have to check out the cause of the headaches. After a few hours, she began crying uncontrollably. We took her to the closest hospital, which was less than half an hour ride from home. Upon reaching the hospital, Jerodene was still crying. We registered her and were told to sit and wait for her name to be called. After a few minutes, they called us and we rushed in to see the doctor.

After explaining to the doctor the diagnosis, she turned to us and said *"well, when it is at stage 4 there is nothing much that we can do"* with a matter-of-fact attitude. When she said that, I shook my head and looked at her. I was so upset! O God, I wished that I could have slapped her for saying that. I was asking *"Like seriously doctor?!"* She said it as if she was not talking about a human life

- a little child. Anyway, they told us that they had to admit her and that was when I learnt about the pain medication, morphine. I tried to remember the name because I needed to add it to my vocabulary, and do some reading on it.

During the admission, we were briefed on the visiting hours, et cetera. They informed us that the visiting hours were throughout the day but visitors had to leave by 10:00 p.m. We started questioning ourselves because we had no idea how that would work because of Jerodene's attachment to us. It was the total opposite at the previous hospital but because Jerodene had been crying, she was tired. So shortly after the IV and morphine were administered, she fell asleep minutes before 7:00 p.m. We used the opportunity to go home early. If she had not gone to bed, she would have cried so much that the other children may not have been able to sleep and we would have been heartbroken. For the entire night we struggled to sleep because our minds were on her. Each time we dozed off it was as if we could hear her crying in our minds. When I remembered that at the other hospital, I was able to stay with her, it really pained my heart. My mom had to come by to help us out with Rasheed because Jermaine and I had to make daily trips to the hospital.

The next day we got up, packed a little bag with clothes and made breakfast for her. When we got to the hospital, her bed screen was drawn. I began wondering what was wrong with her and found out that when a screen was drawn, it either meant that the patient was very ill or had transitioned. All kinds of thoughts were going through my head. Knowing that when we left the night before, Jerodene was asleep and relieved of the excruciating pain she was in, my heart pounded and my head instantly began to hurt when I saw the screen drawn. I aggressively pulled the screen and to my surprise, it was another child who was there. Unfortunately, that child had transitioned. I started to panic and as I stepped back, I heard a nurse telling me that I was not allowed to interfere whenever a screen was drawn. It took the grace of God for me not to react. I knew that if they were going to relocate a patient, the child's parents should have been notified and told of the changes if they were not present. The nurse apologised after realising that I was angry. She tried to calm me down then told me that Jerodene cried all night when she awoke and did not see any of her parents. I told her that it was expected since she was not accustomed to not having her parents around. Jerodene was so happy to see us and we shared the same sentiment. She told us that she was feeling much better than the day before. She told us that on our next visit we should bring her toys because she got bored.

Shortly after we met with the doctors, they told us that we would have to do a CT scan on her brain. They also said it would have to be done at a private facility since unfortunately, the hospital did not have one of those machines. A private facility was very close, which worked out to be the cheapest, so we were sent to make the necessary payment. The cost was J$15,000.00. It was a good thing that Jermaine had just collected from a job he had completed so we were able to take care of that bill. The lab was not able to facilitate us that day but could the following day.

When we went the next day, we had travelled in the ambulance to have the procedure done at the private facility. We were both anxious and concerned at the same time. When the procedure was completed, we asked the attendant what the result was. She said it was against the rules to disclose the result, even though we were the parents. She said we would have to wait for the doctor to read the result and he could explain to us exactly what the reading was. We prayed the entire time asking God that if there was anything that was not of Him, he should reverse it because we knew that there was nothing too hard for Him to do. We lifted our faith to Him and encouraged ourselves that all would be well. When we got back to the hospital, the doctors were in a meeting, so we had to wait for their availability. After a few hours, we were still waiting because the meeting went on for a long time. Sometime after, they called us aside and told us that the result showed that the legions had gone to Jerodene's brain and that was the cause of the severe headaches that she was experiencing. Oh my God, what else could one family bear? *Are you seeing right?* I asked the doctor with tears rolling down my face. My husband looked at me and told me that God was still able. We sat there dazed for a while due to disbelief. That was not the news we wanted to hear.

## *Jerodene's 5th Birthday*

Jerodene's birthday was a few days away and we came to the understanding that she would be spending her 5th birthday in the hospital. We all knew that would not be any fun. The doctors told us that with the chemotherapy that Jerodene would be getting, it might be able to reduce or clear up what was there. We decided to leave it all in God's hands. We knew that a lot of prayers were going up for her and we believed that she would be fine. Now and then tears would flow but we did not lose faith. Later that night as it drew near for us to leave her for home, we felt feelings of sadness and pain. We anticipated that she would fall asleep very early like the previous evening, so we waited. Unfortunately, even after visiting hours were up, her eyes were still wide open. We had to find a way to leave without her realising. We were told the next day that she cried when we did.

At that point, we were told about a lady by the name of Kerlyn Brown. We did not know her personally, but I had always seen her reading the news on a well-known television station. We were told that she had a program by the name of 'Inspire Jamaica'. When we inquired from a friend we were told that she would seek for children who were very sick and highlight their conditions on the program, so that persons would be able to know about the different kinds of illness that can plague our children. We inquired about the timing of the program. We thought to ourselves that there was no way that we could have gotten in touch with her. She must be very busy, I thought. However, we were able to view the program and luckily, that same night, the child who was being interviewed, I realised his mother was an associate of mine. I got in contact with the mother within a few days, attempting to get a contact number for Kerlyn Brown. I was unable to speak to her directly but was able to do so through that lady. I explained Jerodene's situation to the lady and she passed all the information on to Kerlyn Brown. We were so happy when we got in touch with her because we knew that she would be able to help us. We waited for a few days to hear from her. When I saw a message from the lady, I got very excited. Unfortunately, the message we received was not what we expected. She said that Kerlyn was not able to air Jerodene's story at the time because she was switching her focus from cancer and was highlighting other rare illnesses. We felt so disappointed because we had our hopes up that Jerodene's story would be aired and that we might have gotten some help to purchase the chemotherapy drugs. We crossed her off our list.

The doctors at the hospital were not able to tell us how long Jerodene would have been admitted. One particular day while I was there after Jermaine had gone to work, all her teachers came to visit her, including her principal and her class teacher. Jerodene was overjoyed to see them. She always spoke highly of her principal and told us how she loved her. Jerodene showed them her toys and told them that she was tired of the hospital and she wanted to go home. She wanted to play with her little brother knowing that children were not allowed on the ward so he was not able to visit her at the hospital. They took a gift for her and she was very happy especially when she saw that it was one of her favourite character books, Mickey and Minnie Mouse. She was excited because that was her very first book with them. She promised to take good care of it because it became her favourite book of all times. Her principal got really emotional because it was so hard seeing Jerodene in that situation. As tears rolled down her face she walked away knowing that one of her students was diagnosed with such a critical illness. I realised then, that she was not handling the situation well. They left shortly afterwards telling us that they would be back to visit at another time. Jerodene hugged them and told them to be safe. She then got very sad when she remembered that she might not see them for a while. Jerodene told them to say hi to her friends and to tell them that she missed them and that she would see them soon. That same night, her teacher Ms. Green came back and sent us home telling us that she would stay with Jerodene for a few hours until visiting hours were up. Ms. Green took a very heavy load off our shoulders as she really sent us home to rest. We really appreciated her kind and thoughtful gesture. She read to Jerodene story after story. She also took her tablet with her so that Jerodene could play games and enjoy them. Ms. Green even promised her that next time around she would download new games and stories for her. Jerodene told her that it would make her very happy for her to do so.

The following day, Ms. Green called to tell us that she read bedtime stories until Jerodene fell asleep. Again we told her how much we appreciated what she did. Her response while smiling was *"No problem, Mrs. Bailey. I wish I could do more"*. Jermaine was unable to accompany me the next morning to visit her, but promised that he would come by after he was through working. I arrived at the hospital at 6:30 a.m. because that was the normal time she expected us. When I got to the hospital, the nurses told us that last night was the best she had since her admission. They said they had no idea what her teacher did to her but whatever she did, she did it well. All I did was smile because I felt pleased. The doctors told us that morning that they still were not able to send her home and that they still had to keep her under observation and that they would still be giving her morphine to control the pain. I researched the pain medication (morphine) and found out that some of the side effects were constipation, drowsiness, loss of appetite, among many others. We really wanted them to withdraw from the morphine as soon as possible. They told us that they were not able to stop the medication suddenly but probably over a period of time they could reduce it. We understood but still prayed for a miracle.

That same evening her grandaunt, Sis. Charmaine and my mom came to visit her. She was very happy to see them both because Jerodene loved and spoke of them highly. They stayed with us for a while and encouraged us letting us know that God was still able. Before they left, they told us that they would pray with us, so we sang some choruses, and then it was time to pray. Before they prayed, my mom told Jerodene that she should pray first. Knowing Jerodene to be that brave little girl she was, she gladly took the challenge. She asked if we could close our eyes in reverence and agreement. She started to pray and in the midst of her prayer, I heard her saying these words, **"God, Lazarus was dead for four days until he started smelling, and God I am not dead and I know you can heal me in Jesus name"**. By the time she was through praying, my mom and Sis. Charmaine were in awe, knowing that Jerodene prayed such a powerful prayer. My husband and I knew that she had it in her from a tender age, so did Auntie Charmaine, but it was the first they heard her praying.

Her teacher, Ms. Green kept her promise and came to spend a few hours with her. She also downloaded most of the girl apps that Jerodene loved. Earlier I made mention of Simone Mason. When I told her about Jerodene's situation, it ripped her apart knowing the bond that Jerodene and her son shared and that no one could separate them. She called a few times, asking if Jerodene was still hospitalised and when I told her yes, she said she was close by so she would be there in a few minutes. Upon reaching the hospital, I could tell that she was putting her best outside. Jerodene was so happy to see her she gave her a big hug. Simone mentioned something to her about her son, Raheem and Jerodene with her little sassy self, told her to pronounce her son's name properly. She reminded her that his name has the letter H and that the letter H makes the tired sound. We all had a good laugh. Shortly after that Jerodene started crying in pain. She cried saying **"Mommy, do something, please help me"**. By the time I looked, Simone stormed off the ward crying. The porters tried to stop her to find out what the problem was, but she was so distraught by what she saw that she could not answer.

The doctors administered the morphine and she began feeling a little better. Shortly after, my aunt Sandra and her friend, Mrs. Oliver came to visit. I was happy to see them and was happier that they did not come when Jerodene was in pain. Jerodene's friend, Jestina, Mrs. Oliver's daughter, also came to visit. Jerodene and Jestina always enjoyed playing games and reading stories together. Jestina was the elder, hence she would be the reader and Jerodene the listener. It was a pleasure having them knowing that Jerodene and Aunt Sandra had such a bond. Jerodene was very happy to see her. Jerodene got the most visitors. She had almost everyone's support from near and far.

Jerodene was brave, spunky, jovial and sassy. A little girl who loved to correct her peers and always behaved as if she was always the eldest. She loved singing so I always jokingly said to her, *"Please have your mother's voice and not your father's"*.

A few days later she was discharged and that was the happiest day of our lives. When they told us, we quickly packed her stuff without hesitation since we were anticipating that day. When we got home Jerodene was overjoyed to see her brother. She started to play with him instantly and was telling him that she had missed him. Within a few days of being home, Jerodene told us she was healed. She said to us **"Mommy and Daddy, I am healed because my body is feeling different than how it was."** Tears rolled down my face, her dad stood in shock hearing our then 5-year old daughter telling us that she was healed. Jermaine and I then came to the conclusion that we would contact the doctors at the University Hospital and have them set an appointment to redo the CT scan on the brain. They did as we requested but she had to be admitted in order for the scan to be done. She was admitted two days before the scan was done. On the day of the scan she got an injection on her leg, I think to keep her calm during the procedure. The scan was done hence she was discharged. We were told we would be called when the result was ready.

When we were leaving the hospital, Jerodene was barely able to walk. When I brought it to the attention of the doctor, I was told it was nothing threatening but because Jerodene really wanted to go home she told me she could manage to walk. That was one of the most difficult situations I had to deal with. She cried for most of the time especially, while we were on the bus from Kingston to Mandeville. I had to pay for an extra seat for her comfort. Normally she would sit on my lap but due to the fact she was in so much pain, I had no choice but to make her as comfortable as possible.

However, when we got to Mandeville, Jerodene was unable to walk due to the terrible pain she was still having. She cried the entire time. I felt so helpless. All I could do was carry her. We went to Payless Shoe Store to get her a pair of shoes for school in September. She was in so much pain to the point where we could not purchase the shoes. I called a taxi driver named Raymond to pick us up at the store. When the taxi came it was difficult to put her in the car because I had to be careful of the position in which I held her. The taxis in my area carried five passengers: one on the front passenger seat and four to the back. The two passengers were getting emotional since they could not help either. The passenger in the front told the driver that she would pay for the extra two seats since the child needs to go home. Jerodene cried continuously, I wished that there was something that I could have done to ease the pain. With the assurance of payment for the other two seats, the driver left immediately.

When the driver got on the highway, the ride was pretty smooth but she cried just the same. The driver was very patient with us because I had explained the situation to him. He drove very slowly and was very understanding. As we exited the highway, I started to worry because the rest of the journey would be bumpy due to the road surface. Jerodene cried harder and louder when the taxi would navigate a pothole. O my God, there was nothing else that the driver could have done.

Each time the car would enter a pothole she would yell. I figured she was crying for her father whom she did not see for a few days. Instead she shouted, *"Satannnn you are a liar, Satannnn I say you are a liar"*. Honestly, tears started rolling down my face, and when I looked at the two passengers they too were crying. The lady said to me, *"Miss I have never seen anything like this before"*. My only concern was for us to reach home safely then I would be able to hold and cuddle her. I could only imagine the pain that she was feeling. Even Raymond got really emotional. Men on a whole normally tend to hide their emotions, but the driver could not hold it in any longer. I tried so hard to comfort her but unfortunately that did not help and that was when I broke down. In a matter of minutes, we reached home, and I gave her some pain medicine and almost immediately she fell asleep. I really thanked God that she felt better after a while.

We believed that God would have healed Jerodene and we went ahead and got her school uniforms made so that she could continue her basic school years. Jerodene was looking forward to wearing her new school bag, shoes, new hair accessories, and seeing her friends that she had not seen for a while. Even though sports day was a few months away she was already planning to run even better than she did in the first year. While she was in K1 she ran at sports day and got a few certificates because she was successful in all her races. She told her dad, **"I am going to get more certificates Daddy"**. We really believed in her and knew that she could do it.

In September 2015, Jerodene marched out for school in her full uniform. Her hair was well done by my hairdresser, Mervalyn Osbourne. She really started with a bang and we looked forward to her finishing the year in full swing. September ended and Jerodene was back to normal. She was not feeling any pain. She was still jovial and in high spirits. In other words, she was back to the happy child that she once was. The doctors from the University Hospital had called us into a meeting and informed us that the results showed that the legions that were in Jerodene's brain were not as many as before. We started thanking God for healing her. We truly believed that she was healed.

## *The Herbal Way*

In mid-October 2015, Jerodene again started to feel pains. We gave her pain medication that we had received from the doctors. We then learnt that there might be another way that the cancer could be treated instead of using the chemotherapy treatments. After learning about the side effects of the chemotherapy, Jermaine and I decided that we would take the herbal route by using natural herbs as medicine. We inquired and found an herbal doctor and took her there. The doctor recommended that Jerodene do a body detoxification. There were several things we had to remove from her diet, for example chicken and some of her favourite snacks. At first, we did not know how to break the news to her, when we finally did, she cried. Her new diet consisted mostly of fruits, vegetables, and nuts. We eventually cooked and packed her lunch for school. Having her take her lunch to school daily was a struggle because what we prepared for her was different from her previous meals. She was not enjoying the food and sometimes would not eat it and returned home with a packed lunch dish. Some days, she would tell us that her Principal, Miss Anderson, fed her, which we did not mind because we knew she cared for Jerodene.

One night, all four of us were at home when Jerodene began complaining about pains she was experiencing. At the time it was not in her head that she felt pain but in her legs. Her legs? We never saw that one coming. The following morning, we received an ointment that we were told would help to relieve the pain. That night she began experiencing pain again and before we knew it, it got worse. She cried hopelessly while her dad rubbed her legs. As she screamed in pain she cried **"Mommy, Daddy help me, help me, do something 'cause I can't take it anymore."** We both looked confused since we did not know what else to do. That night seemed like the longest night we ever had throughout the devastating situation.

Many questions came to our minds when we realised that the ointment was not helping. We were out of options. We had no idea what else to do. That Wednesday night, no one slept. We took turns rubbing her legs and trying to comfort her as best we knew how. By morning, Jerodene's eyes were swollen because she cried almost the entire night and got no rest. It was customary that when Jerodene woke up each morning you could hear her saying her prayers then greeted us with a *"good morning"*. However, that morning was different. When she woke up, she began singing **"You've been in a storm it seems like forever, ride out your storm"**. When I heard her, my heart melted. I thought *"Oh my God, is this child for real? Am I hearing clearly?"* I rushed to call her dad who was preparing breakfast. We both were speechless. This was another sign that this child was special. Even at that time we stood by our decision that she would not get any more chemotherapy treatment because we knew that God was bigger than cancer and all our situations.

A few days went by, and she was pain free. We believed God that her healing had come through. We went to church that Sunday and she told me that she wanted to testify. She then went to the rostrum and told the pastor. He handed her the microphone shortly after. She started to talk of God's goodness and that she was healed in the name of Jesus in the presence of over 100 persons who were in the congregation. Jerodene was not too shy or scared to talk about Jesus. She was very brave and happy to do so.

The following Sunday we all stayed home since she complained of feeling tired. At about noon, Jerodene complained of not feeling well. I cooked our regular Sunday dinner that consisted of rice and peas with chicken and vegetables. When she was served dinner, she did not eat as much as she would normally eat. After a while, she rushed to the bathroom feeling the urge to throw up. She vomited. By the time her father took her to the bedroom, I had to rush with a bucket because she wanted to throw up again. We thought that the meal might have been too heavy on her stomach, so we made some vegetable soup. She drank it and when we thought that she was fine, she threw up again. Sighing, her dad and I held hands and prayed that Satan would take his filthy hands off her. We reminded Satan that Jerodene was one of God's chosen girls. After our prayer, Jerodene began feeling better. She slept in our bed that night while her dad slept on her bed. She always loved when I hugged and cuddled her. During the night when I woke to check on her, surprisingly I realised that the bed was wet including her underwear. We were very shocked because she was potty-trained before she was three years old. We questioned ourselves asking what went wrong. We woke her up and I said to her, *"Jerodene you peed the bed"*. She replied, **"No Mommy"**. I then asked *"Jerodene, how did you know that you peed the bed"*? She said, **"Mommy because you just told me"**. Her dad and I looked at each other in total shock. I used a thick bath towel to cover the wet area with the intention of changing the sheets in the morning. Jermaine and I then went back to bed, clueless. We dozed off for a while then she peed again. I exclaimed *"Oh my God, this cannot be real!"* Tears rolled down my face as I stared at my husband as we both looked on in disbelief. *"My God, what next?"* we asked. What have we done to deserve this terrible situation bestowed upon our household? The following morning, which was November 1, 2015, we took her back to the herbal doctor. He advised us that there was no way he could help. By then her abdomen began swelling and she cried in a weak voice, **"My belly, my belly"**.

## Readmission To Mandeville Hospital

We hurriedly took her back to the hospital, wondering what they could do for her. We started to panic as she cried openly **"mi belly, mi belly, mommy and daddy help me, do something"** she cried beseechingly. Helpless as we were, we started praying. The doctor attended to us, and we hurriedly told him what had transpired, while Jerodene cried on top of her lungs. By that time her abdomen was distended, one could hardly touch it. The doctor instructed the nurse exactly what to do. We were ushered into an examination room. She undressed Jerodene's lower garments, reached for a bag and a pair of gloves. I inquired what was in the bag and the nurse told me it was a catheter. I had to ask more questions because I never knew what a catheter was. She explained the purpose and how it was used. It was to drain the backed-up urine from Jerodene's bladder, which caused her abdomen to be distended. She further explained that it was inserted into her vagina. The procedure took longer than I thought it would. Only one parent was allowed in the examination room, so her dad waited in the waiting area with our son, Rasheed. He sat there clueless and because the cellular reception was very poor in that area, I could not call him to let him know what was going on. I told the nurse that I would be back shortly, and I went to give him an update. He then said to me, *"Don't worry because Jerodene is healed"*. By the time I got back to the room, she fell asleep although the procedure was not complete. After a few more minutes, the procedure was finished. The urine bag was almost full. The doctor then advised me that Jerodene would be admitted because they wanted to find out what caused her not to be able to pass her urine. We were curious as well. Within a few hours, Jerodene passed stool on herself. *"What could have caused all of this now?"* I asked. First, it was urine and then this. Jerodene told us that she did not feel the stool coming.

We decided at that point that since Jerodene would be admitted, it would be impossible for Rasheed to stay at home. We did not have anyone to stay with him and knew that he would need attention since he was just over one year old. With mommy being a pastor and daddy an active member of the church it would have been a little difficult on their part, to keep Rasheed. We then recalled that my brothers' wife, Keysha, was not working at the time. We called, explained the situation, and asked if they could keep Rasheed since we were not sure how long Jerodene would be in the hospital. They gladly accepted the proposal. My mom and dad came for Rasheed, took him to their home in Clarendon where my brother and his wife would pick him up; they lived in St. Ann, Jamaica.

Prior to the admission, we noticed that a bump was growing on Jerodene's chest close to her neck. Upon showing the doctors they told us that the cancer caused it. I have grown to hate that word! They told us that only the chemotherapy could make it go away. We still insisted that she would not be doing any more treatments and if God could not remove it then nothing else could. That admission was not as bad as the first one. Jerodene was a bit calmer. She did not cry for the duration. She now understood that the only time we would leave her side was because we did not have any other choice. We went home after the visiting hours were up. When we went to the hospital the next morning, we got good news about her from the nurses. The doctors told us that they would have to do an x-ray on her spine to find out what was the cause of her not being able to feel when she wants to pass her stool and having difficulty passing her urine. The test was scheduled to be done the same day because the machine happened to be working at the time, unlike other times. I went with her when she was called because I knew that she would need some assurance that everything would be okay and that mommy and daddy would always be by her side, no matter what. The x-ray was done and again we had to wait on the doctors for the test results. The doctors came later that day to have a meeting with us. They told us that the cancer affected the spine, which also affected the bladder area and was the reason that Jerodene did not have any urge to go to the bathroom. At that point I asked for the way forward. They advised us that Jerodene would have to remain in the hospital for a few more days. They assured us that it would not be as long as the first time. Within a few days, they had retrained her bladder and sent her home Sunday evening.

## *Discharge From Mandeville Hospital*

Upon learning of Jerodene's discharge, Jermaine called our then pastor and told him and he said he would do us the honour of taking us home. That same Sunday night the church was hosting a healing and deliverance meeting, which is an annual convocation. On the evening of Jerodene's discharge, it rained heavily but by the time we got home, the rain stopped. Jerodene insisted that she wanted to go to church for the Healing and Deliverance meeting. We told her that it would not be possible because she was just discharged from the hospital and we were sure if the rain would continue into the night. She was very disappointed and started crying. We had to call our pastor and ask him to talk to her because she would not be consoled. She cried and told us, **"Pastor will be upset with me, because I told him that I will be coming to church tonight"**. Pastor called and spoke with her, and that was when she conceded. To cheer her up, we called my brother, Ryan, so that she could talk to Rasheed, although he could barely speak at the time. A few hours passed and having not gotten any proper sleep since Jerodene was in the hospital, we were looking forward to having a well-rested night. Close to 10:00 p.m., Jerodene began crying for her tummy. *"My belly, my belly"* she bawled openly. When we checked her we realised that the same thing reoccurred. Her abdomen was again distended, and she passed stool on herself. *"Jesussss!"* I cried out, *"Not again!"* The situation was becoming unbearable. She told me that she did not want to urinate. But at the same time her underwear was wet, and her abdomen was even more distended. My husband and I decided that we would have to take her back to the hospital. I literally cried when I saw all that was happening before my eyes and there was nothing that we could do to help her. We then called a taxi to take us to the hospital.

## *Readmission To Hospital*

Upon reaching the hospital we did not go to the Accident & Emergency (A&E), because that would have taken too long to get registered, furthermore Jerodene was in much discomfort. We went directly to the ward that she was on a few hours before. We explained to them what transpired since we left. On examination, they realised that the same thing reoccurred. I started to panic because I had no idea what next they would tell us. Unfortunately, they told us that she would have to wear the catheter for a while, and not only that, but she would have to wear diapers as well. *"Like seriously?"* I asked myself *"Are we hearing correctly? How could this be?"* So many questions remained unanswered. That piece of information hit us like a ton of bricks. *"How do we break this news to her?"* We knew it would be a hard task. Our hearts ached. That was when I was again tempted to ask the questions: *"Why does this have to happen to Jerodene? What have we done to deserve all of this?"* All these questions came to my mind. *"What else could we do and where would we go?"* When we got the courage to break the news to Jerodene, she cried so hard. She told us that she did not want to put the catheter back in and she promised that she was going to know when she wanted to pass her stool and urine. That was so sad because she thought that it was something she could control on her own in this case. She took it hard. We felt so sorry for her. We realised that we had a lot on our plate and what was on the plate was not delightful. The hospital then informed us that she would have to be readmitted. That was the last thing we wanted to hear, but we had no alternative. Anything they needed to do to help Jerodene feel better, we would just have to accept, except for the chemotherapy. We were still believing that God would continue to work on her.

Since we were naive to the whole catheter situation, we started asking questions. I asked the nurse what the cleaning procedure was. She told me she would take me through the procedure the following day. Jermaine had to go to work but told me he would come in the evening. I got to the hospital early in the morning to ensure Jerodene got a proper meal. I got up very early to make breakfast for her. When I got there, she was very happy to see me as was I. She ate the breakfast and enjoyed it and commented that it tasted better than the hospital food. We played some games, and she was able to watch her favourite cartoon, Mickey Mouse on the television. A few hours went by, and she came to me and told me that she smelled faeces but she was not sure if it was hers. A sense of sadness came over me when I realised that our daughter had gone back to the stage of being a baby, the only difference was that she was able to talk. I called the nurse and told her; she came with some gauze, a pair of sterile gloves and some brownish colour liquid. When I asked her what it was, she told me that it was Betadine. Not knowing the purpose of it, she drew the screen and told me that she was going to demonstrate the cleaning process. I did not grasp everything at first but knew that I would catch on to it. Later that evening, her dad came as promised and brought her favourite fruit. Oh, how happy she was to see him (she was daddy's princess). At that time, Jerodene was admitted for about two weeks. Every day I visited and would spend at least 14 hours with her. I ended up spending most of the time with her since Jermaine had to go to work but his evening visits were sure.

One Sunday morning I was not able to visit her because after all those long hours I was totally drained, I was weak and tired. My husband told me to stay home and get some rest, and he would go and spend the day with her. I was overjoyed when he made that proposal. He saw that I was not able to make it. I planned that I would get some deserved rest for the day. During the day Jermaine called telling me that a doctor came to Jerodene's bedside. He said that the doctor did not have the courtesy to say good morning. Jermaine said that the doctor just passed him and stood at her bedside. He said the doctor looked at Jerodene then looked at the team of doctors and said in an aggressive tone. *"What is she still doing here? What is she still doing here? She is supposed to go home. She is supposed to go home."* Jermaine sat there shocked and figured that it was because we decided that we did not want her to get anymore chemotherapy treatment. Tears came to Jermaine's eyes knowing that the doctor made such a remark and there was no way that Jerodene could have gone home, because by then she was barely able to walk.

By then we had to be buying packs of pampers and wipes for our five year old daughter. How hard could this be? We then started to wonder to ourselves *"would Jerodene be wearing this big urine bag so that everyone could see?"* How would that be possible? And most of all, how would Jerodene feel knowing that people would be looking at her wearing a urine bag? Shortly afterwards, her paternal grandmother, Doreen, who was overseas called and I was telling her about the current situation. She told me that she would not have to wear the big bag. She told me to go to the pharmacy and asked if they had any urinary leg bag. She told me that the urinary leg bag would be private, and people would not have to know that she was wearing one. Jermaine went to the pharmacy but unfortunately, they did not have it in stock. They recommended another pharmacy. We continued to ask, *"How could our daughter be wearing a catheter?"* This must be uncomfortable. *"How would she be able to walk comfortably wearing that thing?"* Jermaine finally purchased one and brought it back. We gave it to the nurse who made the switch. Thank God! That felt a thousand times better. We were happy that we learnt of the urinary leg bag through my mother-in-law because the medical team did not share that information with us. It was much easier to handle since all the nurse did was to strap it to her leg. At that point, we realised that she would not be able to wear shorts or short dresses anymore. Instead, she had to wear long pants to disguise the leg bag. Jerodene cried and said she did not want any of her friends to know that she was wearing it. She then asked us to pinky-promise her that we would not tell her friends and we did. Shortly after that, we left for home and promised her that by God's will, we would be back the next day.

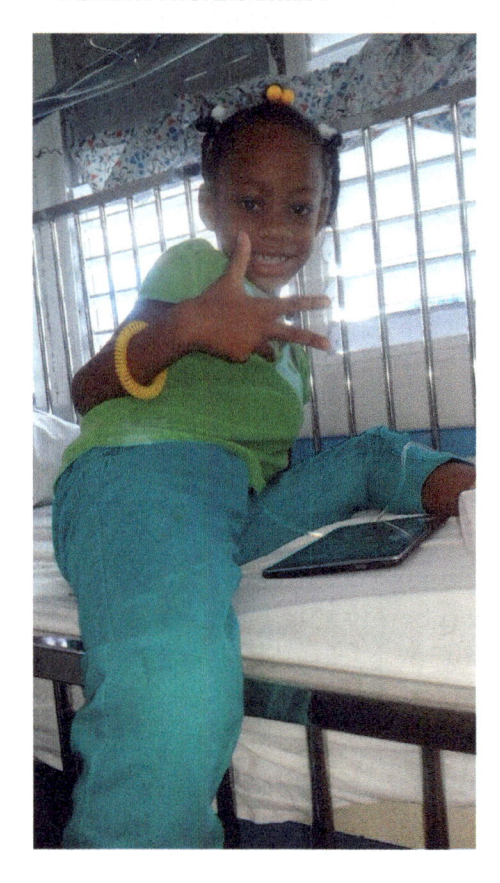

## The Angelic Dream

That same night, I saw Jerodene in a dream and she was in a carriage. She was an angel, and she was sleeping in the carriage all dressed in white. Other angels were pulling the carriage. I turned to the angel and was about to ask the angel where she was going with my daughter, but I woke from my dream. I called my mom and told her the dream. She said maybe I was not supposed to ask the angel anything. That dream bothered me for months because I did not understand it. Who am I to be interpreting dreams? My own dream at that.

## A Strange Telephone Call

About an hour before I left home for the regular hospital visit, Jermaine's phone rang. Upon answering, the person on the other end asked if the phone belonged to Jermaine Bailey, I replied "*Yes*". The person then told me that she was a janitor at the hospital and a little girl begged her to call her dad. She said that the little girl gave her the number to call. The lady was shocked when she realised that the number really belonged to Jermaine, the child's father. She said that she thought that the child made up the number out of nowhere and that she did not know that a child so young could be so smart and sensible. Jerodene then told me to take her shampoo and conditioner along with her beads, because she wanted me to wash her hair. We did and within a few hours after I got to the hospital, Jerodene was all dolled up with her multi-colour beads. She was so happy, and her face glowed with delight. She said, **"Mommy I feel pretty"** and I replied, "*yes baby, you look beautiful*". She was still unable to walk like she used to but there was a slight improvement. We believed God that within a few days she would have been discharged.

Her friend, Raheem, and his mother, Simone, came to visit. He was, however, unable to go on the ward because he was underage. I went and told Jerodene that she had visitors as she was watching her favourite cartoon. When she heard that it was Raheem, she got so excited and forgot about the cartoon. She whispered in my ear, *"Mommy please go and get my bath towel so I can wrap it around my lower body because I can't let Raheem know that I am wearing catheter"*. I did as she asked, and she then walked slowly whilst leaning against the wall after a few steps, to balance herself. If she was able to run, I knew she would have sprinted off, but because she was barely able to walk, she had to go slow. They embraced each other and laughed heartily; they were very happy to see each other. They had a lot to catch up on because Jerodene was out of school for a while. Jerodene wanted to find out what was being taught at school. What did he have for lunch and the most important question - when was Sports Day? Jerodene told almost everybody that Raheem was her cousin, and nobody could tell them otherwise. They really loved each other, and they were inseparable. Raheem's mom and I walked a little distance away from them to give them some privacy. After all, we did not know when they would be able to see each other again. They spent over an hour with us and when it was time for them to leave, Jerodene cried so much that I had to comfort her. They really enjoyed each other's company. Raheem, of course, promised that he would come again to visit. Jerodene sat on the bench and waited until they left because she did not want them to know that she was wearing a catheter.

The following day as I went to visit her, I had to go back on the road to purchase diapers. While there, I saw one of my neighbours who told me she saw Jerodene in a dream the night before. She said Jerodene was journeying on a lonely road, and when she asked Jerodene where she was going, she did not answer her. The lady told Jerodene that wherever she was going, she would follow her because she had to find out where she was going. By the time the lady looked she saw an angel dressed in full white coming out of the sky and took Jerodene away. I questioned: another dream within a two-week period? Who am I to interpret the dream? I asked myself, *"What could these dreams mean*?" I never shared the dream I had with the neighbour. I asked God to show or tell me the meaning of these dreams, because I would love to know the meaning.

Within a few weeks Jerodene's condition started to deteriorate. The severe pain started all over again. We thought her walking ability was improving, instead, it was the total opposite. Everything started to take a negative turn. My husband and I found ourselves between a rock and a hard place because we knew that we had to come to a mutual agreement. The doctors were there but obviously there was nothing much that they could do because we had decided that there would be no more chemotherapy. We were at the point where we needed Divine intervention because Jerodene was very sick.

## *Big Decision*

My husband and I prayed about it earnestly right there and then, when we realised that we were cornered. That was when we gave in and told them we changed our minds about the chemotherapy treatment. The following morning before I got to the hospital, we decided to call the Oncologist at the University Hospital of the West Indies (UHWI). We felt bad knowing that since we left there we never looked back. We both knew that we had to call them because Jerodene's life was at stake. Jermaine made the call to Kingston early the following morning, and the Oncologist told us to take Jerodene to them and they would work on her as best as possible. The UHWI contacted the Mandeville Regional Hospital and told them of the decision. They then wrote up a transfer sheet for Jerodene to go to Kingston and by the following morning we were rushed to the UHWI in an ambulance.

## *Readmission To The University Hospital*

When we got to the hospital, we were placed on Ward 15. Jerodene was so disappointed because she was not familiar with any of the nurses on that ward. She started to cry because she really wanted to go back to Ward 16. Nonetheless, Jerodene met two wonderful nurses there: Nurse Halstead and Nurse Lewis. Even though the team at the Mandeville Hospital already did their tests on Jerodene, the UHWI had to redo the tests and scans for them to have a better understanding of what was going on in Jerodene's now frail body. Later that afternoon, the doctors came and started asking me the reason for bringing her back to the hospital. I explained it all to them and they told me that they would be sending her to the X-ray Department to check the condition of the spine, etc. We did not wait long for the test to be done, since the doctors had informed them to create a space for her. By the time we got back to Ward 15, Nurse Halstead introduced herself to us and showed us to Jerodene's bed. Jerodene cried to Nurse Halstead saying that she "does not want to be on that ward". Nurse Halstead responded, "Nothing is wrong with this ward; it is a nice ward." She continued "No, it's not a nice ward because my friends are not over there." The nurse inquired who her friend was and Jerodene told her that Nurse Martin and Nurse Robotham were her friends. Nurse Halstead tried to calm her down even as Jerodene behaved badly because she did not get what she wanted. Nurse Halstead told her that Nurse Robotham was not there because she was in school. Jerodene cried even more, telling her that she did not care, she still wanted to go back on Ward 16. Nurse Halstead tried so hard to be Jerodene's friend, but Jerodene was just being difficult. Nurse Halstead and Jerodene eventually became friends. She then promised Jerodene that she would make sure she would request a transfer to Ward 16. When we got back from the X-Ray Department, I called a friend, Pierre, who had loaned me a folding bed on our last admission. I recalled that he told me previously that if I ever needed the bed, I should feel free to call. When I called, Pierre said that he was planning on going overseas the following day, and he would send the bed right away with a bearer. We were given the bed as a gift. Of course, God knew how grateful and happy I was because that was where my journey at the University Hospital truly began.

That night was not as difficult as previous ones in the past when I had to sleep on tough wooden chairs. The sleeping arrangement, however, was the least of my problems. My main concern was to see Jerodene stabilised and able to walk. The following day, Jerodene got her desire. Yes, she got the transfer. There was much delight on her face. It was as if she won a million dollars. When we got to that ward, the nurses were happy to see her but not in the state that she was in. They greeted us and showed us to the bed assigned to her. Of course, Nurse Robotham was not there as Nurse Halstead had told us. That time, Jerodene was placed on bed 18, closer to the nurses' and doctors' station. I figured that was a good idea since Jerodene would be getting first class treatment. Across from our bed, on bed 20, I noticed that a patient and a lady were there. The little girl seemed to be about eight or nine years old at the time. She had a few balloons at her bedside. I figured it was unfortunate for her to be spending her birthday in the hospital and thought to myself that that could never happen to Jerodene because that would be no fun. No fun at all. At that point, it was the holiday season in December 2015 and the ward was packed with patients and their parents. In my head, those children should be home enjoying their holidays and having fun instead of getting needles.

The doctors came and informed me that the results were the same as it was in Mandeville, based on the information shared. Around that time, Jermaine called me very distraught. He was instructing me to not let them administer the three (3) chemotherapy drugs to Jerodene. He believed that it would be too harsh for her being as young as she was. He did not believe that her frail body could handle everything at once and neither did I. I told the doctors my husband's request; they said they understood our plight and they would work with our decision. Within a few days, Jerodene and I tried to adjust to the new situation. Jerodene started meeting new friends in her age group while I met other parents from all walks of life. It was not difficult for Jerodene to make new friends and get attached to the nurses because she was very friendly, brave, vibrant, outspoken, confident, inspiring, strong, intelligent, strong-willed, talented, caring and overall she was just 'a power-pack'. Even though she was feeling so sick, she still tried her best to present all these qualities. It was obvious, however, that she was not well because all these qualities were almost non-existent.

We got a prescription to fill and that was when the reality really hit me that Jerodene had cancer. I filled the prescription, and the treatment was administered within a few hours. I was very curious. I wanted to see the good that the first round of treatment would have done to her. *"Would she be able to walk again? Will her hair fall out*?" were some of the questions I was asking myself. I was not working at the time, and I was happy because I was able to always be by her side. As a matter of fact, if I were employed, I would have had to quit the job to be by my child's side since she would be priority number one.

By that time, our relatives knew that Jerodene was transferred to the UHWI, and they knew that her condition had worsened. My cousin, Iyonie, was already doing some research trying to find out if there were any hospitals overseas that would be able to treat Jerodene's condition. She then told me about St. Jude's Hospital. I was told that they did not refuse anyone. I told Jermaine immediately. We were so elated because at least we knew that she stood a chance of surviving. I said it to the doctor; they promised they would send a referral.

A few days went by, and to my surprise it was close to Christmas and children were being discharged. We prayed and hoped that Jerodene's name was on the list, who by then, was able to walk again, although she was still wearing the catheter and diaper. Regardless of the challenges we faced, we were glad she was still with us. The jam-packed ward became partially empty. Two days before Christmas 2015, our relatives called and invited us to a Christmas dinner at my brother's house in St. Catherine. We asked the doctors if they could give us a one-day discharge for Christmas Day. We were overjoyed knowing that Jerodene would get the chance to see her brother who was still in St. Ann with my brother and his wife. Unfortunately, my dad, Anthony, and my adopted brother, Melbourne, were not able to attend since they had another engagement. Jermaine, my brother, Ryan, and his wife came along with Rasheed; my mom and aunt came as well. We had a wonderful Christmas dinner. We laughed, joked, and had a lot of fun. We wished that day would not end but all good things must come to an end. The day after Christmas we were asked to return to the hospital by 5:00 p.m. When my brother took us back to the hospital, Jerodene cried because she did not want to go back into the hospital. She really enjoyed her time with her brother, Rasheed and cousin, Xariah. I had to console her and told her that she would get the chance to see them again soon.

## *Life At The Hospital*

I had to make a personal shower roster because there was only one bathroom to facilitate all the parents on all three wards. At times, I would go in the early mornings to beat the crowd.

Sometimes, though, there would be a long queue, so I had to get used to that situation. That was nothing anyone wanted to get used to. During the days at the hospital, I would go to a nearby restaurant to purchase meals. I used to purchase enough to share for Jerodene and myself, since Jerodene would complain that the hospital meals were not tasty.

The day before my birthday, I sat on the ward verandah, since I had nothing to do at the time. The lady I mentioned before, whose child was on bed 20, was seated there on the bench. I introduced myself to her. She told me her name was Janet. We started a conversation sharing our children's illnesses and that was when I learnt that her child's name was Jada. A few minutes later, I heard her on the telephone calling relatives asking them to donate blood for Jada because she needed blood. I listened to her conversation but behaved as if I was not.

The following day, I saw her again on my 31st birthday. I told her *"Whenever it is someone's birthday, we are all anticipating gifts from friends and family"*. She smiled but I could see the pain behind her smile. She replied, *"Of course"*. I then told her, *"Today is my birthday and I am about to give"*. She looked at me in confusion, then asked, *"What are you talking about?"* It was at that time I told her that I was going to the blood lab to donate some blood for her daughter, Jada. Tears of joy fell from her eyes knowing that a total stranger was going the extra mile to do such a generous act. She told me thanks about a million times. I went to the lab, and they tested my blood count to see if I was eligible. As nervous as I was, I felt so happy within myself, because if Jerodene was in that same situation, I would have wanted someone to donate for her. Since that day Janet and I became very good friends and so did Jerodene and Jada. Sometimes when Jerodene was bored, she would get a chair and sit at Jada's bedside and vice versa, while they played on their tablets.

Jermaine was not able to visit us as often as he would have loved to due to the distance. He, however, would come as often as possible. He had to work and would send money to my account whenever I would run low on cash. It was very costly being at the hospital, but there was no way I would have left Jerodene's side, and I did not know how long we would be there. Gradually, Jerodene improved, and we truly gave God the glory.

Whenever supplies such as toiletries and snacks for Jerodene ran low, I would ask a nurse to watch her so that I could go to Papine to do a little shopping. Likewise, if Janet ran out of stuff, she gave me money to do a little shopping for her or vice versa. If both girls were joyful and in high spirits, we both would run a quick errand. Other parents were there as well but Janet and I grew very close.

As 2015 ended, unfortunately Jerodene and I knew that we would spend the start of the New Year in the hospital. I did not mind though; we only needed to know that Jerodene was doing better than when we first arrived. She got more frustrated as the days went by. She wanted to know when she would be able to go home and when she would be out of the catheter and the diaper. Sadly, I was unable to answer those questions and the doctors were also unable to say because it would take some time for her to be stabilised. We prayed and waited for the day to hear that we were discharged. As the months passed, patients were discharged and readmitted and we were still there. It was difficult to deal with. Jerodene grew even more frustrated.

## Release For Home

January 2016 went by quickly and then came February when we began to hear positive news that we could be going home within a few days. I was so happy that I shared the good news with Jerodene and her dad because I was overly excited and could not keep it to myself. After a few days, we got discharged and we were ecstatic. Words could not express the joy! When Jerodene was discharged, she still had the catheter in and was still wearing a diaper. Jerodene did not mind because she just wanted to go home to her family. We packed our stuff and left. Our home was two hours away, so we had to move as quickly as possible when we got downtown Kingston, Jamaica. We headed to the bus park. We hurried because night was fast approaching. While we were only a few minutes away from the bus park, Jerodene was dragging behind. I got upset because we had no time to waste. She then pulled her hand out of mine, so I turned around to see what was happening. Before I could utter a word to her, I saw her looking to the skies. Her mouth was moving, but I could not hear what she was saying. I told her to speak louder because I was not hearing what she was saying. She then said, *"Mommy I am not talking to you."* I started to consider that no one was close by so who could she be speaking to? I then saw her close her eyes and started to pray. Her prayer was *"Oh God, thank you for letting me get discharged. Oh God, thank you for allowing me to go home to my family. God, you are the best yaw man"*. I got emotional hearing that prayer, because of all the times she has prayed, I never heard her pray like that before. That child was truly special. She really knew how to express her feelings to God. By the time we got to the bus park, there was only one bus with one seat. I gladly went in and carried Jerodene on my lap. About halfway through the journey, Jerodene started complaining that she was feeling nauseous. I hurriedly took out a plastic bag from her handbag in time for her to throw up. The entire journey was very rough for Jerodene because she vomited quite a few times. We got home after 8:00 p.m. but we thanked God that we got home safely.

It felt good to be home. For the past few months, we were not able to sleep in our own beds and it felt great. A few days later, we sent for Rasheed so he could be with his sister. They were so happy to see each other; it had been a few months since they last saw each other. They played a lot and had lots of fun. Jerodene learnt a few things based on how often they did a full body examination when she was admitted, and she was demonstrating on Rasheed. Rasheed cried because he grew frustrated with what his sister was doing. He probably felt like he was being punished. Within a few weeks, it was the Easter holidays and Jermaine went shopping. He wanted to know that we had enough bun and cheese to last for the rest of the holiday. That was the children' favourite. As the holiday was coming to an end, we planned to send Jerodene back to school. A few days before school reopened, I received a call that I was not expecting, not even in a thousand years. The news was that Jerodene's Principal was just murdered, the same lady whom Jerodene loved and spoke of so dearly. Oh God, seriously? As tears rolled down my face, and I screamed out, Jerodene came asking, *"Mommy what's wrong?"* I just told her that I received some bad news. "How could I explain to her what I just heard?" I asked myself. I knew that I did not want her to hear otherwise. Jermaine was at work, so I called him and told him, and we both had the same concern. This Principal, Ms. Anderson, Jerodene loved her so much, and we decided not to tell her until when we deemed it was the right time.

Jerodene was looking forward to going back, so a few days went by and eventually we broke the news to her. And just as we thought, she did not take it well. She had so many questions. *"Mommy, why was she murdered? Daddy, who did it? Why would someone kill my principal?"* Her eyes became red, and her tears flowed uncontrollably. We were then informed that the entire staff, students, and parents would be getting a series of counselling. Our other concern was that Jerodene would be travelling in a taxi to and from school, where passengers would be discussing the terrible occurrence. It was on everybody's lips! Jerodene was looking forward to going back to school but not in a manner like this. She eventually resumed school, but things were not the same and would never be the same.

We planned to send Rasheed to stay with my mom and dad whenever Jerodene was readmitted. That way, my parents and my brother, Melbourne and his wife, Kemarie could share in babysitting. It was their pleasure to have him. He was very quiet.

After the Easter holidays, Jerodene had to stay home for a few days. We did not plan to send her to school while she was still wearing the catheter and diaper, especially wearing her uniform. By then, her legs were scarred because we had to keep switching legs to give the legs intermittent rest. Her legs were bruised, and we had to buy an ointment to soothe them. Even though her brother was home with her she was not happy. The situation of her not having any feelings in her bladder area was taking a toll on her. She cried almost every day. Asking me *"why her?"* She said to us that *"I am not happy because all of my friends were going to school, and I had to stay home"*. She said, *"All my friends are happy, and I am not"*. Jermaine and I were broken especially when she asked us *"Why her?"* We had no answer for her questions.

  I vividly remember one day when we were at home. Jerodene was seated on her bed; as she daydreamed, tears rolled down her cheeks, so I turned to her and asked, *"Jero what is the matter?"* She cried harder and said, *"Mommy you wouldn't want to know. When will I be going back to school?"* Honestly, I could not hold back the tears that day. I then said to her, *"Jerodene you won't be able to go to school now. Remember you are wearing diaper and the catheter"*. She then said to me, *"Mommy, please send me to school and put diaper and wipes in my bag, because teacher will clean me when I pass my stool and she will empty the urine bag."* As emotional as I got, it really dawned on me how unpredictable life could be. A child who was born healthy and in good condition was now basically back to baby stage. How worse could this get? As soon as her dad got home, I told him. He said if she insisted then we should let her go. He did not want her to be home worrying only for things to get worst. Shortly after, I called her teacher and told her. I explained everything to her. She told me that we should send her. I knew we had to forgo the uniform tunic and allow her to wear pants with the blouse. By then, most of her outfits included pants, to include her nightwear. Therefore, instead of her sleeping in her girlie nighties, she had to be sleeping in pyjamas. In the decision to send her back to school, pants were the obvious choice to continue to disguise the catheter. We knew that Jerodene would not mind because the most important thing to her was that she was going to school. Sometimes Jerodene's blood count would be lower than normal, making her susceptible to bacteria; therefore, the recommendation was for her to wear a mask to school.

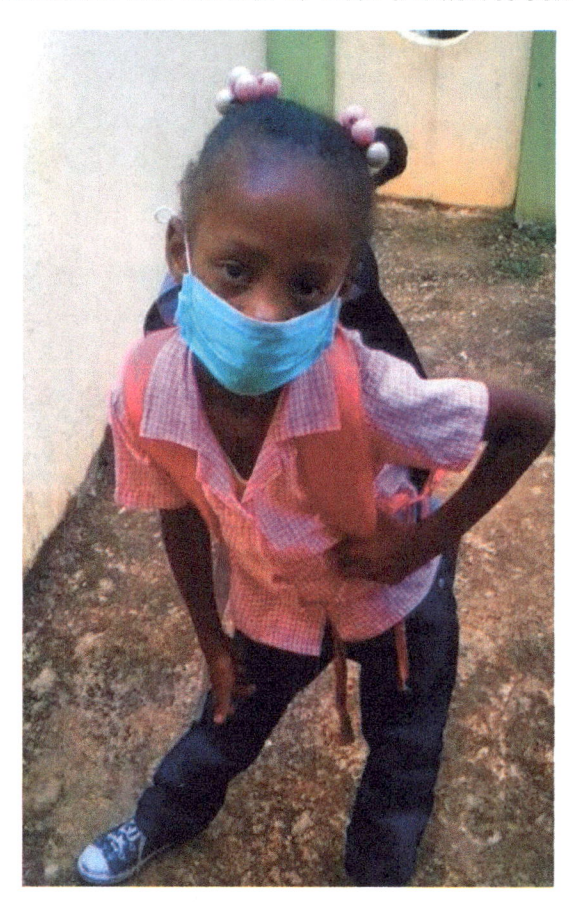

Her teacher had to change her sometimes twice a day and the urine bag was emptied multiple times. On a few occasions, she would come home from school with the bag filled to the point where she would struggle over the hill to get to the house. She came home one day and told me that it seemed as if she had passed her stool and a student shouted out *"I smell faeces"*. She said she felt bad knowing that it could be her, but she had to act as if she knew nothing about what the other students were talking about.

*Readmission*

A few weeks went by and again it was time for readmission. We carried out our plans regarding Rasheed. We journeyed out very early on a Monday morning. When we reached downtown Kingston, Jerodene and I headed to another taxi stand to get a taxi that would take us directly to the Hospital. A few metres away from the taxi stand, there came a vendor walking with her goods to sell, she then bumped into Jerodene because she did not see her. Jerodene then cried out, **"Miss, you hit me with your box"**. The lady then looked and saw Jerodene with her mask over her nose and mouth. The lady then burst into tears when she noticed that Jerodene was ill. She then hugged Jerodene and apologised to her, telling her that the next time she was passing that same spot then she would have a gift for her. When we got to the Hospital a few rounds of chemotherapy were administered, after reading about the side effects of the chemo treatment. The hardest one that hit me was the fact that Jerodene would experience hair loss. How did I not know that? I thought to myself, *"This does not get easier, does it? Another hurdle for us to jump. How do we take the first attempt? A beautiful little girl, with such shiny lovely hair, how do we break it to her? How do we tell her that within a few months she won't have a strand of hair on her head?"* That was another hard task for us. When we broke the devastating news to her, she cried openly, **"Why mommy? Why? Why this have to happen to me?"** She cried as if there was no tomorrow. We tried to comfort her the best way we knew how. We told her that she would look even more beautiful. She told us that it was not true and she was going to look like a boy. We then realised we were not able to answer all of her questions. So Jermaine and I decided we might have to get professional counselling for her and also for us as parents. We never knew how much it would help but we knew that to some extent it would. Jermaine was better at dealing with the situation than I was. On our way back home, Jerodene remembered the vendor's promise so we stopped to speak to the lady. The lady's face lit up when she saw Jerodene, she then hugged Jerodene and handed her a necklace. Jerodene told her thanks and was excited to show it to her dad.

## *Professional Counselling*

Upon our next hospital visit, I mentioned to the doctor that Jerodene's principal was murdered and the situation about her losing her hair. The doctor then told me that there was an office on property that deals with trauma and grief counselling. We made an appointment there and were anticipating the results to come from the counselling process. We were happy when we were advised about the service because it was well needed. Within a few days, the lump that was on her chest disappeared, just as I saw in my dream, it was no longer there. I was so excited to tell Jermaine the good news. When I told him, he started thanking God for healing our daughter. That hospital stay was short in comparison to the previous one. We went home within a short period.

## *Principal's Funeral*

Around that time, it was time for her principal's funeral. Initially, we did not plan to take Jerodene because we believed it would have been difficult for her to handle. However, after a while we decided to take her. Without saying anything to Jerodene, I decided that I would not let her look at the principal. When we got to the funeral, her best friend, Raheem, was there along with his mother. Jerodene's good friend, Tyreka and her sister were also there. They were all happy to see each other in one place. When it was time for the viewing of the body, they wanted Jerodene to go with them to look. I told them no. Jerodene then started to cry and asked, **"Mommy why did you take me to her funeral if you know that you were not going to make me look at her?"** I considered the possibility that seeing her principal may help her get closure and therefore allowed her to go. I was happy that she looked at her because she only spoke of her a few times.

## *Infrequent Church Attendance*

As a Christian family, we were active in church, but since Jerodene's illness we were unable to go as regularly as we were accustomed to, due to her long stay in hospital. We knew that God understood.

## *Pleasant Surprise - Dream Weekend*

A few weeks later, we received a call from Mrs. Hanson of the Optimist Club in Mandeville, Jamaica. She advised us that our family of four was selected to go on a dream weekend to Moon Palace, Ocho Rios, Jamaica with other families whose children were diagnosed with cancer. That was the best news Jerodene heard in a long time and what made it better was that the hotel they were taking us to was my previous place of work. As parents, we were happy too and decided that we would all make full use of the opportunity to relax.

At the time we received the news, Jerodene was admitted. We had to seek permission from the medical team for Jerodene to go. They told us that if she was not admitted at the time of scheduled visit, she could go but if she was admitted she would not be able to go. Thankfully, when time came she was not admitted, and we were able to go. Oh what an experience it was! It was a memorable one, one etched in history. We had a fabulous time! Jerodene and Rasheed made full use of the children's club and the waterslides. We went on the glass bottom boat ride among many other activities. When it was time to go home, yes, you guessed it, they did not want to go. However, we promised Jerodene that we would save some money, with a lot of hard work and then we would be able to make another trip. We said that in faith because we did not know when that would be. Even though Jerodene still had the catheter in and was wearing diapers, she had a lot of fun, she did not let that hold her back.

*Back In Hospital*

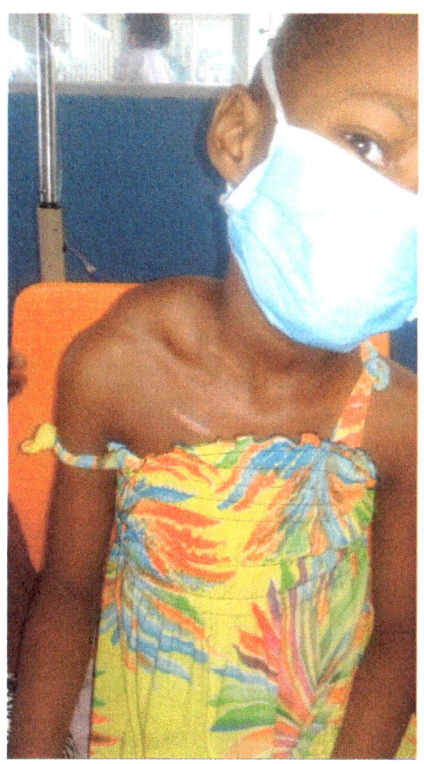

Within a few weeks we were back in the hospital for more chemo treatment and at that time I showed the doctors that Jerodene had a larger lump on her right shoulder, close to her neck. They said that was a matter of concern and only the chemotherapy would get rid of it. Unfortunately, it was larger than the one that was on her chest.

Jerodene was happy that her stays at the hospital were not as long as previous visits. Our next appointment was on a Friday and when we went, they gave her the treatment and she tolerated it well. We were so happy because we got the chance to see Janet and Jada. We spoke for a short while and then I told Jada that I wished she would get well soon. She responded with a little smile because she was not well.

## Homeward Bound

Before we left the hospital, the nurse changed the catheter and told me it had to be changed regularly because she could develop an infection over a period of time. I was happy that she told me so that I could ensure it was changed on every visit. By the time we got home the unthinkable happened, the catheter fell out. We had to rush her to the hospital, closest to us, in order for them to replace it. By the following day, I received a text message that Jada passed on. The phone fell out of my hand and immediately I burst out in tears. I could not control the tears because we had developed a bond that no one could come between. It was hard for me to tell Jerodene but I had to because she would eventually hear. When I told her, she did not take it well but we knew that the ongoing counselling that she was getting would help.

I did not want to imagine what Janet was going through having lost her child to a terminal disease. That must have been a harsh reality to face. What does one tell another parent in a situation like that especially when it is your child? Are there words to console them? I could only imagine the hurt and pain she must have been going through. We prayed for her and asked that God would give her the strength because I knew she had some very rough days ahead. On the day of the funeral, Jerodene was not admitted so I got the chance to go pay my last respects to my friend's daughter.

## *Jerodene's 1st Graduation*

A few weeks went by and Jerodene's graduation was drawing closer. Jerodene was in high spirits because it would have been her first graduation. Even though she was absent from school for quite a while, she was still looking forward to graduation. However, a few days before, she became sick. She had a very high fever. At one point, Jermaine and I had to submerge her into cold water since the fever was 105°, which was very high. We barely slept that night because Jerodene was not coping well and we had to take turns sponging her down. It was as if she was roasting from head to toes. We called my mom and other relatives and asked for prayers on Jerodene's behalf. At one point, we thought she would not be able to attend graduation. The situation got us really frustrated because there was no improvement. We did not know what else to do as we looked at each other in despair. With just a day before the graduation, my Mom came to our house and decided to put this fever and illness away once and for all. The night before the fever had gotten so high that she cried so hard when we submerged her into the cold water. She cried **"Daddy I am cold, I am cold"**. She cried helplessly with her teeth gnashing against each other. We felt sorry for her but we had no choice. When our mom got there, Jerodene was just lying there on the bed. Mom started praying endlessly. She also brought her bottle of consecrated olive oil. We agreed in prayer, believing God on Jerodene's behalf. That night was the best one that we had over the few days she was ill. God really heard our prayers and petitions. By the following morning, Jerodene was a totally different person. The fever was gone and thank God she was able to go to her graduation. Upon arrival at the graduation ceremony, parents, children, teachers, and visitors were all so happy to see her. Most people encouraged her to continue fighting and that God would make her victorious.

My parents and one of Jermaine's cousins, Everton, were at the graduation. My sister, Romayne, from overseas really wanted to be there but unfortunately she was unable to attend but promised Jerodene that as soon as possible she would pay her a visit. Soon, it was time for the handing out of certificates and presentations. When her name was called everyone cheered and gave her a standing ovation, everyone knew all that she had gone through for the past few months.

Everyone was happy for her and cheered her on. Jerodene felt so happy, she was all smiles. Before the graduation was over, they called her in front of the audience and collected donations on her behalf towards her medical expenses. We were very grateful. They then joined in prayer for her. We knew the importance of prayer and so did Jerodene.

After graduation, Jerodene's countenance changed from happy to sad. She was very moody. She did not want to take any family pictures. We asked her what the problem was, but she refused to answer. However, she could not hold it any longer. She burst into tears saying that, **"I am sad because I only got one certificate and my friends got a lot"**. We understood how she felt but there was nothing that we could do. She really took it hard. Her dad tried to console her but it was not easy. It took her days to get over the sadness she felt. Overall, graduation was wonderful, but it was not the same as previous years since the Principal, Ms. Anderson was absent but we were sure she was there in spirit. She was sadly missed.

*Readmission Again*

Jerodene was again admitted and by that time they were having many issues finding her veins. Jerodene, who in the past had no problem with injections, was afraid. It became a nightmare. She began hiding whenever it was time to change the IV. Sometimes even after 10 attempts no vein could be found. I have been in the treatment room on several occasions and seen her cry so much.

It hurt knowing that there was nothing that I could do. Parents were only allowed in the treatment room under certain circumstances. Jerodene was always strong and she fought with all her might. At times, several doctors had to hold her still in the treatment room in order to locate a vein.

As time went by, she was admitted for longer periods at a time. The treatments lasted for five or more days and before we knew it, Jerodene started having vaginal infections. Infections occurred one after the other and caused her 4-5 days chemo treatment to turn into weeks and sometimes months. Even through all of that, Jerodene was determined and told me that she was not going to give up. She had so much resilience. Through it all, Jerodene was a fighter and a very brave one too. With the infection issues, they had to give her multiple antibiotics before treatment could be given and that resulted in more frustration.

### *The Little Prayer Warrior*

Jerodene always loved church since she was a young child. As soon as she was discharged from the hospital, the first thing she would mention was her going to church. We were not always able to go because she only had one ankle length dress and since she was still wearing the catheter that always posed a problem. In spite of all of that, Jerodene always had a testimony and people were always happy to hear her testify that God had healed her from stage 4 cancer. She always testified with authority and power just like her dad always told her to.

*God Be Praised, The Surgery Was Done*

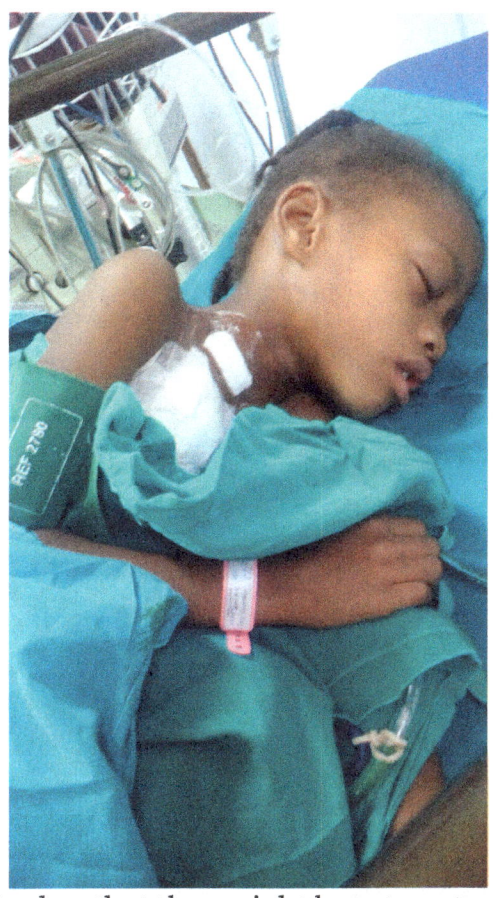

In 2016, the doctors advised us that they might have to put a chemotherapy port in Jerodene and that would lessen the needle jabs and the torture she was going through. They gave us a prescription and told us that there was a specific place in Half-Way-Tree, Kingston, where we would be able to purchase it. We inquired and the cost was close to J$50,000.00. *"Oh my God, were we hearing correctly? Where would we get all that money?"* we asked each other. We were at home one day when I received a text from the family who gave us the bed back in 2015. They were asking about Jerodene's health etc. I then told them about the prescription for the port and they told us not to worry about it because they would stand the cost of financing the port. We were so relieved because that was a ton of weight off our shoulders. Within a few weeks, the surgery was done and we were very happy because the process would become better for Jerodene. The port used a specific needle and for each admission there was a new needle. They cost a little less than J$2,000.00. We were able to buy one at a time and sometimes three depending on our finances at the time. At times, relatives from overseas would send us money to help with Jerodene's medical expenses, when we fell short. Sometimes, we took on the financial struggles on our own.

## *Help From Total Strangers*

One day while we were home and did not have any money, we got an unexpected call. I have a friend, Neiko, whom I met on Facebook (he had recently lost his beautiful wife to cancer). He has a kind heart and is so selfless. A while after he lost his wife, he called me and told me that I should expect a call anytime soon from persons who wanted to help us financially. That day, the call came. The person on the other end identified herself as Patrice and told me she got my number from Neiko and that she heard about Jerodene through him. She said she and her sister, Andrea have never gone through my situation but they empathise with me and my husband. We spoke for a while and I started to share some of Jerodene's testimonies with her and she was blessed. She then told me that they were willing to help with Jerodene's medical expenses (by then Jerodene's hospital bill was very high) and tears started rolling down my face while I was giving praises to God. They could not have known how happy and relieved we were. I told her thanks, on behalf of my husband and I. We were really appreciative of the gesture. They sent the money shortly after. We were able to pay a part for the medical bills and the rest was used to buy the chemo drug. From that day Patrice and her sister Andrea became our friends.

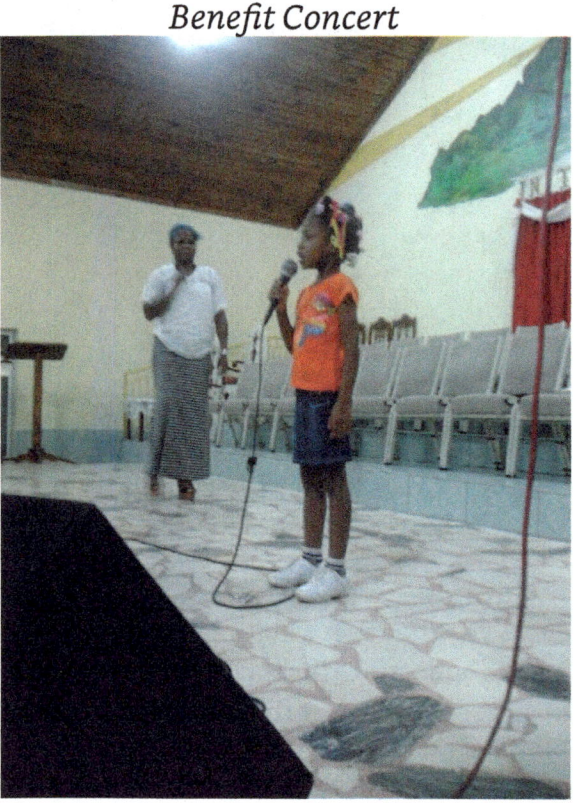

## Benefit Concert

We hosted a gospel concert in Kellits, Clarendon that featured the Kazak Ministry from Ocho Rios. This concert was a fund-raising event to help with Jerodene's medical expenses. Each time that we went to the hospital, the bill assessor would walk the ward and present us with our bill. Jerodene's favourite song was "Nobody Greater" by Vashawn Mitchell, a song I taught her. It was a bit challenging for her to learn and sing the song, but she pulled through and delivered in front of a large audience of family members, friends and strangers. They all attended to hear Jerodene pray and encourage others. Kimoy May and Shaurna-Kay Christian drove from Spanish Town, which was almost two hours' drive from the venue. They were happy that they were able to attend and so was I. They told me they would not have missed the event for anything. The concert was not well attended but the people who went really enjoyed themselves. For those who never met her before had the golden opportunity to at the concert.

## Back To School Preparations

September 2016 was fast approaching and we had already made the necessary preparations for her to go to a new school. At that time, Rasheed was two years old. We asked the dressmaker to make her uniform a little longer than usual because of the catheter. We also asked her to make the bloomers a little longer than the ordinary. Jermaine and I decided that we would send Rasheed to a daycare on a daily basis so that I would be able to accompany Jerodene to school and stay with her. I planned to take the necessary diaper and wipes to clean her and empty her urine bag. Bear in mind that she would be moving into Grade 1. We were very excited because Jerodene was about to climb another milestone in her life. She was very brilliant.

Unfortunately Jerodene was not able to commence her new school because upon admission she started to spike a high fever. When they checked her temperature, it was 102°. She was not the jovial, happy child that we all knew. It was obvious that she was not feeling well. The doctors ordered a urine test and culture, the results showed that she had another vaginal infection due to the wearing of the catheter. That time, they had to prescribe stronger antibiotics because it was occurring too often.

## *Making Friends*

A few days before school began Jerodene was admitted for more chemo treatment. Based on our calculation of the days, we knew that she would have gotten discharged by the first day of school. At that time, I met another lady by the name of Dainia along with her daughter, Jhordania. It was unfortunate the way we met, under circumstances like that. She became a very good friend of mine since Janet left. Dainia and I connected soon after we met and so did Jerodene and Jhordania. They had so much in common. They both loved the same cartoon character. At times, one would see both of them in their beds and having their imaginary phone calls and playing with the doll house. Hospital became home for us. They had to make do with what they had in order to not get bored. Sometimes their blood count got so low that they were told to wear masks. As close as they were, they were not allowed to touch or play with each other as they normally would. Dainia and I are Christians; we cried, laughed and prayed together, acknowledging the power of prayer. As rough as our situations were, our children being diagnosed with critical illnesses, we still had to encourage each other when the doctors would come with sad news.

## *One Of Jerodene's Healing Experiences*

I remember clearly when we went in for that admission, I took 15 diapers with us and after a few days during the 14 days of antibiotics she said to me, *"Mommy, please don't put any diaper on me"*. I looked at her in awe knowing that she could not do without them. I then said to her, *"why would you say that?"* She then said, *"Because I can feel when I want to pass my stool"*. I was so happy that the urge was back and could not wait to tell Jermaine the good news. I then told her that the same God that helped her to get that feeling back was the same God who would allow her to regain the urge to urinate again. She nodded her head and said, *"I believe you Mom, I believe."* She called her dad and told him, his response was a big *"Hallelujah"* then he started thanking God. Her dad had planned to visit her the following day, surprisingly, he came that same day. She was overjoyed to see him and he brought her favourite hot and spicy KFC chicken. He stayed with us for a few hours and then left to get back home before dark.

## *Jerodene Loved By One And All*

By that time, all the nurses had gotten to know Jerodene and most of the doctors as well. However, because the doctors were on rotation every month, they only spent a short time on the ward. They all loved Jerodene. If she was ever missing, one could check the nurses' or doctors' station or even in the doctors' office to find her. She was also learning a lot as time went by. I was fortunate to have caught her on camera giving one of the doctors a massage. She was having a lot of fun even though she was not well. Jerodene got along basically with everybody, both young and old.

## *Jerodene Made Another Friend*

Her youngest friend was merely one year old. They met one day, when the doctors sent us to another hospital to do an echocardiogram test, while we were in the ambulance. That was when they became friends. The little girl played with Jerodene's necklace as we journeyed to and from the hospital. Over a period of time, Jerodene and the little girl became very close. Sometimes, Jerodene would ask my permission to go to visit her by the side room. The toddler was also battling a critical illness and as friends they planned to fight with all their might.

## *That Unexpected Call*

Getting discharged was our happiest moment. September 2016 was Childhood Cancer Awareness Month. After we were discharged and on our way home, I received a call from the Oncologist, Dr. Reece-Mills, from the hospital. She told me about Childhood Cancer Awareness month and that Kerlyn Brown from a popular television station wanted to interview families of children who were diagnosed with cancer. Knowing Jerodene's personality, she thought it was a good idea for us to do the interview, so she called to find out if it was okay for her to give Kerlyn Brown my telephone number. Without hesitation I gladly said *"yes"* remembering that we tried to get her before but it did not work out.

Jermaine was very overjoyed to hear the news. Within a few days, my phone rang and on the other end of the line was Kerlyn Brown. I felt so privileged to hear from her. She made my day. A date was set at the same time and happily Jerodene was not in hospital. Prior to the interview day, Kerlyn had asked me to find out from Jerodene what made her sad. Jerodene told me that the catheter made her sad and she did not want anyone to know about it. I told her that even though it was just Auntie Kerlyn and her cameraman who were going to be there, she should not mention anything about it because her story was going to be aired on television.

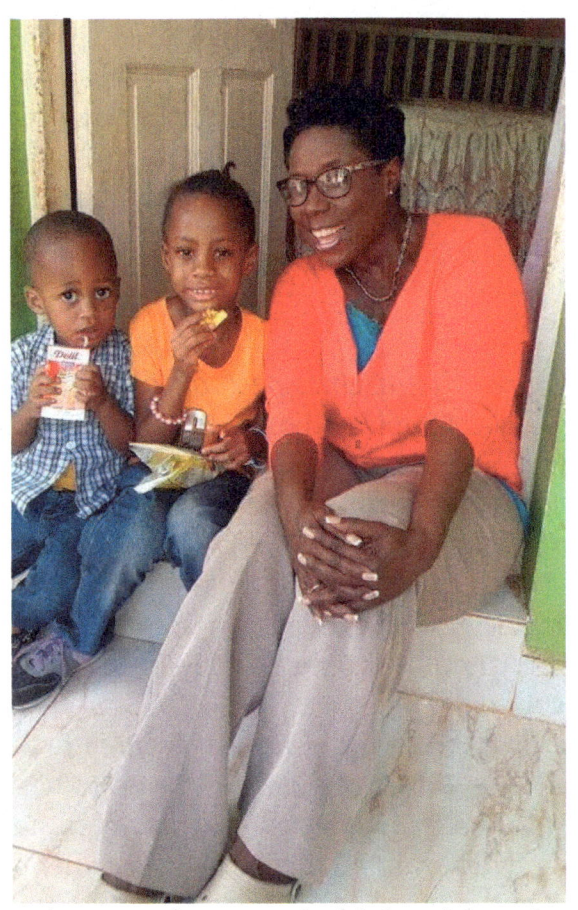

On the day of the interview, Jerodene was in high spirits. She was happy and bubbly, you name it! We were all excited to meet Kerlyn Brown and hosting her in our own home was a pleasure. It was a very successful interview and Jerodene really enjoyed showing her books, toys and talking about her diagnosis. Jerodene also prayed at the end of the interview. The prayer really touched Kerlyn's heart. She was stunned to know that a six year old was able to pray such a powerful prayer. We all got emotional, including the cameraman. A part of her prayer was that she wanted God to heal all the children who were diagnosed with cancer and she wanted them to be healed the same way God was healing her. A few days after our interview was aired on CVM television station, Jerodene was excited to see herself on television. She screamed for joy knowing that all of her friends were going to see her.

Her name was on almost everybody's lips. Persons who were not able to watch her on television were able to do so on social media. By then, other videos were placed on Facebook and people began to follow her on her journey. Even when she went on the road, people were excited and overjoyed to see her. She was a sassy little princess, people really loved her and were drawn to her because of her warrior spirit.

## *Another Encounter*

During the time when Jerodene was still getting chemotherapy treatment, we found out that Rasheed, who was then two years old, had a lump on the side of his neck. That was one of the scariest things that could have ever happened. Knowing that Jerodene's diagnosis all started with a lump, my mind was all over the place. I wanted to scream my heart out. We then mentioned it to our relatives and everyone was in disbelief. We prayed and hoped for the best. We knew that he would eventually have to go to see a Paediatrician but I knew I would not be able to take him. I could not manage anything else. *"Not another one Lord. Not another one"*. The Lord knew how our hearts felt. He knew what the outcome would have been. Time was moving swiftly and we could not delay. Jermaine then told me that I would have to take him to see the doctor. I prayed and hoped that he was not serious. He was. I felt as if I was about to pass out. I literally cried before I left the house to go see the doctor not knowing what the outcome would be. When I went to their Paediatrician, she sent Rasheed to do some blood tests. All of them came back okay. The doctor then advised us that Rasheed was well. We lifted our hands to God and thanked Him for the diagnosis.

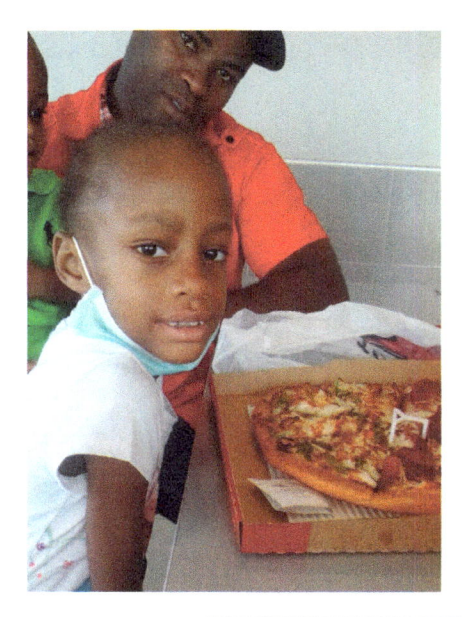

## *A Celebratory Mood*

The same day that Rasheed did the blood tests we remembered vividly because it was also Jerodene's 6th birthday. We took them to Pizza Hut in Mandeville, Jamaica for a treat and bought her a birthday cake. We met some people from overseas, who saw Jerodene with the mask covering her nose and mouth, and then they asked us what was wrong with her. After we told them, they prayed for her and gave her US$40. That was a happy day for us because we were in a celebratory mood. Jermaine then took us to the photo studio where we did a few family pictures. Those photographs have been framed and are on display to date. Those we will have for a lifetime. We enjoyed our time at home. One late night, Jermaine had to charter a taxi to the hospital because the catheter slipped out again. It really got frustrating for Jerodene especially but we tried to encourage her as each day went by. We told her that it would not be like that always.

## *Admitted Again*

In October 2016, there we were again packed and heading back to the hospital for another round of chemotherapy treatment. By then, they found out that she still had the infection on and off but it was not as serious as previous times. Sometimes, the scent of the urine was bad when I had to empty the bag. I could smell the antibiotics in her urine. On one or two occasions, the bag was not screwed tightly enough and the urine drained on the hem of her pants foot causing her to feel uncomfortable.

She looked at me one day while she was in pain and told me that *"Mommy it's not what the doctors say, and at the end of the day it is what God says."* She was just very mature for her age, and she knew exactly what she was talking about. As time went by, Jerodene found new friends, mainly nurses, doctors and even the student doctors. They loved and cared for her dearly. They would spoil her on numerous occasions - taking her sweets, cupcakes and all those treats. She was loved and great care was given to her.

*Jerodene's #1 Cheerleader*

On several occasions, Jerodene got a lot of visitors but her dad was her number one favourite. She got visits from other relatives and friends, including Josh and Daniel, whose parents and I are very good friends. When her dad came to visit, she would take him to the nurses and doctors station for a short introduction. Then she would spend the rest of the time cuddling in his arms because she wanted to tell him everything that took place while he was away. Besides Jerodene's dad, she really enjoyed when her brother and grandad would come to visit her at the hospital. They both cried when it was time for Rasheed to leave so we always assured them that they'd see each other soon.

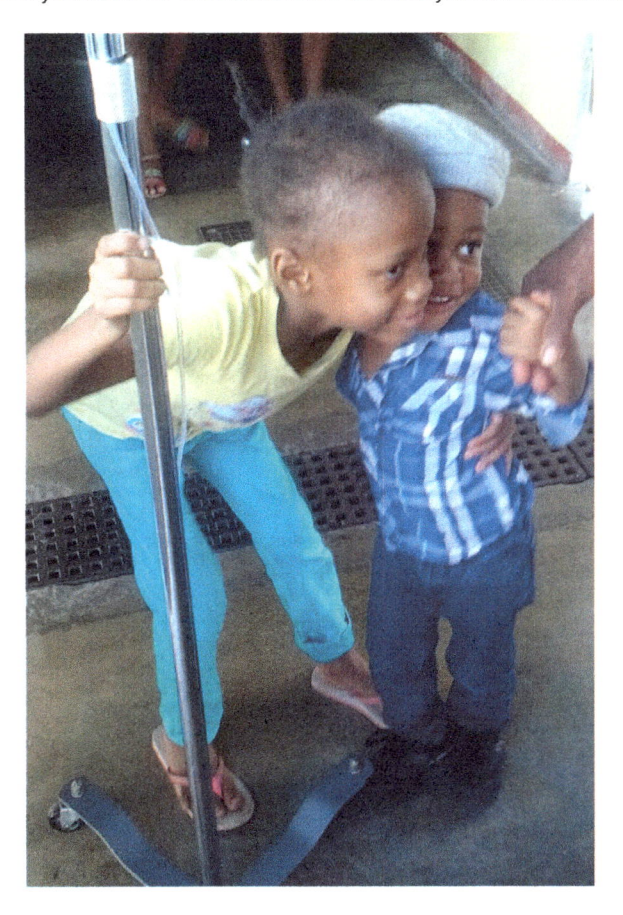

*Faith In Action*

While she was in the hospital in October 2016, I remembered that the November that followed would have made it one year since Jerodene had been wearing the catheter. I was praying that it would not make it to one year. I remember telling a female doctor that I was praying that Jerodene would not continue wearing the catheter as we approached the one year mark. In a few days, the thought came to me that I should find out from the doctors and nurses if it was a possibility for them to teach me how to 'pass the catheter'. By then her 14 days of antibiotics treatment was coming to an end. Due to the fact that she was going to get discharged soon and to lessen her risk of getting more infections, I thought that would have been the right thing. When I asked one of the nurses, she told me that she would have to get permission from the doctor before she could give me the go ahead. I waited patiently for the answer. Knowing how much we had gone through with her at home while wearing the catheter, on numerous occasions we had to charter a taxi to rush her to Mandeville Hospital in the late hours of the night because the catheter would often fall out, causing her lots of pain. If they would give me the chance to learn how to do it, I could help Jerodene better.

*YESSSSS!!! God Did It Again*

Eventually, the nurses agreed to teach me how to 'pass the catheter' and the lesson began immediately. It was an easy task for me because I saw them do it multiple times before. I was very happy. The following day was October 2, 2016 and we were scheduled to get discharged within a few days. Before we were sent home, I was given a box with all things needed for the procedure to be carried out successfully at home. They gave the correct size catheter, betadine, sterile gloves, gauze, gel et cetera. They also gave me a specific catheter (the in/out) and told me that during the nights we should let her sleep in the regular catheter but we should just use the in/out one during the days. I was cautioned to always remember that it was a sterile procedure, we did not want any recurrence of infections.

We went home on the last day in October. Immediately, I washed my hands and got sterile, then I deflated the catheter that she had in. She was so happy and felt as free as a bird. She jumped and screamed for a long while telling me that she felt free as if she was out of bondage. She rushed to get her prettiest dress that she had not worn for almost a year because it was shorter than where the catheter was. She rolled and split on the bed because she was so happy she could not control herself.

A few hours went by and at about 5:00 p.m., Jerodene called me and said *"Mommy please come and catheterize me now because I am afraid that my belly would start to hurt me again"*. I went to get my hands washed. I laid out all the items needed to do the procedure. I washed my hands again then followed the instructions given to me. After draining her bladder, she resumed playing with her brother whom she missed a lot. About two hours later, her dad came home from work and we were all at home. I was on the telephone with my aunt when Jerodene came to tell me that she was ready to go to bed. She asked if I could come and replace the catheter and I should remember what the nurse told me (she should have it in for the entire night). I then told her that I was on a call and that I would be with her shortly. During that time she was listening to Glacia Robinson's testimony (the curse of death) on her dad's phone and she lifted her faith to God and shouted on top of her lungs. If Glacia shouted Jesus 10 times, Jerodene did the same with authority and power. When Glacia said, "I don't need a wheelchair anymore", Jerodene shouted, *"I don't need a catheter anymore"*, again with more power and authority! She began shouting for a period of time, calling on the name of Jesus telling him thanks for healing her. I heard her shouting my name very loudly, by then I ended the call that I was on. She shouted *"Mommy!"* again. Then she shouted with excitement *"Mommy I feel something coming down and what I feel is not faeces, it is urine"*. By the time I pulled down her underwear to examine her, her underwear was soaked with urine. Jerodene shouted, jumped and cried tears of joy as her dad and I started worshipping God with her. We were so excited and elated. As my husband and I carried her to the bathroom, she cried out *"Mommy it's my time now! Mommy God decide that it's my time now"*. We did not bother to put her on the toilet seat, we got the potty for her because we really wanted to see with our own eyes. Even when she was on the potty we were all shouting and worshipping God with her. At about 10:00 p.m. when she got off the potty, there was urine. Oh my God, what are we seeing? Within a few hours less than a year, God came through for Jerodene!

We ran up and down, in and out, because we were giving God thanks and praise. There was nothing anyone could have said to make us sad. Rasheed was in his crib at the time when the deliverance took place, he was a little over two years old at the time. As young as he was, he wanted to be giving thanks too; therefore, we had to take him out of the crib. Bless God! That was a wonderful feeling knowing that God still worked miracles especially on our daughter. To God be the glory! We prayed to God and told Him that we did not want the situation to extend to a year. That was a miracle! He came through for us just a few hours before the New Year. Who could it be? We went to church the following day (Sunday) and shared our testimony with the church. The church was on fire when our testimony was shared; everyone was happy to hear.

## *Chemotherapy Not Helping*

We prayed earnestly to God and hoped that she would be taken off the chemo sooner than later. Based on the amount of treatment she got, there should have been some positive results by that time. We were told that Jerodene might have to do some radiation treatment because the chemotherapy treatment was not helping where the tumour was growing on her shoulder. We were sent to do a radiation assessment off the hospital property. We went and did the assessment and I asked the doctor if she was getting back to back chemo treatment and radiation what would be her chance of survival? He told me that it was very slim and that we should prepare ourselves because she would not be making it. *"Oh my God, am I hearing clearly*?" I asked myself. *"Is he talking about my child*?" I asked myself over and over. It really hit me like a ton of bricks but I braced myself and remembered that God was our only source. I also remembered how Jerodene told us that *"It was not what the doctors say, but at the end of the day God has the final say"*.

## *The Frantic Scare*

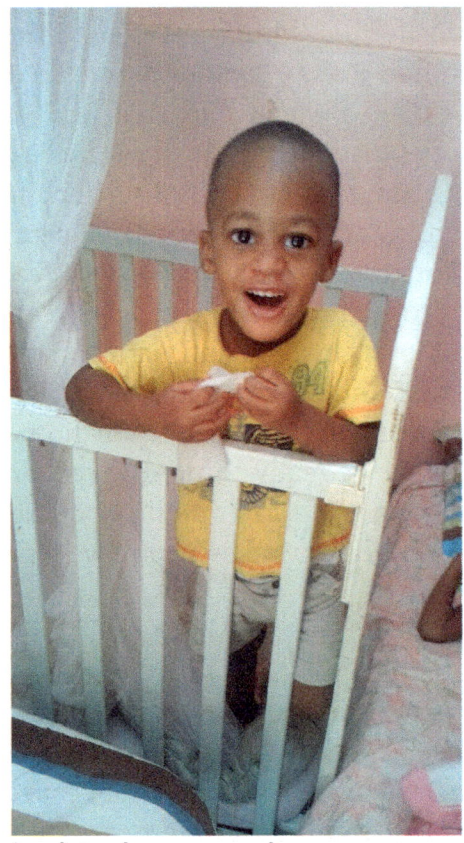

A few days after Jerodene's victorious experience, we were at home, I was in the kitchen, while the children were in our bedroom. I am unable to say what happened but I heard a loud sound, my heart skipped a beat and by the time I rushed in I saw Rasheed on the floor. I grabbed him up in fright, because I was so frightened. My heart felt as if it was pumping through my chest; that was how frightened I was. I called his name but he did not answer. It took a while before he cried out. I felt so helpless and weak not knowing what my next move should be and my husband was not at home. Rasheed started crying, holding onto the side of his head, which was when I realised that he had hit his head. When I told Jermaine, we decided that I should take him to the hospital. Upon arrival at the hospital, I explained what happened. They ordered an x-ray immediately. The results showed that there was a crack on his skull but they said he would not have to do any surgery, but it would eventually heal by itself over a period of time. We were so happy that it was not anything more severe. To God be the glory!

## *Jerodene Losing Her Hair*

Jerodene was out of hospital for a few weeks because her health had greatly improved. She had a bitter/sweet moment because she was out of the hospital, which made her happy but she was sad because her mind was at school instead of her actually being there. We always encouraged her that things would go back to normal soon.

One day while I was washing Jerodene's hair, the unthinkable happened. Jerodene's hair started coming out in patches into my hands. The reality of the side effects of chemotherapy hit me. I wished that I could have put it back in but I just had to face the reality of the situation. When Jerodene saw what had happened she got very angry and started to cry uncontrollably. I knew that this day was going to come, but when it came we were not prepared for it. My mind went blank. I managed to calm her down with a lot of work. I had to use a pair of scissors to cut the rest of her hair to give it a neat look. I am not a barber but I knew that I had to do something. After a few hours, Jermaine came home from work and I was able to tell him what transpired. The unfortunate thing was that it was evident that Jerodene's head was getting bald. It was just a very sad situation and that was the part that we were scared to face.

*Jerodene Accepting Her Hair Loss*

The thought was, do we get a wig made for her? What do we do? We got our relatives involved and the majority said that we should go ahead with the wig. After a while, unfortunately, the rest of her hair fell off. Within a few weeks Jerodene even forgot that her hair was gone. She accepted the situation and often modelled her bald head with her favourite colour headband and until it did not matter to her if she had on a headband or not. She actually told us that she really enjoyed her new look. Her aunt 'Yanto' helped to build her confidence by surprising Jerodene with a selfless act. When she learnt that Jerodene had lost her hair, she went to the barber and cut her hair as well. She told me that she did not want Jerodene to feel alone. One day, Jerodene received a video call from her aunt and oh how excited Jerodene was! She said, *"Aunty Yanto, you did your hair just like mine"*. They both smiled at each other and continued their conversation.

## Christmas 2016

Christmas 2016 was fast approaching and Jerodene was still admitted. We really prayed that she would be discharged by Christmas because we remembered that in 2015 we were admitted at that time as well. Our prayer was for her to be sent home, if it was even for the day. We would have been grateful. Two days before Christmas, I was at the hospital with her and Jermaine had to take Rasheed to my parents' home. I asked one of the nurses to watch Jerodene so I could rush to Papine to pick up some toiletries and a few snacks for her. When I got back to the ward, Jerodene was with the nurses at the nurse's desk. We still were not told if we were going home. Other children were being discharged but unfortunately we were not on the list. Jermaine's plan was to spend Christmas day with us at the hospital, because I refused to leave her. It was not easy being there at the hospital day and night but that was the sacrifice I had to make while Jermaine had to be at work.

## *Becoming Ill*

On the night of Christmas Eve while Jerodene was sleeping, as I sat in the wooden chair trying to get some sleep, I became ill. I started to feel very sick, exhausted, tired, dizzy and nauseous. I felt so weak. I was not able to reach the bathroom, I had to reach for the vomit bowl that was placed under Jerodene's bed and utilised it. I was barely able to call the nurse to my aid. Nonetheless, she heard me and rushed to my assistance. At that time my mother was at home praying for me because a few minutes before that took place I had informed her that I was not feeling well. I figured that the lack of sleep, not eating properly nor on time had all contributed to me falling ill. However, I decided not to leave Jerodene's side at all no matter what. After I told Jermaine about what happened, he told me that I should come home and he would spend a few days with Jerodene, while I recuperated at home. I was so happy for the relief, and so was Jerodene. She did not have a problem because she was her daddy's little girl. She was happy. The difference with me being there and her dad was that the Patient Care Assistant would have to give her a bath twice a day. When I was there I used to bathe her. Jermaine would not bathe her but he would feed her.

## *Jerodene The Optimist*

While I was at home on Christmas day, my phone rang and when I looked, it was Jermaine calling. He told me that he met a lady by the name of Donna, whose son was admitted on the same ward. He said he was seated at Jerodene's bedside and the lady ran to him very excitedly, hugged him and said *"Daddy thank you for your daughter, thank you for your daughter"*. Jermaine then looked at her and asked, *"What are you talking about?"* She then told him that she was seated on the ward verandah when Jerodene approached her and asked her what was wrong with her son. She then answered Jerodene and told her that her son's childrenney was bad and he was very ill. She said Jerodene looked at her in awe then asked, **"So is that the reason why your face is looking like that? Fix your face because the doctors say that I have stage 4 muscle cancer, and look at my face (smiling) and look at yours"**. Jerodene wanted to compare their facial expressions because Jerodene wanted to tell her that she (Jerodene) was in a worse situation. Therefore, Donna's face was supposed to be more pleasant. He also told me that an Evangelist had come the same day to visit another patient. Before he left, he called a few patients and relatives to join hands in prayer, including Jermaine, Jerodene and Donna, who had already asked Jermaine if he could allow Jerodene in the prayer. Upon getting the go ahead, they joined hands and as the Evangelist was about to pray, Jerodene told her dad that she would be the first one to pray. She prayed and the evangelist was in shock and uttered *"a little child shall lead them"*.

Despite the fact that Jerodene was admitted, thankfully she was not bedridden. She was able to move around with her IV stand. She was so independent and if any issues arose, she would bring it to the nurse's attention to rectify them. She seemed to be the 'mother' of the ward. She really missed home but tried to find things to occupy her time to distract her mind from home. She really enjoyed playing in the playground, and going to ward 15 to look for Nurse Halstead and her other nurse friends, whom she loved dearly.

She always spoke highly about the nurses, Patient Care Assistant, doctors who were on ward 16. She loved them dearly and would defend them at any given time. They would go all out for Jerodene no matter what the situation was. They laughed, they played, and they even joked around together. She would sometimes be seen on Dr. Swaby's back being a jockey. Even though some of the doctors were rotated on a monthly basis, Jerodene was attached to a couple of them.

*Jerodene Meets Danique*

There were days when some volunteers would come and take their tablets and gadgets with them so that the children would feel happy and playful. One such who stood out was Danique Williams. The first day she saw Jerodene, she sat and watched her for a while then they got the chance to know each other. They developed a bond and always remembered their first conversation. Jerodene asked her what she was doing with such a huge bag. Until this day, Danique still jokes about it. They really loved each other. At that time, Danique was a student at that Hospital campus and for most times after classes Danique would come and visit before she headed home. When admitted, Jerodene always looked forward to seeing her and so did Danique.

## *My 2nd Birthday In The Hospital*

It was again nearing my birthday and since Jerodene was admitted, it meant spending a second birthday at the hospital. Jerodene felt sad, because she wanted me to be home so that she, along with her daddy and Rasheed could treat me like a queen.

She, however, had to face the reality that she and I would be together. To my surprise, she went around quietly and told all the doctors and nurses on the ward that it was my birthday. They wrote birthday greetings on a decorative paper and all the doctors and nurses signed it. Jerodene told me that she really wanted me to feel special knowing that I took the time to spend my birthday at the hospital with her. I told her that I would have done it all over again. I just wanted to know that she would be okay.

## *Jerodene Sought Refuge*

Around that same time, Jerodene was having a fever on and off. She was vomiting and was constipated. They were not able to say what was causing the fever, but we knew that the vomiting and constipation were side effects from the chemotherapy treatments. Eventually, they had to do a blood test. Unfortunately, they told me that they would not be able to take the blood from the chemotherapy port because there was a blockage, instead, they would have to draw it from her veins. I was angry because that was the reason we got the port in the first place and we knew how terrified Jerodene was of the needles. She started to cry immediately and stuck her head under the pillow giving me the indication that she did not want any more needle pricks. They then asked me to take her to the treatment room. By the time I took her to the treatment room, she slipped out and ran to the bathroom, seeking refuge. I had to run as fast as I could to catch her before she could lock herself in. I had to lift her, in order to take her back to the treatment room with a lot of screaming, kicking and crying. All eyes were on us because Jerodene was screaming on top of her lungs. When we got back to the room, what made me feel guilty was that I had to hold her down while the doctors stuck her several times trying to find her veins. When they pricked her a few times unsuccessfully, I had to walk out of the room with tears running down my face. There was no way I would be able to witness another needle prick, because in my opinion, that was straight torture. I walked off the ward because hearing her scream my name, I felt as if I was going to explode knowing that there was nothing I could do to help her. Had I not taken that walk, I knew that I would have just grabbed her and walked away. After a few attempts, they were successful. They then came back within a matter of minutes and told me they would have to make an attempt in pulling some blood from the chemo port. They had to perform a minor procedure to clear the blocked port because she had developed another infection. The situation proved to be difficult for us to cope because it was not yet a year since they had placed the port in. However, Jerodene ended up doing a surgery that could have been avoided. That meant a lot of needle pricks for Jerodene. It was not as difficult as before though because by then most of her veins had developed since the time that she had the chemo port in.

## *E COLI (Urine Infection)*

They then did that and the results came back saying that she had an infection in her blood, 'Escherichia coli (e coli)' to be exact and that they would have to start treating her with antibiotics right away. They would also have to isolate her from all the other patients. They would have loved to put us in the side room, that way she would have been out of the reach of everyone, but unfortunately that space was already occupied. That was when they decided that they would have to move our belongings to the back of the ward and place a screen around us. We were told that Jerodene would be on 14 days worth of antibiotics. That meant that for 14 days she would not be able to physically interact with her friends, especially her two new friends, Akayden and Aaliyah, whom she had met recently.

It pained Jerodene so much since she was only allowed to see them through the window while they played on the outside. How painful that must have been for her. Jerodene took it hard because she was not even allowed to go use the bathroom. She had to use the bedpan on a daily basis and each time she had to use the bedpan, eat or drink we had to tell the Patient Care Assistant present in order for them to chart it. During this time, a doctor went to her bedside to flush her port, which was done on a daily basis. Jerodene looked at the doctor and asked, **"Doctor, do you love God?"** The doctor responded in a timely manner, *"of course I love God, Jero, as a matter of fact everybody loves God"*. Jerodene then looked at him and boldly replied **"Doctor, Satan hates God, and you know that I am telling you the truth."** The doctor looked at her and smiled but could not respond to her because he was in shock. Within a matter of days she was cleared of the infection and was able to get more chemotherapy treatment.

*Jerodene And Her Friends*

Jerodene, Akayden and Aaliyah got along very well. Akayden was from Grenada, five years old and diagnosed with Wilms' tumour. He and Jerodene bonded very well and so did us as parents. Almost everywhere on the ward one would go they would see Jerodene and Akayden. They really looked out for each other. They had their differences just like other children would, and instances where they would not speak to each other for a short while. It was a good thing that Akayden's mom, Akili, and I really understood them. Being mature as parents, we allowed them to sort out their differences and within a few minutes they were friends again. Aaliyah was from Jamaica, nine years old and was diagnosed with leukemia. Aaliyah was not admitted as often as Jerodene and Akayden at the time. All the parents that I met including Aaliyah's mom, Simodel, all bonded together as if we knew each other from before.

Each time that we got discharged, I would leave all of my stuff at my brother, Randal's house. He would leave work and willingly take them to his house until the next admission he would take them back to the hospital for us. I really give thanks for him and the rest of our relatives who really stood with us and often would call to check up on us to see how things were going.

*Easter At Home*

On Holy Thursday in 2017, we were so happy because Jerodene got discharged. We were happy because we were able to go home and spend Easter holidays together as a family. By the time we got the discharge slip, it was getting very late. We hurried to the bus stop and were fortunate enough to catch one of the Jamaican Urban Transit Company (JUTC) buses. We had a comfortable ride heading Downtown, Kingston, Jamaica.

## *The Big Fright*

By the time we got Downtown, the bus stopped and the driver of the bus got out while the passengers were getting off. The bus was packed and there were a lot of passengers behind and before us. We all were basically crawling out of the bus. I held on to Jerodene's hand as she walked in front of me. As I stepped on the last step and Jerodene was outside holding on to my hand, the driver drove off. I was still inside the bus while Jerodene was outside. The automatic door hit me on my hand and I cried out. A lady had to hold onto Jerodene because it was impossible for me to jump from the moving vehicle. As the passengers screamed out to the driver, he stopped abruptly. I eventually got off the bus and rushed to retrieve Jerodene from the 'Good Samaritan'. I then walked back to where the bus stopped. That was when I realised that the drivers must have switched, because it was a male driver who was now around the steering wheel and not the female who was driving it before. I then frightfully explained to him what transpired. He looked at me in anger and shouted *"You all must know how long it will take you to get off the bus"*. At that time Jerodene was still crying and it got worse when she heard the driver shout at me. We were both scared. I hurriedly held Jerodene's hand and headed to my other bus stop because downtown can be very violent at times. That was not the place to stand and argue with anyone. We were frightened but gave God thanks that the situation was not worse.

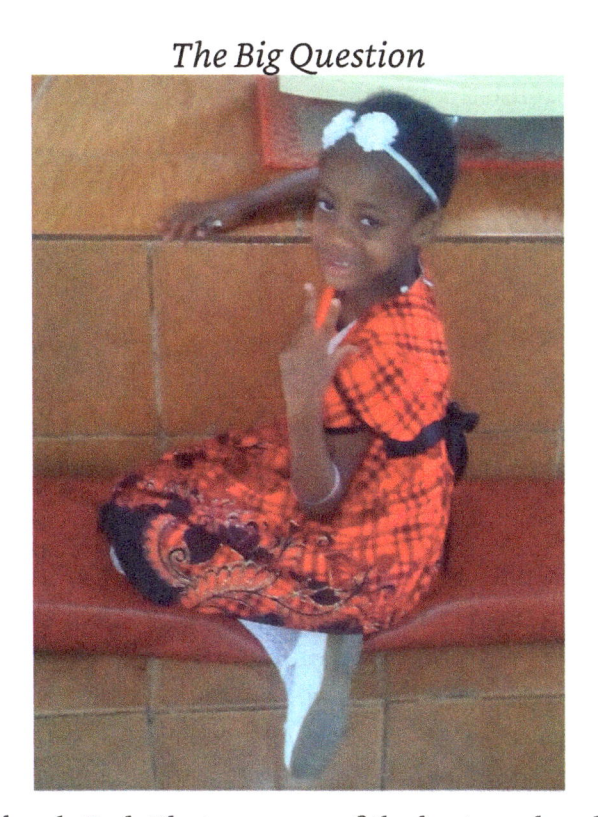

## *The Big Question*

We got home safely, thank God. That was one of the best weekends we had in a long time. We went to church. However, before we left for church Jerodene told her father and I that she wanted to ask us something. We then asked her what it was. Then she uttered, **"Mommy and Daddy, what** *are you both waiting on to give me my water baptism?"* We both were in shock and asked her, what did you say? She repeated. I then asked her, *"Jerodene when someone gets baptised, what does that mean?"* Her response was, *"Mommy, when somebody gets baptised, it means they get saved. They stop doing the bad things they used to do. They are not disobedient, they don't steal and they don't tell lies. The next thing is they start following Jesus' footsteps".* We then knew that we had something to consider. We knew that it would not take much consideration because we tried our best to raise her and Rasheed the best way we knew with God's help. We had been setting great examples for them to know that Jesus was the only way. When we arrived at church, we told our pastor and he said that whenever we were ready for her to be baptised we should let him know. They called on her to give her testimony and she gladly went. She started to sing one of her favourite songs, 'whose side are you leaning on'? She then gave her testimony telling the members about her experience at the hospital and she knew that God was healing her. She knew that the Devil could not kill her because she was fully covered by the blood of Jesus. Before ending her testimony, she prayed and all were in awe just listening to that six year old girl pray.

We were scheduled to go back to the hospital the following day. So in preparation to do so, Jerodene started crying, telling us that she did not want to go back to the hospital. She cried very much. We felt sorry for her but God knew that it was beyond our control and there was nothing that we could do. In the process of crying, she took out her pink diary and drew a picture of a sad little girl with tears rolling down her face and a broken heart beside her. We felt sad and helpless. I then showed it to her dad. You could have seen the gloominess on his face. We both were very emotional knowing that we had to take her back. We wished we could have done otherwise. We did not have a vehicle for ourselves so each time we had to go for admission, we had to take public transportation. We encouraged her and told her that all of this would be over soon and she would get back to her normal lifestyle. She was not convinced though, she told us that she was getting frustrated and tired of the hospital, the needles and that she wanted to be home with her family.

The following morning while we were on our way to the hospital from downtown to Papine, the taxi that we were in met in a minor accident. The other driver of a van must have dosed off only to see his van climbing on the bumper of our vehicle on the side that Jerodene and I were on. To God be the glory nobody was hurt. We were very frightened and scared. I had to comfort Jerodene because her heart was pounding so rapidly.

## *Admission Again*

During that admission period we were expecting to hear some positive news. Instead, I realised that the mass on Jerodene's shoulder was getting bigger. I brought it to the doctors' attention and that was when they told us that we should consider radiation as soon as possible and informed us that St. Jude had denied us. That was the second time that St. Jude denied us. They were not doing any clinical trials at that moment. Even though we were very disappointed, we still believed that she would be accepted, whenever the time was right. We thought that the radiation would only be on her shoulder but to discover that she would have to do four rounds of radiation treatment. That included her shoulder, brain, abdomen and pelvis.

Upon hearing that information, I had to take a seat. The radiation would have to be done privately. There was a hospital that would have done it but we were told that they had a long list of names and that Jerodene had a long wait. When we inquired about the cost for the radiation we were told that it was in excess of JM$1.5 million. We had no idea where we would get all that money. We told the doctor that since my husband was not present I would have to discuss it with him first before we would know the way forward.

## Testing Of Faith

Another time, when we were headed home, her fingers were slammed in the car door while we were boarding the taxi. I heard when she cried out loudly, *"Mommy my finger, my finger!"* That was when I realised that the passenger at the front of the car closed her door and Jerodene's fingers got caught between. The taxi driver hurriedly opened the door. Jerodene was in excruciating pain and was screaming very loudly. I was livid and started arguing with the lady but she did not pay me any attention. She barely grumbled under her breath, *"sorry"*. I was extremely upset! I had to thank God that He changed me or there would have been an altercation for sure. Jerodene's fingers felt better after a while because the driver was very considerate and got some water to cool the injury.

## The Third Dream

Mommy told us that one of our church members had a dream. In the dream the lady said they were at Mommy's church, while church was in session. She saw Mommy and Jerodene walking in behind each other and they were both dressed in full white. Jerodene had a cross in her hand and when Jerodene saw me she then said *"Mommy, don't worry I am just an angel"* That had me wondering because that was the third dream since Jerodene was diagnosed. This really had us thinking and asking ourselves a lot of questions. We did not prolong it because we knew that sooner or later God would send someone to interpret all three dreams. *"Is Jerodene an angel?"* I asked myself.

## New Friends From Canada

Along Jerodene's journey, she made 14 new friends from Canada. They were all children around Jerodene's age group. I met a lady years before named Michelle and we kept in touch even though we had only seen each other once. When I told her about Jerodene's condition she was saddened by the news, considering Jerodene was so young and had to go through so much. Michelle was the teacher for all those children and that was how they bonded. Jerodene wrote all 14 of them letters and they wrote her in return. Within a few months, Michelle came to Jamaica on her vacation and she managed to carry 14 teddy bears from Jerodene's friends. We knew that their friendship would last a lifetime. Even while Jerodene was in the hospital, Michelle came back to Jamaica to visit family and friends and she took the time out to come visit us in the hospital. We were elated to see her. Jerodene was overjoyed and inquired about her new friends. Jerodene and Michelle were singing *"Sammy plant peas and corn dung a gully"* and they both had fun. As the saying goes "all good things must come to an end" and eventually Michelle had to leave because she was due to fly home back to Canada the following day.

### *Jerodene's Followers*

Around that time, Kerlyn Brown had a follow-up segment on the Inspire Jamaica program. All of Jerodene's videos from church when she was praying and her fun moments at home, were all uploaded to the Inspire Jamaica page on Facebook. Thousands of people started to follow Jerodene's story and all were inspired by her bravery. By then, people tracked me down on Facebook and a lot of requests were being sent to me. A lot of people wanted to message me and let me know in what way their lives had been touched by our daughter. People in Jamaica, Africa, Canada, U.S.A, England, Cayman, and all over were really touched by our little girl, Jerodene.

### *Love In A Cheque*

I remember once when I went on Facebook and met a lady named Portia Davis. We spoke for a while, then I told her about Jerodene's situation and she got very emotional. She was trying her best for Jerodene to go overseas for better treatment. Unfortunately that did not work out. I told her about the radiation that was supposed to be done and that we had no clue what would be our next step financially. She then advised us that there was a foundation that might be able to help and that she would try her best to see if they could help. She messaged me within a few days and told me that the foundation was willing to stand the cost of JM$1.5 million for radiation. When I broke the news to Jermaine we both broke down in tears, giving God thanks for sending help from a stranger. She later became family. She requested all the information that was needed and filled out the online forms and before we knew it the forms were accepted and it was official. Jerodene would be able to do the radiation; we were just awaiting a date to begin. That was when we became family. Sometimes, Jerodene would video call her on Whatsapp or send her voice notes. She also did that with Patrice and her sister, Andrea. It is amazing to have strangers who become family. God really works in mysterious ways.

### *Bonding*

I got the chance to meet many other parents. I met this other lady named Trudy-Ann. She had a son by the name of Rashaun. The one thing all these children had in common was that they were fighting to survive that dreaded disease. They all were battling that dreaded disease 'CANCER'. All those children, coincidentally, were born around the same time between July and August. The same way they all looked out for each other, they played together, they really enjoyed each other's company. The same way those children bonded, the same thing happened to us as parents. We cried together, we prayed and laughed together. We all knew that we were home away from home and all we had was each other. We all looked out for each other's children. Besides those parents, I came across a lot more.

### *Hospital Visit Turns To Admission*

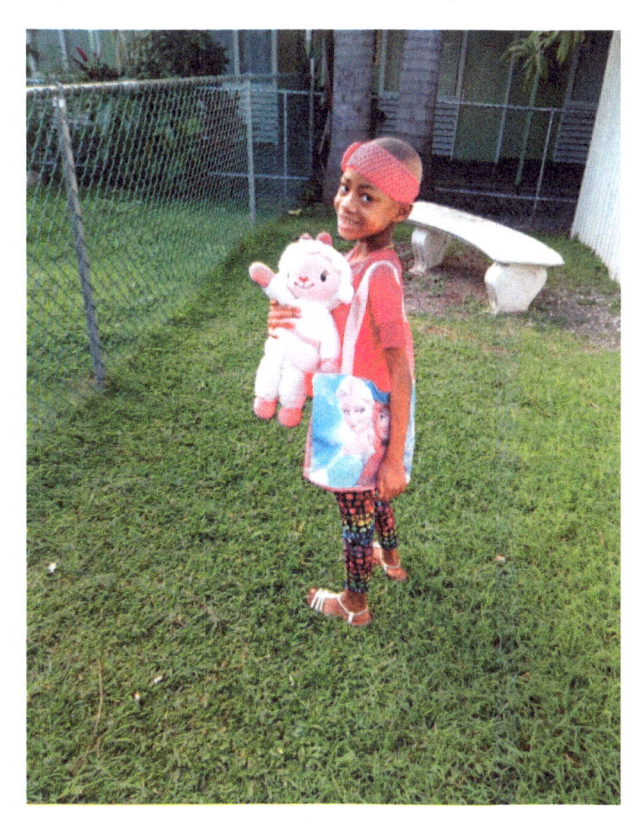

We were scheduled to be at the hospital for a dose of *Vincristine* and then we would be able to return home the same day. Upon reaching the hospital, the doctors ordered her to do a blood test. The results came back and her blood count was at two. The doctors started questioning me to find out if Jerodene had fainted or was even feeling nauseous. I told them that she was feeling okay. They were still in shock because they said that with such a low blood count, anything was likely to happen. We knew that God was in control and He would not allow anything to happen to Jerodene. In order for her not to catch an infection she had to be placed in the side room and had to wear a mask. She hated the mask but had to wear it since she was having problems breathing properly. We told her it was just for a while. Since we had only gone there for the day, I had to leave her at the hospital and rushed to Mandeville, which was two hours away, to get clothes etc. for admission.

Shortly after that, the little baby girl, who she met the last time she was admitted, died. Jerodene was admitted at that time but it was her dad who was there with her. Jerodene had a difficult time accepting it. She cried very much knowing that she had lost another friend. The good thing was that Jerodene did not know that both of them were diagnosed with cancer. I am happy that Jerodene had no idea because I know that she would have had a lot of questions to ask. When I went the following day to release Jermaine, Jerodene broke down and told me that she saw the little girl's parents crying. She thought they were tears of joy because they were going home and would not have to be in the hospital anymore. However, when she looked and saw that the little girl was in a white sheet and not in her parents' arms was when she realised that she had died. Jerodene had to get more professional counselling because she had a hard time dealing with the death of her friend. She told me that she wanted to talk to the little girl's mother to encourage her because she knew that it was the lady's only daughter. She also wanted to pray for her. I sent a message to the mother but she never responded to me.

*Radiation Procedure*

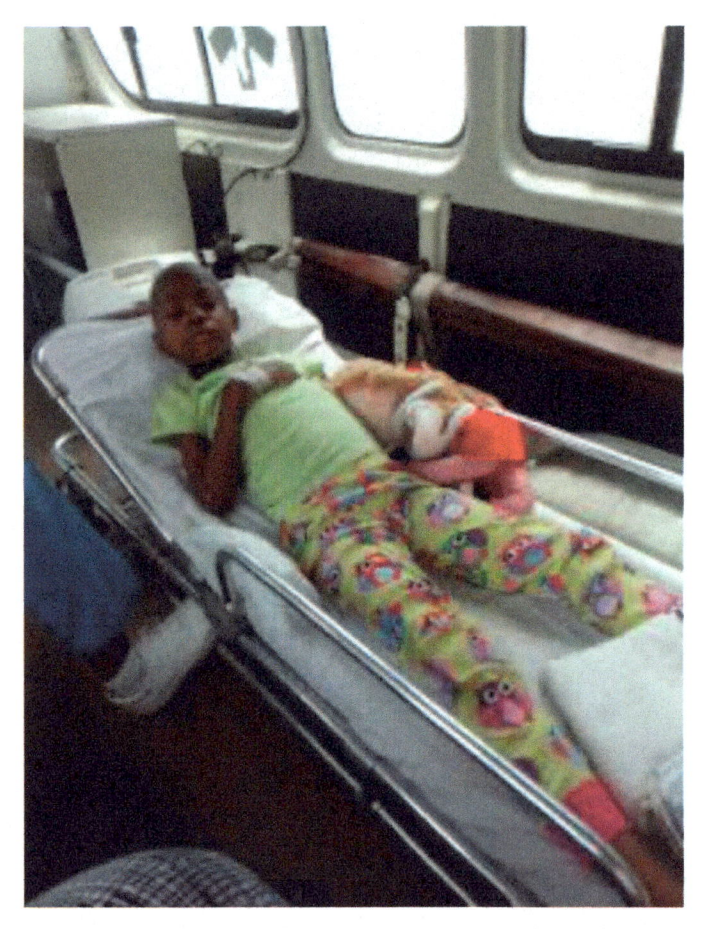

The time finally came for Jerodene to start the radiation process and the scheduled time was only on weekdays. I asked for permission for us to go home on the weekends. We were so excited and overjoyed when the consultant, Dr. Olugbuyi, affectionately called Dr. O, gave us the go ahead. The radiation was done at a private facility so everyday, Jerodene and I, along with a Patient Care Assistant or a nurse would travel in an ambulance to Ripon Road, Kingston 5. Jerodene enjoyed the ambulance ride on most instances, especially when other vehicles had to give way at the sound of the siren. She just loved the excitement. I was so happy when we were able to return home on weekends. Jerodene was going through a lot and being with her family together even for a day or two, made a huge difference. She especially loved seeing her baby brother, whom she loved very much.

I remember after getting discharged on a particular weekend, we stayed home for the entire time because Jerodene and her brother had not seen each other for quite a while. We did not want them to miss out on that quality time to bond. On Monday morning, while we were on our way back to the hospital, it was raining heavily, but by the time we got to our stop the rain stopped. I was relieved because we were told that water was supposed to touch the area that a person was doing radiation on. Sometimes, depending on the weather or if we just wanted to relax, my brother, Randal, would pick us up and take us to his house. Jerodene would have fun playing with her cousin, Xariah. They both bonded so well. One main thing they had in common was they both loved to pose for the camera. At one point, when we got discharged, it was too late to go home, so my brother came to get us and took us to a restaurant to eat. Both Jerodene and her cousin, Xariah, had fun eating their ice cream and cupcakes. Jerodene definitely ordered her favourite colour topping on her cupcake. Jerodene really had fun, she laughed so much and forgot about all the pain and torture that she endured at the hospital.

It was soon time for her to go back to the hospital. The first round of radiation went well. Jerodene met some new friends in the staff at the Radiation Office. They had no issue with Jerodene because she was sociable. Even the patients who were present at the Radiation Office on a daily basis always looked forward to seeing Jerodene. At that time, people remembered seeing her on the local Television program, Inspire Jamaica and also from some of her videos on Facebook.

### *Jerodene Meeting Mr. Chance*

Jerodene became friends with the porters who went to the ward on a daily basis to pick her up and transport her to the ambulance. One day, she met one of the drivers of the ambulance by the name of Mr. Chance. Over a period of time, they were both buddies, and they both looked forward to seeing each other on a daily basis. Mr. Chance always looked out for Jerodene and most times, would joke around with her and Jero liked it. From time to time, Mr. Chance would just randomly take a walk on the ward where Jerodene was just to say hello to her. If she happened to be in pain, he would normally turn away because hated the thought of her crying in pain.

### *Jerodene's Biggest Disappointment*

Back in July 2016, the children and I planned a little surprise birthday for Jermaine. It was a big surprise for him and he had no clue. It was just the four of us and that was all we needed. In July 2017, when his birthday was coming up, it was so unfortunate that we were in the hospital. I asked the doctors if Jero would be discharged by then, if all was well with her. Jerodene was so excited about the possibility of spending her dad's birthday with him. A few days prior to that, we were told that her treatment would have ended the day before her dad's birthday. On July 27, 2017, Jerodene had called her dad to wish him Happy Birthday. She did not tell him that we were coming home because we wanted it to be a big surprise. While we were there packing our things to go home I noticed that she had some red spots on the inner part of her lips. I brought it to the doctors' attention because I wanted them to attend to it before we left for home. I had no idea what might have caused it, and as a caring mother I wanted to be on the safe side. When I showed it to the doctors, they then told me that they would have to do a blood test in order for them to tell me exactly what the situation was. The blood test was done and unfortunately it showed that her blood count was at two. They explained to me that it was very low and all that was due to the side effects of the chemotherapy treatments that she was getting. I did not know how to break such sad news to Jerodene knowing that we would not be able to go home for her dad's birthday celebration. When I conjured up the courage and told her, she was very upset at me saying that I was to be blamed. She cried so much and told me that I should not have showed her lips to the doctor and if I had not done that we would have already been on our way. Even though I was being blamed, I knew I did the right thing. Had I not done so then I had no idea what would have happened on our way home. She was very disappointed and still blamed me for what happened. They had to keep her back at the hospital for a few more days until her blood count stabilised.

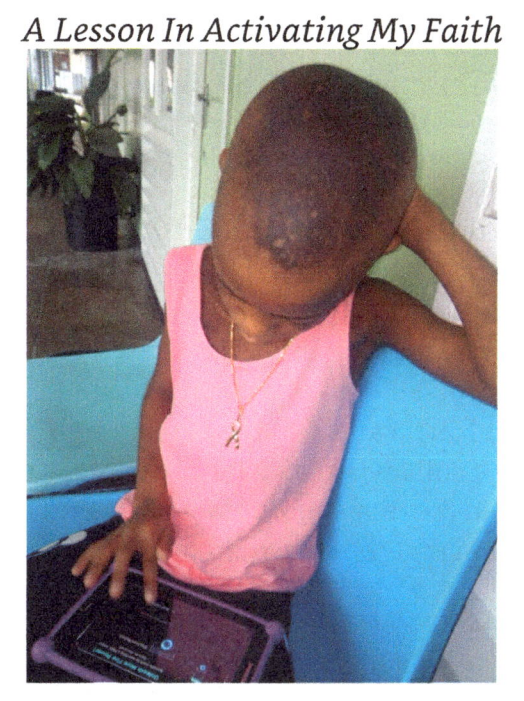

*A Lesson In Activating My Faith*

Being at the hospital, the happiest moment for Jerodene was when it was time for her to get discharged. That particular weekend when we got our discharge slip, Jerodene was on cloud 9. She skipped and danced to how happy she was. She got an early appointment at the Radiation Office, so instead of going to my brother's house we planned to go home. The journey was so long that by the time we got to Mandeville we had to make a quick stop in the town. Shortly afterwards, we took a taxi and decided to head home which was roughly 20 minutes away. While we were in the taxi on the Winston Jones Highway heading home, the rain started drizzling. With five passengers in the car, I prayed openly saying, *"Lord please help me that when I reach home there's no rain because I don't want any water to touch the area that Jerodene is doing the radiation on."* As we continued our journey it started to rain heavily. At that time, I repeated that same prayer but this time I did so a little bit louder. By the time I was through praying, I heard Jerodene shout at me, **"Mommy, God heard you already! It's because you are not listening."** I was so frightened that I looked at her in shock, and she just stared back at me. By then, all the passengers were looking at me. I felt as though I was about to sink, hearing my then seven year old daughter telling me to listen to the voice of God. I felt so bad that I was speechless. By the time we got home, the place was dry. There was no rain at home. I was startled, and Jerodene then looked at me with a bright smile on her face saying, **"Mommy, see? I told you that God answered your prayer, so why are you making God look so small?"** All I did was smile back at her and shake my head. I was able to share that testimony with everyone that I came across letting them know that it is always important to pause and listen to the voice of God. It took my then seven year old daughter to remind me of the importance.

### *We Reached Out To Glacia Robinson*

I recall having gone on Facebook and deciding to randomly send our own International Gospel singer and songwriter, Glacia Robinson, a message telling her about Jerodene's testimony of deliverance through her song "The Curse of Death". I imagined how busy she would have been so I was not expecting to hear from her anytime soon. I thought it would have been best to share it with her over a phone call as opposed to sending to her in a text, so I left my telephone number in her inbox and hoped that I would hear from her at some point. Within a few days, whilst at home, my phone rang and to my surprise on the other end of the line was Glacia Robinson. *"Oh my God, is this for real?"*, I asked myself. I was so excited to hear her voice and also to share Jerodene's testimony with her. She was elated that her testimony had such a great impact on our daughter's life. She told us that we made her day with such great news.

### *Jerodene's Favourite Gospel Artistes*

Jerodene's favourite gospel artistes were Jodian Pantry and Kevin Downswell. She loved their songs dearly and hoped that she would have met them someday. I messaged Jodian a few times and told her about Jerodene's situation and that Jerodene wanted to meet her in person. When Jodian was a child she did a song entitled, 'I'll Give My Heart'. Ever since Jerodene heard that song, she fell in love with her and her song. She wanted me to explain to her how it was that she saw Jodian singing that song on YouTube as a child when in actuality she was now a grown woman. Jodian had responded to my message and told me that she would have planned a day to pay us a visit. Jerodene waited and waited but we had faith that Jodian would have kept her promise. Another of Jerodene's favourite songs was 'Heaven's Playground' sung by Pastor Shirley Caesar. Ever since I let Jerodene watch the video, that song became one of her favourites too.

### *Jerodene's Message To Usain Bolt*

Jerodene's next wish was to meet the World's fastest man, our very own Usain Bolt. To be frank we knew that her meeting him might have not been possible because of his tight schedule. In July 2017, while Jerodene was admitted, the thought of her meeting Usain Bolt came back to me, and that was when we decided to do a video. We had no idea how far the video would reach but we did it anyway. While I stood to videotape her, this was what she uttered, *"Hi everyone, how are you? I am a big fan of Usain Bolt. So Usain Bolt, if you are hearing me right now, I wish I could see you in real life. I am a very big fan of yours. When you run so fast it's like something moving so fast. Everybody and Usain Bolt, I am in the hospital and I am very ill so can you put up prayers for me please?"* After I was through videoing her, I then sent it to Aunty Kerlyn Brown, and she posted it on the Inspire Jamaica page on Facebook. To our surprise that video went viral more than my husband and I could ever imagine. By the following day over 3,000 persons had already shared the video on their pages. Viewers from all over the globe commented on our daughter's video. They were all sending up prayers for her as she had requested. A lot of people were crying and really shared her pain. Each time we'd be walking on the street, people were very happy to see her, some would be in groups talking among themselves, *"There's the little girl who sent the video to Usain Bolt."* All were elated to see her. We prayed earnestly that the video would have at least reached one of his family members, then we knew that it would have reached his ears.

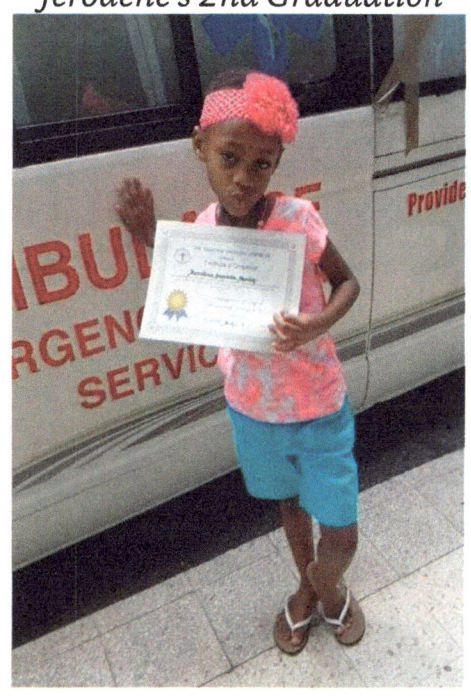

*Jerodene's 2nd Graduation*

On the day that Jerodene was through with the radiation treatment on her shoulder, the staff there had planned a graduation ceremony for her just as they would have done for all the other patients. That day was just a special day, the sun came out in all its glory. We were happy as we drove in the back of the ambulance off to Ripon Road to the Radiation office. Jerodene received her certificate of completion and the staff had commended her for her bravery, but before the little ceremony was through she was asked by the staff members to give a speech. Jerodene stood boldly in front of 10 other patients who were present and encouraged them telling them that by the grace of God they would be graduating the same way that God allowed her to do so and that they will be well in Jesus' name. Before she was through with her speech, she did what she does best and that was to pray. She prayed on everyone's behalf asking God to give the patients' strength to overcome and that she was depending on Him for constant healing.

Everyone was left in tears, knowing that a little girl had just encoUraged and prayed for them even better than some adults would pray. A lady cried and told me that ever since she laid her eyes on Jerodene, she knew that she was a special child sent from God. The ambulance came and we went back to the hospital. Jerodene left smiling because she had accomplished and earned her Graduation certificate. We were overwhelmed that the round of radiation was through, we were so happy to share the good news with her dad who was home taking care of our son.

*More Chemotherapy Treatment*

After the round of radiation we hoped to hear some good news but after a few more tests were done, we were told that Jerodene would have to continue with more chemotherapy treatment. We were not able to go home on weekends like before. Jerodene was very disappointed but came to an understanding after a while. One particular afternoon, I realised that the wash area was empty so I rushed to get our dirty clothes to do some laundry. At that time we were at bed nine, which was at the back of the ward, so I had asked Aaliyah's mom, Simodel, to watch Jerodene for me. That was the way we as parents looked out for each other in each other's absence. Jerodene complained several times that the hospital meal was not appealing but each time I purchased meals at a nearby restaurant, she enjoyed it. As I was there washing, a parent rushed to tell me that Jerodene was not feeling good. By the time I got to her bedside, Jerodene vomited in her bed and was lying there helplessly. I was frightened. Besides the fact that she was very weak, she was not looking too good. I brought it to the nurse's attention and took her out of her bed and requested a change of sheets. The nurse then told me not to give her anything else to eat or drink.

It was hard for me to see Jerodene so helpless, I was not used to seeing her like that. I believed that the God we serve surely would deliver. A lot of prayers from all over were going up to heaven for our baby girl and we believed and lifted our faith to God that He would see her through. That night, I went to the bathroom and by the time I got back to her bedside and tried picking a conversation with her I realised that Jerodene was hallucinating. It was hard for me to process all that was going on because she was not able to tell me her name or where she was. It was hard for me to know that our talkative and smart daughter was not able to utter a proper sentence. At that time I had to call one of the Patient Care Assistants, Ms. McDonald, who was on duty. Being a strong woman of God, she immediately prayed for Jerodene. I also called my husband, my mom and other close relatives and asked for special prayers for Jerodene. I called one of the doctors who was on duty and mentioned it to her. To my understanding, it must have been the side effects of one of the medicines that she might have gotten because I saw the exact thing happen to another child before. There was hardly any explanation from the doctor as to what might have caused that.

## *Where Is The Urgency?*

The following day was August 3, and after such a rough night, I arose and gave Jerodene her early morning bath as usual. That morning though, I had to do so at her bedside because she was too weak to make it to the bathroom. Shortly afterwards, she complained of having a severe headache. I did not hesitate. I went straight to one of the senior nurses and informed her and the nurse told me that she would bring her some pain medication soon. I then went back to her bedside but by then Jerodene was crying loudly: *"My head Mommy, my head… it's hurting badly."* She sobbed openly. I then went back to the nurse and reported the matter for the second time, this time with my eyes filled with tears. The nurse then told me that she was looking for Jerodene's cardex. By that time I was angry because Jerodene was crying uncontrollably and I was helpless. I then went back to her bedside and tried comforting her but that was not helping at all because Jerodene still had not got the pain medication. She cried out even louder, *"Mommy help me! My head! My head!"* I went back to the nurse for the third time, and decided that I was not going to leave the nurse's station until I saw her coming with the pain medication. I stood at the nurse's station waiting for her. For those who know me well, they know I am not a loud or obnoxious person but at that time I was about to raise my voice, just to get some attention from someone or anyone for that matter.

While standing at the nurse's station and looking in the direction of Jerodene's bed, another parent close to our bedside then beckoned to me that I should come to Jerodene's attention. As I took off hastily I heard the same parent saying, *"Why is it that Jerodene has to be doing that to herself?"* Hearing her say that made me move even faster, when I got to the bedside, Jerodene was helpless in her bed she was also in an awkward position. Immediately my heart skipped a beat. Her head was tilted backwards while her eyes were pulped and rolling over. I shouted her name once and there was no movement whatsoever nor pulse. The second time I shouted her name even louder and by that time all eyes were on me. There still was no response and that was when I shouted, *"HELP, SOMEBODY HELP!"* That was when the doctors rushed to my aid.

By the time the doctors got to her bedside, I stormed outside bawling because I thought that Jerodene was dead. Upon hearing the uproar, all the parents from the other wards were already out on the corridors looking in my direction. I fainted, and the next thing I knew was that I was in the Nurse's Lounge. When I came to my senses, I was handed some water while another nurse was reassuring me that everything was going to be okay. *"But how could everything be okay when I knew what I saw?"* I thought to myself. As I sat in the Lounge I was so scared to face reality. That was when I was told by the doctor that Jerodene was not dead and that she had a seizure. Seizure? I thought to myself, I remembered seeing another patient who had an episode, which was an awful experience but never thought in a thousand years that something like that would have happened to our daughter. No, not at all. The doctors then told me that they would have to do some scans to see exactly what was taking place in her body. They went on to say that she was revived and was now talking. I was told that I should go be with her by her bedside because she was asking for me.

I was a bit scared and shaky to go see her because even though they told me that she was conscious I still did not know what to expect. The position that I saw her in earlier could not leave my mind. I somehow managed to wipe my tears and went back to the ward. I then noticed that they had moved her from the back of the ward and placed her at bed one, which was right next to the doctors' and nurses' station where they could monitor her better. I cannot recall her first words to me but I remember that she went to sleep right away. That was the scariest moment of my life. I wished I could erase it all. It all happened so quickly, within that short time I knew that my blood pressure spiked. My entire body felt as if it was lent to me, or I felt as if I was trapped in someone else's body. I was so weak and helpless. I felt so empty and broken and wished that my husband was there with us but then I remembered that he had to be there for our son, Rasheed, as well.

I stood by her bedside and would not leave her because I feared that the same thing would reoccur. I prayed to God that it would not. About the same time, the doctors were doing their ward rounds. They stayed at Jerodene's bedside for a while discussing her situation. They told me that the scans were scheduled within the next half hour. As I pulled down the bed rail and stood there for a short while, another seizure attack occurred. I panicked and Jerodene nearly fell out of her bed. Luckily, the doctors were not far from our bed so they were able to attend to her immediately.

Shortly afterwards, the CT scans were done and I was told that she has **hydrocephalus**. My brain was still in shock and I could not even think straight. I was told that she had excess fluid surrounding her brain, and that they had limited information to provide me with at the time. They further stated that the team that specialises in that area, would be there shortly to guide me through for me to have a better understanding. The doctors on the ward also told me that a surgery might have to be done on her brain and a shunt might have to be placed in her brain in order to drain the excess fluid. *"A shunt? How could little Jerodene manage all of this?"* I thought to myself, *"The Bible says in all things we give thanks but wow, in sickness? How does one give thanks when his or her child is sick?"* I had so many questions left unanswered. I wondered what more could one child go through. What more could one family go through? When would Jerodene be healed? When would Jerodene go back to living a normal life? I always heard people saying never to question God but I had to. Where was God in all of this? We put all our trust in Him and really hoped that He would come through for us. But it is not our timing, but His.

The same day, the doctors put her on a stretcher with IV attached all over her body then got the ambulance to take her to do radiation scanning. When we reached the office, the person in charge examined her and told us that she was not stable enough to do the scans. So we had to go back to the hospital.

## *The Unexpected News*

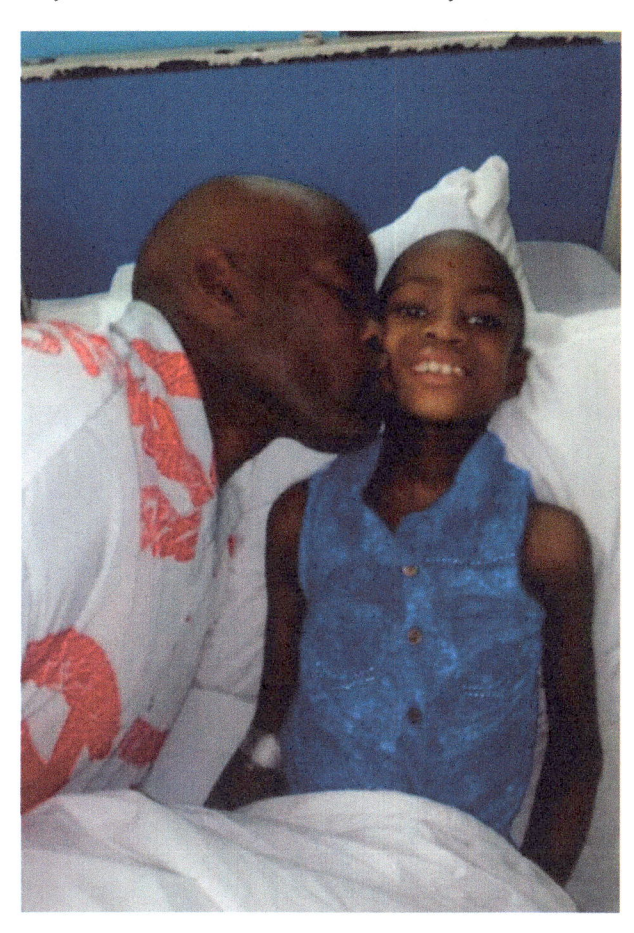

When we got back to the hospital, I realised that things had gotten very serious. The oncologist called me into her office and told me to call my husband and ask him to come to the hospital as soon as possible. She told me that things were not looking positive for Jerodene; she might not make it. *"Am I hearing correctly?"* I thought to myself. Jerodene's favourite part of all her prayers was, ***"I shall not die but live and declare the works of the Lord."*** I started repeating that in my head, *"Jerodene shall not die but she shall live and declare the works of the Lord! Jerodene shall not die but she shall live and declare the works of the Lord!"* We knew that Jerodene was a brave and resilient little girl and with the help of God she would pull through. I then told myself that no matter what they said we still had hope in God that He would work things out. The doctor also told me that I should call all our relatives who wished to see her and that they too should come. My cousin, Natasha, and her family were visiting from England and they came to visit us the same evening. My dad, my brother, Randal, and his family came too. Other relatives wanted to come visit Jero too but due to the distance and the time when I was told, it was not possible. For relatives who were not able to make it, they were home praying for healing for Jerodene.

Eventually Jermaine got to the hospital, he was in total shock when I told him about the rough ordeal that Jero had gone through. He held on to hope and told me that everything would be okay. I felt stronger now having our relatives with us. I literally gained strength. After a while, the rest of the family had to leave because visiting hours ended. It was a pleasure having them, though. Everyone left feeling emotional because of the situation. The hospital's rule was that only one parent per child could stay after visiting hours but this time due to the intensity of Jerodene's situation both of us were allowed to stay with her. Even though Jerodene was very weak and was not very talkative, we saw a smile on her face when she realised that both of us were by her bedside. She was very family oriented; she often spoke highly of her love for her family.

By then, the team of doctors came and questioned me about what had transpired earlier. It was difficult to relive the moment but I had to. They then told me that in order to place a shunt in a patient's brain, there had to be evidence that the patient was unaware of one's surroundings and oneself. They advised that the team would conduct check-ups on Jerodene and question her to confirm her awareness. They did as they advised on a number of days but Jerodene was always ready to answer all the questions. I recalled her on one of the many days questioning one of the specialists, *"You came and asked me the same questions yesterday already."* The doctor then looked at her and smiled, then left, never to return. We knew that God had answered our prayers because Jerodene did not need the shunt after all. Jermaine stayed with us for a few days and we were grateful to be together. During the nights, we took turns watching her, hoping that she would not have another seizure episode. Jerodene had IV accesses all over her body; she was getting medications to prevent the seizures among others.

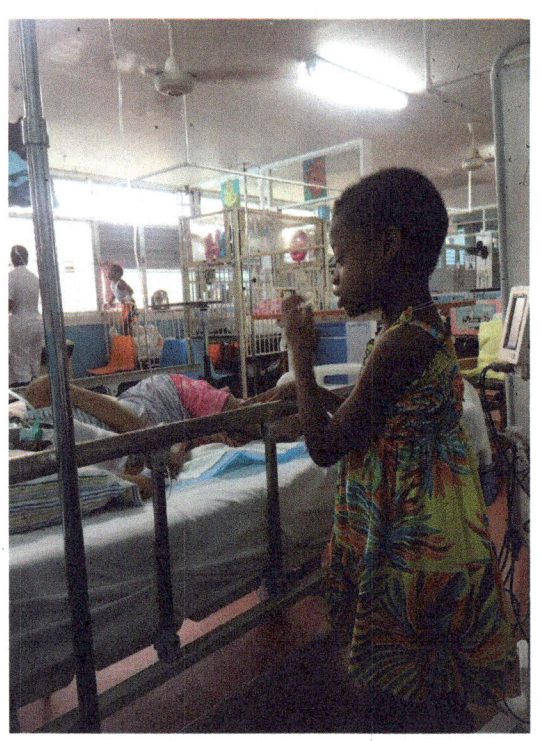

*The Sick Jerodene Praying For Amielle*

    The following Sunday, there was a little girl who was a patient there with her bed opposite ours. Jerodene was seated in the bedside chair. She then looked across and saw the little girl, Jerodene then said to me, *"Mommy, I want to pray for that little girl."* I then told her that the little girl's mother was right by her bedside and that she might have to get the mother's permission first before praying for the little girl. Knowing Jerodene, she easily got frustrated at times and I had thought that time would have been one of those times. To my surprise, it was not. Instead of her becoming frustrated, Jerodene reached for our bottle of consecrated olive oil that was on a little table right by our Hospital bedside. She poured a little in her hand then anointed her own forehead, I then took the bottle back from her to replace it and by the time I turned back around Jerodene was not there. I then looked by the little girl's bedside and Jerodene was standing right in front of the little girl's mother staring into her eyes. I then heard Jerodene utter, *"Miss can I pray for your daughter?"* The lady then responded by telling her yes. Immediately, Jerodene clasped her hands and began praying for little Amielle. The little girl's mom took her phone out to capture the moment of Jerodene praying. I remembered that prayer as if it was prayed yesterday. I recalled Jerodene praying, *"God I want You to heal her the same way that You are healing me, and God I ask that You give the doctors wisdom, knowledge and understanding as they help us as children to feel better."* We listened in reverence as we got teary eyed. At the end of her prayer, the little girl's mother was in shock because Jerodene was just 6 years old at the time and was able to pray such a powerful prayer. That was when both families met officially. We were no more strangers but strangers that became one family. We then learnt that the little girl's name was Amielle Brown. We met Amielle's parents, Mr. and Mrs. Brown, her grandmother and one of her aunts. They were such a lovely family.

## *The Out Of Body Experience*

That same day, around 5 pm, Jermaine and I were seated by Jerodene's bedside while she was seated in her bed. Jerodene then said to both of us, *"Mommy and Daddy, there's something that I have to tell both of you. Daddy, if it wasn't for Jesus I don't know what would have happened to me, and as a matter of fact, I wouldn't want to know either."* She then continued, *"Something happened to me the other day while I was very very sick."* When she said that, both of us were stunned because we knew within ourselves that she could in no way remember anything that transpired. Nonetheless, we really wanted to hear. She said, *"When I was very sick a few days ago, I felt someone pushed me on a stretcher into an operating theatre room and all my limbs were off and my blood was gushing out. Some of the doctors were there and they were all confused asking among themselves 'what would they do to replace all the blood I was losing. Mommy and Daddy, I heard everything that the doctors were saying but I was unable to speak."*

Jermaine and I sat in awe, because what she was saying was very deep. Because we remembered that on the day, when the scary situation had occurred, she was sent to do a CT scan, I then responded to her saying, *"Jerodene, are you sure that it wasn't the CT scan that you had gone to do?"* But the expression on her face was confirming that she knew exactly what she was talking about. She then responded, *"Mommy, no it was not a CT scan that I had gone to do."* She then went on to say, *"Mommy, could you play the video of Shirley Caesar's song, Heaven's Playground, and then I will show you what I am talking about."* I then immediately found the song on YouTube and started playing while all three of us watched. When we got to the part of the video where the doctors were in an operating theatre room dressed in their gowns and proper gears, etc that was when she asked us to pause the video then she shouted, *"Mommy and Daddy look! That was where I was."* That was when things got way deeper beyond our imagination. Her dad then asked her to repeat everything that she had just said. I then got my phone then recorded her entire message. She repeated it all word for word. I immediately sent the recording to my mom and after she was through listening, she told us that Jerodene had an out of the body experience. "An out of the body experience?" we thought to ourselves.

We still think about it at times. As she went to bed, she had asked me to play one of her favourite songs "Heaven's Playground" on her tablet. I did what she asked but I could not sleep that night. Each time I dozed off, I woke up in fright just to see if she was still breathing. I could not fathom why she wanted to hear that song while she was not well. Again Jerodene's favourite scripture came back to me, *"I shall not die but live and declare the works of the Lord."* Oh what a night that was.

*Jerodene, The Little Celebrity*

By that time, a lot more people had shared the video with her wanting to meet Usain Bolt, and people at the hospital would ask her on several occasions if her icon came to see her or if she heard from him. Of course, she wished that she heard from him and we knew that with so many people sharing her video both on Facebook and Instagram most likely it would get to him somehow.

## *One Of Her Special Friends*

By then, a lot of friend requests were coming to me on Facebook from people all over the world. Most of them were strangers and that was where I met a young man by the name of Adrian Cameron from overseas. He then told me that he had been following Jerodene's story on the Inspire Jamaica Program and how much she had touched and changed his life in so many positive ways. He went on to say that he was very happy that I had accepted his friend request and that he wanted to reach out to us for a long time. However, it took him a while to search and find us on Facebook. He asked to speak with Jerodene on numerous occasions and from time to time they sent voice notes to each other via whatsapp and Jerodene would give him advice. It was a pleasure listening to those voice notes sent to and fro. Within a few days, they became great friends. At one point in time, when his dad was visiting Jamaica, Adrian sent a beautiful doll for her and that doll became her favourite of all times. I videotaped her while she gladly unwrapped it from its box and you should have seen the expression on her face. Adrian was overwhelmed to see how happy and appreciative Jerodene was for her treasured gift. Adrian further went on to say that he anticipated the day that he would get the chance to meet Jerodene – the precious little angel that made him a hero.

## *Little Television Icon*

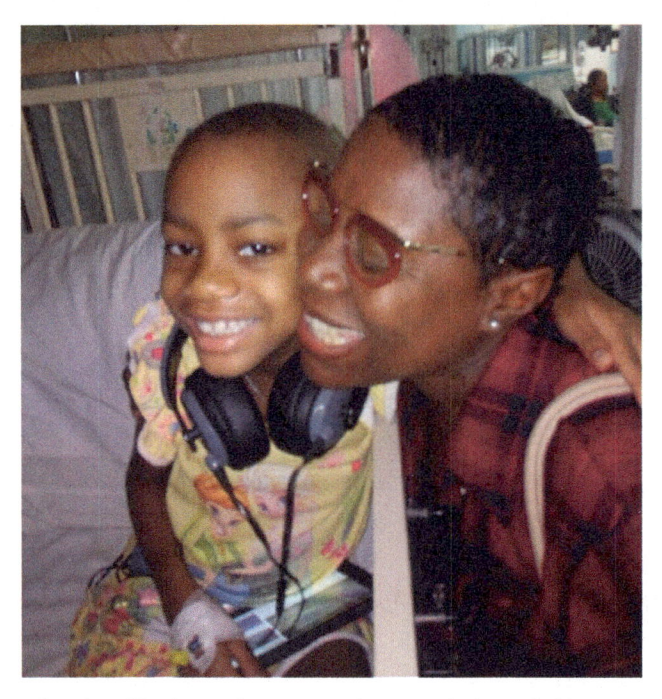

Aunty Kerlyn Brown had called as she was always doing follow-ups on Jerodene's story and would update her story on the Inspire Jamaica Program. People always looked forward to seeing our little princess on their television screens. Jerodene was more excited to see herself on television more than anyone else, especially whenever she was admitted at the hospital when the nurses and doctors on duty and other patients were able to see her.

*Deep Sigh!! What If?*

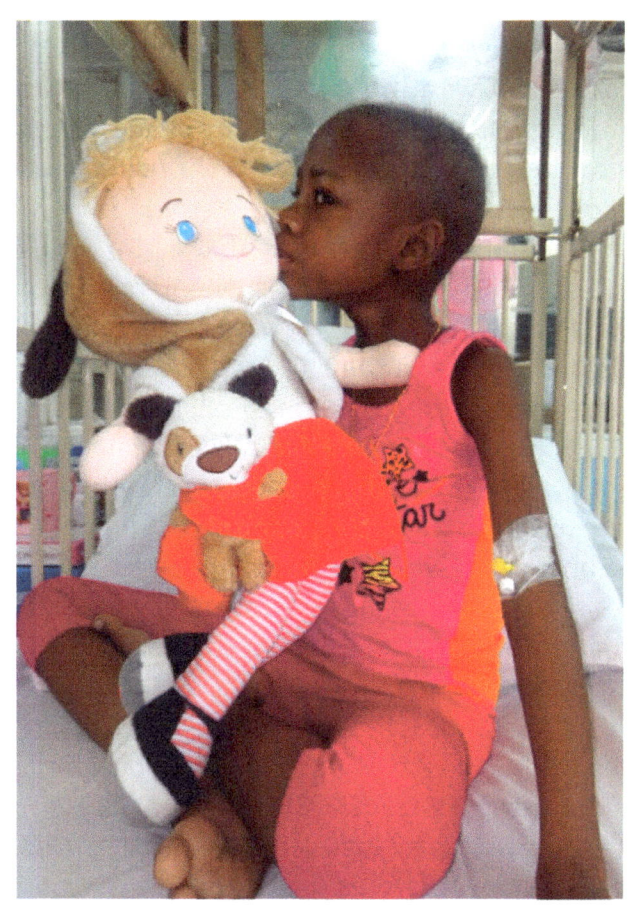

A few days after the seizure episode, my mom came to visit us at the hospital. By then, Kerlyn Brown had heard about our terrible ordeal, and came to visit us as well. I had asked my mom to sit in for me while I left from the ward to do the interview at another section of the hospital. We gave God thanks for the continual healing of Jerodene's body, we never underestimated the power of our Almighty God. We knew that He would come through for us. Jerodene was transferred from bed 1 back to bed 9 due to the fact that she made a drastic change, she made great improvements back to her normal self. That interview was a very touching and emotional one because of the scary seizure episode and the days leading up to the interview were very rough to deal with. As I was being interviewed, tears ran down my face as Kerlyn asked me the unexpected question, *"What if?"* That question I was unable to answer because it had never come across my thoughts. What if Jerodene dies? That had never crossed our minds, because we still believed that God would heal her. We knew that He was still in the healing business and could do what no other could do. When people saw that interview on the Inspire Jamaica Program, some sent messages and even called us crying as a result of the "What if?" question that was asked.

## That Unforgettable Approach

A few days afterwards, whilst Jerodene was still admitted, I almost ran out of supplies for both of us. I had asked one of the nurses to watch her closely while I ran an errand downtown to pick up a few things. While I was there in the busy heart of Downtown Kingston, in one of the wholesales, a man approached me from behind. He was not dressed as an average man. He had scars all over his face and seemed to be one of the volatile types. In a very rough tone of voice he then said to me, "I am selling you a gold chain, are you buying it?" Honestly I was a bit shaken up due to his appearance and tone of voice, I then nervously answered, *"No I am not buying that gold chain."* He then stared into my eyes and repeated the question. I then nervously gave him an explanation of the reason for me not wanting to purchase his necklace. By then his response was, *"No man, your voice sounds too familiar."* I then asked him what he was talking about. Then only to hear him respond, *"Was it your daughter that I saw on the television? The little brown girl who has cancer?"* That was when I let out a sigh of relief and I then told him yes. He told me that he had not shed a tear since his mother died but Jerodene's story made him cry. He then shook my hand and told me to say hello to her for him. He insisted that I say hello to her for him. He then said, *"Tell her to continue fighting that dreaded sickness and that God will come through for her. And tell her to continue believing in God."* He repeated it four times. I then asked him to tell me his name so that I could tell Jerodene specifically who sent her the greetings. He then stepped closer to me then in a very soft tone uttered, *"I don't normally tell people my name, but tell her Donovan says to tell her hello."* He then left, I stood and watched him walk away until I could see the back of his shirt no more. I picked up the things that I wanted then hurried back to the hospital to tell Jerodene about my encounter. She had a lot of questions to ask, ones that I was not able to answer.

    We wanted people to hear about my ordeal and how Jerodene had touched the vilest of sinner's hearts even in her sick state. So I told Kerlyn about the encounter and she told me that I should do a video saying exactly what happened. I did as I was encouraged to but the thought also came to my mind that I should get Jerodene involved. Therefore, I asked Jerodene to say a prayer but before she prayed, these were her words to the young man, **"I would love to say God bless him, God keep him and God cover him under His blood."** And then her prayer was, **"Oh Father God bless that young man who Mommy came across a few days ago. God, You know that he is a nice young man. God cover us under your blood. Jesus cover all of these people under Your blood that You make, save him oh Jesus. God bless him and sanctify him God, in Your name, Amen."** Within a few minutes, Kerlyn posted it on the Inspire Jamaica Page, and that was another video that went viral on Facebook. People literally cried after hearing Jerodene's prayer and encouraging words for that man. For people who had just gotten the chance to meet Jerodene on social media, they were in awe just watching and listening to our little princess, Jerodene. Oh what a prayer that was!

    Few days had gone by and our baby girl's birthday was fast approaching. Due to the fact that Jerodene wasn't as stable as before and she was recovering from the seizure episode, we knew that she would be spending her big seven in the hospital. We all know that spending one's birthday in a hospital was no fun.

## *Relay For Life 2017*

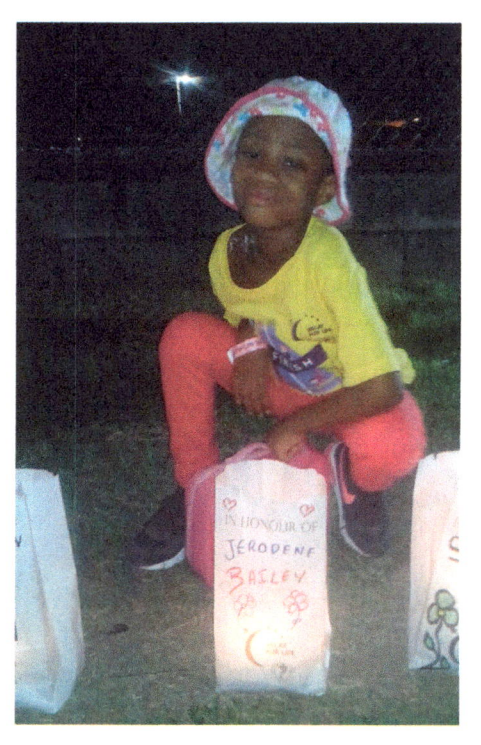

The doctors told us about a function, which would be held about 20 minutes away from the hospital. That event was called the 'Relay for Life'. It was an annual event held for persons who were battling, who survived and even those who have died from the dreaded disease, cancer. Of course we believed God that one day soon Jerodene would be on the survivor's list. The good thing was that it was scheduled to be held on a weekend and we would get the chance to attend because Jerodene was back on weekend discharges. For children who were admitted to the hospital during that time, transportation was organised to and from the event for them and their parents. Therefore we attended the Relay for Life 2017 all in our beautiful colours in support of our brave and courageous children.

Some doctors and nurses were present as well. All of us, both children and parents alike, were seated around a huge table. The children were happy being away from the hospital. I wondered who would not be happy for a break, if it was even for an hour. I left to go to the bathroom and on my way back inside I saw a man standing right at the entrance of the tent. I had no idea who he was or where he came from. We both smiled and said hello, and for some reason I felt like asking him if he was okay. He then told me no, then I inquired to find out why he was not okay. Then he told me that he was from a popular Radio Station and that he was seeking people to interview but he was unable to find anyone who would agree to one. I then told him that I had a then six year old daughter who was diagnosed with stage 4 cancer and that she was a very polite and outspoken individual.

His face lit up and he then showed me where his booth was and I went inside to get Jerodene. When I told Jerodene, she was very excited to know what she was going to do. We were then interviewed for nearly 10 minutes and it was indeed a successful one. Mr. Foster and his team were in awe hearing such powerful words coming from little Jerodene Bailey. She then told Mr. Foster that she believed in God and that she knew that He was going to heal her. Before the interview was through, Jerodene prayed for the rest of the sick children in radio land. Mr. Foster then asked her what it was that she wanted to say to the other children who were sick. Jerodene then uttered, *"I would tell them that they should continue to believe in God because He is the only healer."* The team was left in tears.

After the interview, we met a young lady who was also a Radio Personality. She and Jerodene both laughed and played together and Jerodene asked her, *"What is your name?"* The young lady then responded saying, *"Shauna Fung Yee."* *"Shauna Fung Yee?"* Jerodene repeated. ***"That's okay, I will go with the Shauna."*** We all laughed so hard until we almost choked. Jerodene said that because she knew she would not remember the lady's last name. Right there and then Mr. Foster, Shauna and Jerodene developed a bond. They had also encouraged Jerodene and told her how much of a fighter she was. We then exchanged telephone numbers and that was where a new friendship started. Jerodene was so excited to tell her dad about her new friends. From time to time they would call and ask to speak with Jerodene. I did not mind at all because I knew that they were some of the persons that God had sent in our corner to embrace us.

### *Jerodene's First Radio Interview*

One of the times while Jerodene was admitted, Mr. Foster had called her to do an interview with him on his radio station. Jerodene was overly excited knowing that the nurses who were on duty would be able to listen to the interview. She was there encouraging and praying for others as she normally did.

### *Jerodene's Big Seven*

Jermaine and I had planned a surprise birthday party for our little princess for her 7th birthday right in the Hospital. She had no idea. She might have thought in the back of her mind that it was going to be another boring day. The plan was that Jermaine, Rasheed, my dad, Aunt Sandra, my brother Randal and his family along with Aunty Kerlyn Brown would have been there. The night before her birthday Jerodene barely slept because she was very excited awaiting the few hours to pass before her 7th birthday. She told me, *"Mommy I am so excited and I am looking forward to my Big seven."*

On the morning of her birthday, she woke up at 5:30 a.m., the nurses did her vital checks as usual and she got her morning medication. Then my phone started to ring off the hook, a lot of birthday greetings were coming in. A lady that we had met prior to Jerodene's birthday, both her daughters were admitted at the same time, she had told her friend, Simone Clarke-Cooper, who was a Television personality, to give a shout out to Jerodene on her big day. Jerodene was elated and by then the nurses were changing shifts. They all hugged Jero and wished her a very happy birthday. I gave her an early morning shower then dressed her in her favourite denim dress and her pink headband.

### *The Response From Usain Bolt*

A friend of mine then sent me a video via Whatsapp. When I viewed it, to my surprise it was Usain Bolt himself sending out a message to Jerodene saying, *"Hi Jerodene, Usain here I saw the video that you sent out. I'm happy to know that I'm your favourite athlete and you look up to me and all. I see that you are sick, I'm sorry to see that. I know it's your birthday so I just want to wish you a happy birthday. I hope all your wishes come true, hope you get all the presents and I wish nothing but happiness for you. When I come to Jamaica I will try and come see you. So have a wonderful birthday."* Jerodene had no idea that Usain had gotten her video much less to be responding to it, so when I showed her the video, she jumped and screamed so loudly that everyone who was present paused what they were doing and all eyes were on Jerodene. She screamed and hugged me saying, *"Mommy he called my name, he called my name, and he said that he would come see me when he gets back to Jamaica!"* She took the phone from my hand and ran all over on the ward and showed it to her nurse friends who were present. She was so elated, words were not enough to express her feelings. She then called her dad and told him the good news. By then, doctors, nurses, PCAs and everyone else who were on the ward heard about and saw the video and were all celebrating with our Princess Jerodene. Her seeing the video, we knew that her birthday started off with a bang and would end on a splendid note.

## *Two Birthday Parties*

Soon it was time for her to go get her radiation treatment at Ripon Road. I always travelled with her in the ambulance to and fro on a daily basis. But just this one day I chose not to go just because we wanted to put her little surprise party together. A while before the ambulance came to pick up Jerodene her granddad and Rasheed came to pay her a visit. Their visit made her even happier. She introduced her little brother to almost the entire staff because she loved and spoke so highly of him. If only you knew. They played so much because they wanted to catch up on lost times. She then asked one of her favourite nurses, Nurse Halstead, if she could open the play area so that she could play on the swing with her brother because she missed playing with him so much. Her request was granted and you should have seen the look on their faces! By then, Aunt Sandra had arrived. Before she came, Jerodene had told Aunt Sandra that she needed a pair of binoculars for her birthday because she had never owned one before. She had no clue that Aunt would have gotten her one, so that too was a surprise. Jerodene was so happy having her family around her on such a special day. Her dad had a surprise for her and that was he was going to be present for her big day. I could just imagine the look on her face when she saw him.

The ambulance had arrived and it was time for her to go do the radiation. Nurse Chin was scheduled to journey with her, her entire countenance had changed, because she now realised that she would have to leave her brother. She also hated the fact that she would have to go do the radiation without me accompanying her and she thought that by the time she got back to the hospital Rasheed would have already gone. But I reassured her that he would still be there when she got back. As soon as Jerodene left we started preparing. Aunt Sandra and Akili (Akayden's mom) went Downtown, Kingston to pick up a few more things that were needed for the party. We had gotten a few items needed for the party from the lady whose two daughters were admitted but we were still in need of a few more items. Jerodene wanted a tutu, she had to describe it to me because I did not know what it was. Luckily, Aunt Sandra knew what it was. It came with a wand and a set of princess wings. Everything was in place.

Kerlyn knew all the plans that were in place and she had some plans of her own as well. Her planning to be at Jerodene's party was also a surprise. In the midst of the preparation, I received a call from one of the staff members of the Radiation Office saying that they planned a surprise party for Jerodene at the Office and that I needed to be present. That was when I told them that I was at the hospital making preparations for a surprise party for her as well. None of us had any idea that each was planning a birthday party for our Jerodene. I wondered how I would pull that off but nonetheless a few parents and staff members fit in for me while I left for Ripon Road until Aunty Sandra got back from off the road. For that I was grateful. Jermaine was not there as yet but he told me that he would have been there shortly.

Kerlyn and I both met up at the Radiation Office at Ripon Road, and by the time we got inside, balloons, banners, and other decorations were all over. All the staff members and quite a few patients were there and all had smiles on their faces. The birthday girl ran and hugged me and was just laughing, obviously she could not contain herself. By then, she was just glowing, she had that ear to ear smile. She was so happy to see Aunty Kerlyn because she had not seen her for a while. Overall, Jerodene was just so happy, she sang and danced and had loads of fun with the staff at the Radiation Oncology Center. They all loved and cared for her. Cameras flashed and phones were recording as Jerodene hit the dance floor. Jerodene really loved it. Oh did I mention that they had a big gold colour helium balloon with the number 7 representing her 7th birthday? All was well put together and it was evident Jerodene was having fun. When it was time for her to blow out her candles, she blew them out with a smile then said, **"My one and only wish is that I wish my daddy was here with me as well."** But little did she know that he was already on his way. After her fun filled party, Jerodene gave her speech then prayed openly thanking God for such a beautiful day.

After her first party, Nurse Chin, Kerlyn, myself and the birthday girl left in one transportation. We stopped at Devon House and we got a huge bucket of Ice cream from the Manager as a gift for the birthday girl. I had called Aunty Sandra and she told me that all was in place at the Hospital, and that they were all anticipating the birthday girl. We took a lot of photos in between as you know one of Jerodene's best friends was the camera. She was just so beautiful.

## *Party At The Hospital*

By the time we got back to the hospital, her dad was already there. You should have seen the smile and heard the laughter as she ran and jumped into his arms as they both embraced each other. That was a priceless moment, one that none will ever forget. Jerodene then saw all the decorations and that was when she realised that it was another birthday party. She asked no questions because she knew that she was the only one on the ward celebrating birthday on that day. She was very excited and at a loss for words.

She saw the decorations, a table well decorated with such a beautiful cake with her favourite cartoon character from Frozen, which was given to her as a gift by one of her favourite doctors, Dr. K. Swaby. Both Jerodene and Dr. Swaby had been friends since Jerodene was first diagnosed in May 2015. Jerodene would always enjoy riding on Dr. Swaby's back around the ward. From time to time, even when other doctors were not able to find Jerodene's vein, Jerodene would have insisted, **"Let Dr. Swaby do it."** Dr. Swaby really knew how to relate to children. She was just awesome.

Shortly afterwards, my brother, Randal and his family came, our dear friends, Kimoy and Aaron came as well. My other two brothers, Melbourne and Ryan were not able to make it, but had promised her that they would have made it up to her. The birthday gifts started rolling in and with Jerodene having us all in her corner with her favourite man there, her Dad, she had nothing but smiles all over her face. Oh wow can you just imagine?! We all smiled because Jerodene was just so funny. Jermaine and I wanted her to have the time of her life because who wants to spend their birthday in the hospital? Jerodene had so much fun, especially having a part of her family around, along with her little brother, Rasheed sharing her special day. When it was time to cut her cake she chose to cut it with Rasheed, he was just three years old at the time. They knew each other better than anyone else did. There she was dressed in her all in one pink and white outfit with her pink fairytale wings and her pink pearl necklace. She had her wand in her hand as she posed for the cameras as if she wanted to work some magic. The cameras rolled and she posed and invented some poses of her own as well.

I told the doctors that I had one request and that was for Jerodene not to get any medication for the latter part of the day and even if the IV slipped out, they should not have it replaced because it was her birthday and the last thing we wanted was for her to be in any discomfort. Even for once, we wanted her to totally forget about the hospital, all the needles and all the torture. Thank God, our wish was granted. We just wanted her to 'let her hair down' and have as much fun as possible. She was so filled with joy and excitement. She was unable to contain herself having family and friends together in one place celebrating with her and knowing that her 7th birthday only comes once in a lifetime. What more could she possibly have asked for? My sister-in-law, Veneica recalled Jerodene telling her, *"Aunty Ven, I am so exhausted! Can you imagine having two birthday parties in one day?"* Overall, it was a day filled with fun and laughter and of course gifts upon gifts started rolling in. Even parents who were there with their children during the party, went and purchased gifts for Jerodene, including our family and friends.

Soon her birthday party was over, her brother Rasheed cried when he realised that it was time for him to go home with his granddad and that he would not be seeing her for a long while. If only I could have calmed him down but no matter what Jermaine and I tried, nothing worked. Soon after Rasheed and his granddad left, we then packed up all her gifts and to our surprise she received a garbage bag of gifts. She was excited to get discharged so that she could get the chance to see and play with them all. Her dad had to take them home because obviously there was no space at her bedside to store them. She kept back just a few items, which included her Icarly perfume that her uncle Randal and his wife presented her with, and a handbag that she got from Shauna and Aaron. She told me that her bag was the perfect size to take her tablet and her girly stuff in when it would be time for her to go to do radiation. She did exactly that. I saw her on numerous occasions using her Icarly perfume spraying a little on her outfit each time she wears them and also some behind her ears smelling all girly and clean. She really loved it.

*Shauna Fung Yee's Visit*

Remember Shauna Fung Yee? Her birthday was in August just as Jerodene's. They both had so much in common and both had wonderful personalities and related well to each other. Shauna came to spend her birthday with Jerodene while she was still admitted. Jerodene wrote her a letter and handed it to her with a tin of Grace Vienna Sausage and told her that she should eat it with another person. Oh how happy they both were! She then told Jerodene thanks for making her day. Shauna spent a few hours with us and I can guarantee that was one of her best birthday gifts because she left smiling. They both loved and cared for each other. Around that same time, Mr. Foster came for a short visit and we were happy that they were able to make it.

*Our Invitation To Kerlyn Brown's Church*

Days had gone by and Jerodene's birthday was in the past. On a particular weekend, I had requested that they not discharge us because Kerlyn had invited us to her church, Worship and Faith International Fellowship (WAFIF). We received a day pass on that Sunday morning and Dr. Swaby told us that if she started having any pain, etc. we should head back straight to the hospital with her. We drove out with Aunty Kerlyn. It was a day well spent in the Lord, worshipping in another church away from our home church. Jerodene was asked to give a testimony, and she did. I recalled her telling the congregation, ***"The doctors say that I have stage 4 cancer but I don't believe them."*** The people in the church started worshipping more and gave God thanks. She told them all that was taking place in her body and that God is the healer, and that we should always continue to believe in Him. As I sat, looked and listened, tears started rolling down my cheeks as my baby girl brought chills to everyone's hearts. Almost all, if not everyone's eyes, were filled with tears. I watched while the pastor stood looking at Jerodene in awe while some sat speechless as Jerodene proclaimed healing even to those who were there and were not feeling well themselves. We all knew and believed God that He would heal her and we all were waiting for that day when she would be cancer free.

### *The Cab Driver's Encounter*

Immediately after church was dismissed, we had to go back to the hospital for the continuation of Jerodene's treatment. On our way back, Aunty Kerlyn had asked a driver, Delroy Smith, to take us back. She told him about Jerodene and in an instance he remembered her and knew exactly who she was. As we continued our journey, he poured out his heart to Jerodene and me. With tears falling from his eyes, he told us of how Jerodene has changed his life ever since he saw her first video on Facebook and that he had been following her on the Inspire Jamaica Program.

Delroy also mentioned that he saw the video that she sent to Usain Bolt. He said that he was thrilled and elated to have met Jerodene in person. As we reached the Hospital, he then asked my permission to take a photo with Jerodene. I told him yes and Jerodene gladly did. Overall, it was a day well spent in the house of the Lord. We were happy that Aunt Kerlyn had invited us.

### *Jodian Pantry's Surprise Visit*

September 2017 came and Jerodene was still admitted in the hospital because she still had some more rounds of radiation treatment to be done. With September being Cancer Awareness Month, plans were already in place for the month. Aunty Kerlyn had organized with local and international Gospel artiste, Jodian Pantry for her to meet Jerodene at the hospital. Timera Brown was another inspiree who was featured previously on the Inspire Jamaica program like Jerodene was. Some months earlier Timera was able to get through to a well-known hospital overseas that caters to children who are diagnosed with cancer. That was the same hospital that denied Jerodene a number of times, unfortunately. Timera and her mother flew to Jamaica the same day and they all planned to meet up at the hospital where Jerodene was admitted. On the visit to the hospital that day were Timera, her parents, Aunty Kerlyn and Jodian Pantry. I knew that Jodian was coming but I did not mention it to Jerodene because we all wanted it to be a great surprise. Jerodene was still at Bed 1 in the section called 'dangerously ill'. Kerlyn called and told me that she was outside of the ward. I was so excited because Jerodene was the one who caused all of this to happen.

I then told Jerodene that she and I were going outside. Of course she inquired the reason and I told her that we would sit and have a mother and daughter talk. By the time we walked off, she ran back to her bedside to get her tablet. When we got outside, Jerodene saw Jodian standing right at the entrance of the door, Jerodene then ran off laughing and screaming all excited and landed in Jodian's arms. They hugged as if there was no tomorrow. They laughed and tears started rolling down my cheeks as I stood and watched them both. Jerodene was so happy that words failed me to explain the moment. Cameras were flashing as the other parents and their children looked on. They enjoyed and welcomed the moment. Kerlyn did an interview afterwhich we all sang Jerodene's favourite song, "*I'll Give My Heart*" They sang and danced happily along with Aunty Kerlyn while Jerodene took a few photos on her own using her tablet. Those were for our keepsake. Jerodene then challenged Jodian with a game called memory. Jerodene won that game and Jodian promised her that she would surely win the game on her next visit.

An interview was done by Kerlyn Brown in order to make an update on the Inspire Jamaica Page and that was when Jodian mentioned that she would be hosting a Gospel Concert entitled, "Jodian Pantry and Friends in Tenacity". It would be held on the 1st of January 2018, and part proceeds would go towards Jerodene's medical expenses. We were happy to hear that because by then Jerodene's medical bill had exceeded J$1 million, and we would be grateful. I could not wait to tell Jermaine the great news. I know that he would be happy like I was. We welcomed the proposal with open arms and we gave God thanks for the new door that He had opened for us.

The evening was well spent, one of joy, happiness and thanksgiving. It was one with a difference for us, especially. Jerodene, being at the hospital surrounded by needles, etc., can get very frustrated, so any little change would have been appreciated. It was time to close the curtains down. Unfortunately, all good things must come to an end. We all had mixed feelings but were overall relieved that Jerodene got her heart's desire. I knew for sure that both Jerodene and Jodian would never forget such a meeting. As they left, Jerodene waved goodbye telling Jodian and Aunty Kerlyn that she would definitely see them soon. She thanked them for coming and the expression on her face told it all. She then told me that was one of her best days ever. She added that she wished that Usain would come as well.

## *The Uncaring and Callous Staff Member*

Around that same time when Jerodene was admitted, I had gone to run an errand. By the time I got back, Jerodene told me that something bad had happened to her while in my absence. When I asked her what took place, she then said that during my absence, the section on her hand where the IV was, got swollen. She then overheard the doctors talking amongst themselves that they would have to replace her IV in order for her to get her required medications. She said upon overhearing that conversation, she ran off seeking to find a hiding spot because she was terrified of the needles more and more as each day went by. She told me that by the time she ran off, a staff member from another department grabbed her by her arm and shouted at her telling her to go sit down and *"take the damn IV"*. Immediately I got upset, and decided to ask her to tell me the second time. She then repeated it another time, word for word. I had so many questions. Why would she do something like that, to a little child, at that? Noone should be treated in such a manner, no matter what the circumstances may be. As angry as I was, I decided not to confront that individual because things might have gotten out of control. Jerodene cried saying, **"Mommy why would she say that to me? And you and Daddy never used the word dam to me or Rasheed. What does she know about me for her to be talking to me like that?"** Upon hearing all those questions from Jerodene I was livid and felt like I would have a physical confrontation with her. That was my daughter whom she hurt and I knew Jerodene would not fabricate such a story. I believed every word that my child told me more than anyone else. That was the first anything like that sort ever happened and I definitely would not let it happen to another child nor would I let it slip. Jerodene was already going through so much already for anyone to be treating her like that. I then told the nurses and the doctors. I knew something must be done, so I did not let it just stop there. I then went to the nurse in charge of all three Paediatric wards. I was then told to write a report of the incident. The good thing was that Jerodene was able to give a full description, even the colour of the uniform that she wore on that day.

I handed them the report and within a day or two, and that particular staff member was then questioned. On one of those early mornings, shortly after the nurses had changed shifts, the nurse in charge brought the same staff member to Jerodene's bedside and then asked Jerodene to tell her exactly what had transpired on the day in question. Jerodene did that but one could see the look on Jerodene's face that she was a bit scared to talk because the staff member was staring right at her. I then told her that everything would be okay and that was when she felt confident to finish her story. The staff member then denied everything just as I thought she would have. Jerodene then shouted nervously, **"But Mommy she is lying!"** Of course, I believed my child. They then left and within a few days the staff member was still working there and so it seemed as if nothing was done. I went back to the person in charge to get some information, then shortly afterwards her contract was revoked. When Jerodene told her dad, he was very angry because he believed in our baby girl the same way I did. We really gave God thanks that justice was served.

### *Being Home Sick*

A few days had passed and our baby girl was still admitted. She was getting more frustrated as each day went by, because the hospital setting and needles were getting to her. She cried from time to time saying, *"Mommy, I want to go home to Rasheed and Daddy. I am tired of the hospital food, I want to go home and eat your and Daddy's cooking because the hospital meals don't taste good."* She told me several times that she was fed up, and each time that she would cry and pour her heart out, it just broke my heart knowing that there was nothing that I could have done to make the situation any better.

### *Veins Nowhere In Sight*

Due to chemotherapy treatment, her veins were becoming less visible each day. I remember at one point in time, when Jerodene's IV had to be replaced, she bit one of the doctors. Normally when children are admitted, the parents were not allowed to be inside the treatment room but with Jerodene it was different. Each time I would have to accompany her inside because on most occasions, she was not cooperative at all. She would cry very loudly when it was time for her to get an injection. Sometimes she would just literally fight her way through. It pained my heart numerous times that I had to hold her down on the bed as she screamed loudly as the doctors would stick her sometimes 10 times just to find her veins. After holding her down on several occasions, I always felt guilty. On a particular day, when holding her down in the treatment room she was screaming out for help, I could not do it anymore. I ran off the ward because I became very emotional and deep inside I felt as if I was doing something wrong. I literally felt as if I was about to faint. Oh God! The hurt and agony that Jerodene and other children had gone through and most instances, us as parents as well.

### *September - Childhood Cancer Awareness Month*

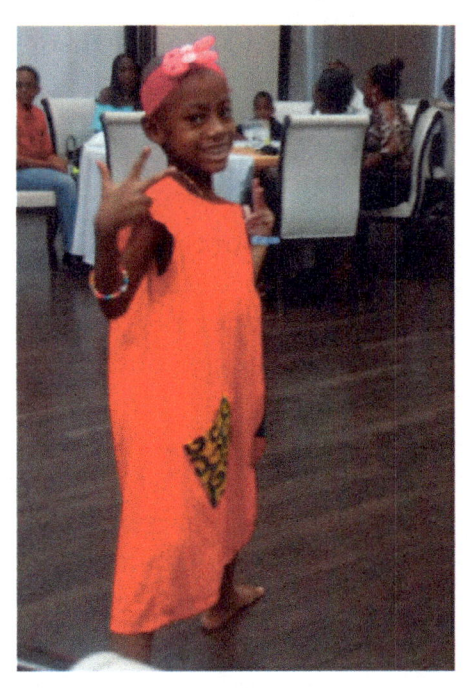

In the month of September quite a number children who were diagnosed with cancer were still admitted. With September being Childhood Cancer Awareness Month, all the children who were diagnosed with cancer were all invited to a function at a particular hotel in Kingston, Jamaica. It was a formal setting and Dr. Reece-Mills, the Paediatric Oncologist, organised a bus to take us to and from the venue. Of course, we as parents had to accompany our children. Oh, you should have seen the look on each children's faces knowing that they were away from the hospital for a few hours! They were just so happy that they all had smiles on their faces. We had fun just seeing our children having fun. Jerodene had never modelled before but she was asked to participate in that part of the program, along with some other little girls in her age group. Jerodene hit the runway in an orange dress, she smiled, waved and blew kisses to the audience. She did extremely well in her other outfits as well. I then thought to myself that Jerodene might consider modelling as a career when she got older but then I remembered her telling her dad and me that she wanted to become a pastor or a nurse. We knew by the grace of God that Jerodene's dream would come true. I sat and watched her as she ate her slice of cheesecake, and felt nothing but genuine love for this child. Words were not enough to explain how happy Jerodene was. One could see that Jerodene totally took her mind off the hospital as the music played, she sang and danced, without a care in the world. The joy in her eyes was evident as the doctors and others looked on.

After a while, Jerodene was asked if there was anything that she would love to do or say, and of course she told them that she would love to encourage the audience. When it was time, she boldly took the microphone from Dr. Michael Abrahams, Master of Ceremonies (MC) and started by singing one of her little songs that she learnt at Sunday School, 'Whose side are you leaning on? Leaning on the Lord's side'. The audience engaged in the song and started singing as well. When she was through singing, she then said, *"I have stage 4 muscle cancer, that is what the doctors diagnosed me with and I don't believe it's true because I know that God is up there healing me. He is covering us, and I want to thank the doctors on Ward 14, 15 and 16. They have been good doctors to us, and I want to thank Dr. Reece-Mills for helping us through our situation. It has been very hard for me and my friends on Ward 14, 15 and 16. So I want to say this from the bottom of my heart, I want all of you to be healed today in Jesus' name, because I know God is up there healing me right now and healing other children out there. So I want to tell God thanks for everything. Thanks for friends and family and also thanks for caring for us and being loving. I want everybody to be kind and friendly to each other, and I want to pray."* She then prayed, *"Oh Holy Father, bless and sanctify us God because You are the only One that we have, You are the One that made us Lord, so cover us and sanctify us while we go through this day. Bless and sanctify this day. Cover the other children Oh God. Cover them under Your blood because I know that You can do it God. Bless and sanctify us God in Your name. Amen."* She then handed back the microphone to the MC. Everyone was brought to tears including the MC when Jerodene was through with her speech and praying. He was stunned and in awe knowing that Jerodene just brought everyone to tears. Jerodene spoke on behalf of all the sick children on all three Paediatric wards. She was not coached on what to say. She opened her mouth and the Almighty God had filled it with the right words to say. She received a pair of headphones as a gift, which was really appreciated. It was time to go back to the hospital and everyone left feeling satisfied.

*National Heroes' Day Weekend*

The month of September was coming to a close and Jerodene was still getting treatment. Thank God that the doctors had given us the chance to go home for the weekend. We were very happy to hear that, and instead of us going to our house in Manchester, Jermaine suggested that all four of us should meet by my Aunty Rose's house in the neighbouring parish. That was a good idea. We were all very elated, especially Jerodene and Rasheed knowing that they had not seen each other since Jerodene's birthday in August. Can you imagine the great reunion? We got there before Jermaine and Rasheed. By then Rasheed had just started Hope Demonstration Basic School and Jermaine had to leave work to pick him up and then travel to Aunt Rose. Unfortunately, we were not home to see him off to school due to circumstances beyond our control. By the time they got there, the children were overwhelmed, seeing each other. They hugged, kissed, they played and laughed. Rasheed was even showing Jerodene how good he was at doing push-ups, and Jerodene was doing them with him. Jerodene was not backing down either. They were just trying to make up for lost times and nothing could stop them.

People always told me that I took too many pictures and that I loved to video too much but I knew that one day I would thank myself for doing so and they might thank me too. As the unofficial family photographer, I snapped more pictures during our weekend together. We had a lovely weekend with Aunty, except at one point when Jerodene started having some discomfort in her abdomen. Luckily, I had gotten some pain medication from the hospital to take with me so that helped. We gave God thanks as usual. There is a saying that I have used quite often in this account, "all good things must come to an end" and unfortunately the time came for us to separate once more. That was one of the hardest times to face, only God knew how we felt. We wished that we did not have to go but unfortunately Jerodene had to go back to the hospital. It was a very sad moment for all of us. I literally cried, I could not control my tears. Letting go ripped our hearts apart. Jerodene and I got out of the taxi first because we had to go catch a bus back to Kingston. The children cried loudly as they waved goodbye to each other. That was an unforgettable weekend.

As Jerodene and I journeyed back to Kingston, I tried to analyse the whole situation, while so many questions were popping up in my head. Instead of us living a happy life, Jerodene had to be in and out of hospital due to this dreaded disease. Why did we not have the chance to live a normal life like other families? I wondered why Jerodene could not have a happy childhood. Jerodene was being tortured with all those needles and had such a fear of hospitals. We deserved to be happy. I thought, there were so many murderers, rapists and robbers are out there living their happy lives and we were never engaged in such activities and we had to be facing all of this. Life was just not fair, I thought to myself. I often heard never question God but I had to ask, why us? What did we do to deserve all this? These were some of the questions I had to ask God and where was God in all this, our crisis?

Oftentimes, when I saw all that Jerodene was going through I told myself that had I known that Jerodene was going to be sick, then Rasheed would not have been in the picture. I said it out of frustration, because it was getting too much to handle. Jerodene has such a bright future ahead of her and she was missing out on a happy and healthy life. She was registered for primary school and her uniforms were made by her dressmaker. She still had the port in her chest area, so we asked her grandmother Doreen to purchase one of those pulley bags because wearing a regular backpack would not be a good idea. It is not as if we did not try. Seeing all the preparations were made for her, we prayed and hoped for the best.

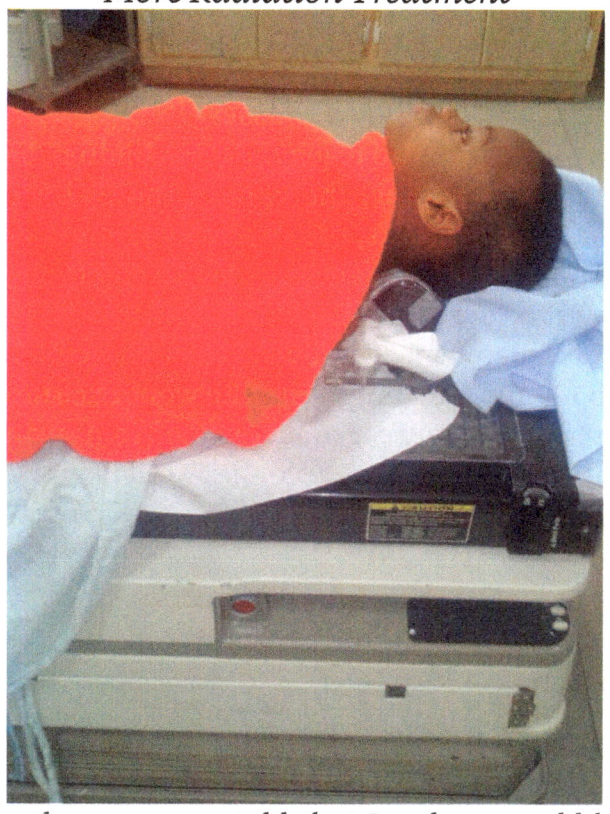

## More Radiation Treatment

October came and by then we were told that Jerodene would have to do added radiation treatments on her abdomen and pelvis. We thought that they would have done both in one in order to speed up the process but they explained that they had to do them at different times. At that time, Jerodene was not able to take a proper shower because no water was supposed to touch the area. After a while, her tolerance for the radiation treatments had improved since the mass that was between her neck and shoulder was gone. We never imagined that the radiation would remove the mass but we knew that God was in the midst of it all. To Him be all the glory and honour. The area was still a little dark but her normal complexion was coming back. Additionally, Jerodene's head had darkened due to the previous radiation treatments done on her brain. Jerodene was light skinned, therefore, the dark areas were easily seen. I saw her a couple of times trying to scrape off the dark area on top of her head but I would stop her in the process and tell her that it would all be gone in time. Her head was so shiny and soft and I had the pleasure rubbing it down with the consecrated olive oil. It felt really good and Jerodene enjoyed every moment of it. The smile on her face was priceless.

## Low Blood Count

When we went back for admission, we were placed in one of the side rooms on ward 16. It had more privacy and I thought that Jerodene would not adjust well to it knowing that she loved being among her friends. On second thought, I figured that it would work out for the best. After a while, Jerodene adjusted to our little room very well and she had her own little bathroom. A few days had passed and Jerodene blood count had fallen and even though we were in the side room Jerodene had to wear a mask. Without a mask, it would have been easy for her to catch any infection lurking around. I was told by the nurses that I had to wear a mask as well. I knew wearing one would have been uncomfortable but I would do anything for our little Jerodene. During that time, there were no visible veins in any of her hands. Unfortunately, they had to place the IV in one of her legs. It was difficult for Jereodene because she had to be hopping on one foot. In most instances, whenever it was time for her to use the bathroom I had to lift her up and take her.

## *Ward Classes*

The hospital garnered two teachers to teach the sick children, because some of the children actually lived at the hospital. For Jerodene, the longest she had ever been admitted was four months without going home, and for others, they had been there much longer. Jerodene enjoyed going to class on a daily basis. Sometimes I had to lift her to and fro and even though at times my back would act up due to my previous spinal injury, I did what I had to. Having the IV in her leg slowed her down by far because Jerodene was always an active child. She loved to run and even though at times I had to shout telling her not to run she would do the opposite. She murmured at times wanting the IV out of her leg because it hindered her from sprinting all over the place. One could see her hopping on one leg while holding onto the IV stand with one hand. Jerodene was just so determined and nothing seemed to hold her back. She was just unstoppable.

*Jerodene Needed Blood*

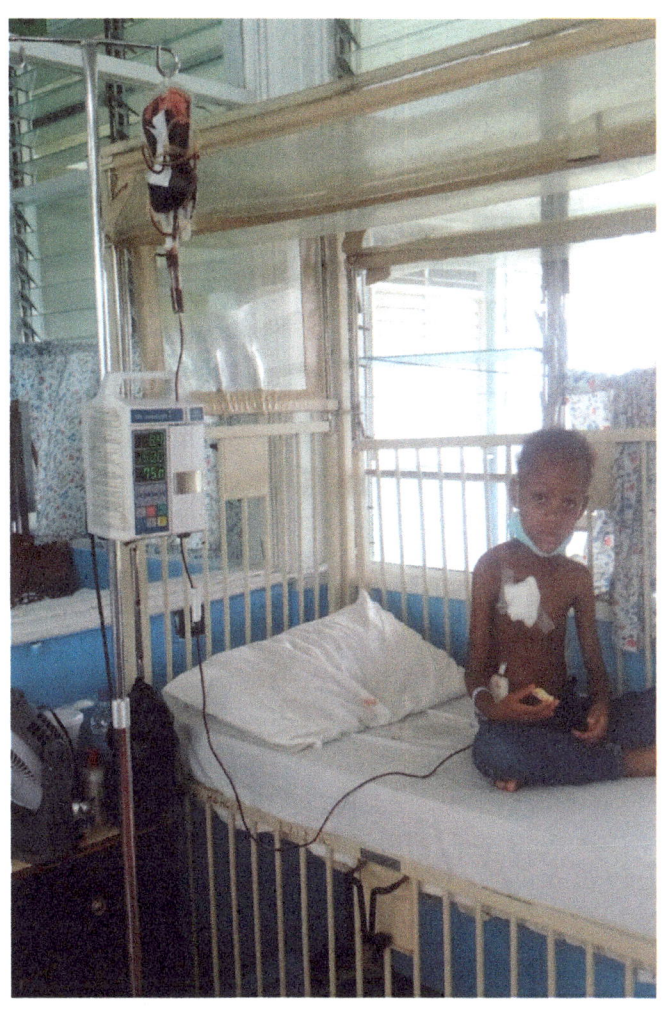

I remembered at another time when Jerodene had a very low blood count and the only option was for them to give her blood. My heart skipped a beat when they told me that because Jerodene had never gotten blood before. I immediately started praying in my mind asking God to let His will be done. They then sent for the blood from the lab. It took a while for them to get it to the ward. It came eventually and the team began the procedure. During the process, all was going well but after a while Jerodene started vomiting and had a very high temperature. They immediately stopped the procedure. That day was also one of the most unforgettable ones, and Jermaine vowed that it would never happen again.

## *Jerodene Sang During Her Pain*

During October 2017, while we were in the side room, Jerodene started having some abdominal pains. I informed the nurses and they gave her some slow release morphine because that was the only medication that would have given her some ease. At one point she was given morphine by injection but the team did not want her to get addicted to it so that was when we were introduced to the slow release morphine tablets. (I did research on all the medications that they had her on. I searched for their side effects. Some of the side effects were hard to deal with but at times we had no choice, therefore we had to ask God to pass all the medications through His Son's blood and let all be well in His name). She cried because she had a lot of discomfort. At times, all I could have done was to give her as much comfort as possible until she felt a little better.

A few hours after crying for abdominal pain, Jerodene started singing a few lines of one of Jermaine Edwards' songs, 'Lord I thank you for sunshine, thank you for rain, thank you for joy, thank you for pain. It's a beautiful day.' I looked at her in shock asking myself, *"Am I hearing correctly? Wasn't Jerodene just experiencing severe pain and then she's thanking God for pain?"* I looked at her then asked her, *"Jerodene, are you really thanking God for pain?"* She looked at me with a little smile on her face then she responded, **"Yes Mommy, I have to thank God for pain because it's not every time things are going to go smoothly, the way we want it to."** I then looked at her and all I could do was smile, that little angel never ceased to amaze us.

## *Remembering Amielle*

Remember Amielle Brown? The same little girl that Jerodene prayed for while she was at bed 1? She was not doing too well for a couple of days, she became very ill. I honestly could not tell Jerodene even though she really insisted on going by her bedside to see her. I had to find some excuse because by then the nurses had already screened her off because the family needed their privacy. I prayed for her and called my mom and her prayer team to pray for Amielle because we knew that God was still able to see her through. Unfortunately, after a few days Amielle passed. I literally cried because I thought that she would have made it due to all the prayers that were made on her behalf. Her death came as a shock to me, a hard pill to swallow. We had asked God for healing and it was at that time it dawned on me that healing comes in two different ways. Obviously, that healing was not the type that we all hoped for. The biggest question I had was, how do I tell Jerodene? How would she react? Would she go into a silent zone? With all those questions I decided not to tell her and the doctors and the nurses all agreed with me as well. They all knew Jerodene very well and knew how sensitive she was and that she would not tolerate such sad news very well. At that time I was very happy that we were in the side room. Had she not been there she would have known or maybe one of her little friends would have mentioned it to her and by then she would have had a lot of questions to ask. So her being in the side room worked out well.

I had to lock her inside the room because I did not want her to have a clue whatsoever. The other thing was the porters would have to walk past our room in order to take away Amielle's body to the morgue. I could not even imagine the pain and the heartache that the family must have been going through. My heart went out to the Brown's family. Tears filled my eyes when I saw the relatives moving her stuff from the bedside to their car, piece by piece and bit by bit and Amielle was nowhere in sight. How does a family deal with such great loss? How do parents move on without their child? From one parent to another, what does one parent tell another to comfort them after the loss of an only child? What were the words of comfort spoken? I knew for sure that there would be rough days ahead. Even though Amielle had passed, I did not let it dampen my faith in God because I knew by the grace of God that Jerodene's healing would come in the other form. Jerodene had so much faith in God and she had so much to share with the world and we really awaited the day when the doctors would tell us that Jerodene was cancer free.

The following day Jerodene had gone on the ward to go see her nurse friends. I went with her because I did not want anyone to mention anything to her about Amielle's passing. Upon reaching the ward, Jerodene realised that Amielle's bed was empty. She then asked me, **"Mommy, where is Amielle, is she gone home?"** I then told her yes. In fact she had gone home but not the home that Jerodene would have thought of. She then told me how happy she was that Amielle had gotten the chance to go home due to the fact that she was admitted for such a long time and that she had gone home to live a normal life. If only Jerodene knew that we had kept Amielle's death a secret.

One of the main reasons I decided to keep Amielle's death a secret from Jerodene was a few days prior to Amielle's death, a lady friend of mine whom Jerodene and I met at the hospital lost her son. Her name was Trudy-Ann and her son, Rashaun was diagnosed with neuroblastoma and he had transitioned a few days before Amielle. His death hit me like a ton of bricks. I felt it so much for Trudy-Ann and her family and could not even imagine the agony that they were in. I knew that God would have given them the added strength to go through their time of grieving. Jerodene and Rashaun were friends; they played together sometimes. At that time Jerodene was in the side room and after his passing I had to let her know because I did not want her to hear from someone else. Telling her would have been one of the hardest tasks, so I had asked the Oncologist to break the news to her. Upon hearing such sad and devastating news, Jerodene sat on the doctor's chair for a few minutes. She was extremely lost and broken. I could have seen the pain in her eyes. Suddenly she rushed out of the office. I ran to get her but then I thought that she might need some alone time to process all that she just heard. I wished that I could have just locked her away from everyone so that she would not be able to hear all the sad news of some of her friends dying.

I waited for a while but she did not return to me, so I told one of the nurses what had transpired and she decided to go find her. I was not too worried about her whereabouts because all three Paediatric wards were secured and she could not have gone beyond the security gate. The nurse found her and she was seated on the outside of Ward 14. The nurse hugged her and lifted her because she wanted to take her back to Ward 16. By the time the nurse lifted her, that was when Jerodene broke down in tears as she wept openly. She cried uncontrollably as the nurse made her way back to the ward. The pain was too much for Jerodene and at that time she cried uncontrollably and loudly as almost everyone looked on. I could not control her then because there was nothing that I could have done to ease her pain. I just wished that there was something that I could have done. As I stood looking at her, tears filled my eyes, fighting to hold them back and trying to console her at the same time but to no avail. She cried so much for Rashaun and there was nothing that I could have done to ease her pain. It was just so sad. It took her quite a while before Jerodene got over Rashaun's death. I am not sure if she ever did. Because of that experience with Rashaun's passing, we did not mention anything to her about Amielle's death. I had planned on being at Amielle's home going celebration but unfortunately Jerodene was not feeling well so I was unable to attend. I was at Jerodene's bedside but my heart and mind was with the Brown's family in their time of bereavement.

## *Rashaun's Homegoing*

At the time it was the time of Rashaun's funeral, Jerodene was still admitted and we were still in the side room but at that time Jerodene was more stable. Therefore, another parent and I decided to go along with a few of the nurses from ward 16. Even though the journey was a long way from the hospital I had asked the nurses to keep a close watch on Jerodene but I had to pay my last respects to the little hero, Rashaun Fearon, who fought so hard. I had to be there in support for the rest of his family. Honestly, if I was the one in their position (and I hoped to God that I would not be in such a situation) I would have wanted as much support as I could have gotten.

As the funeral was in full swing, my phone rang and on the other end was one of Jerodene's doctors. He then told me that Jerodene needed a new IV because the one that she had was infiltrated. They also said upon reaching the room that Jerodene was in, they realised that she locked herself inside the room and was telling them that she was frustrated and tired of all needle sticks and that she did not need any more IV in her leg. I got an instant headache. How could Jerodene have done such a thing? I thought to myself. I am so far away from her. I was on the phone for over 15 minutes trying to convince Jerodene to open the door but all I was saying went on deaf ears. The doctors tried convincing her as well but it seemed as if she had already made up her mind not to open the door. Nothing anyone said to her could have changed her mind. I then told one of the doctors not to select a site for the new IV until I got back from Rashaun's funeral. When Jerodene heard that and with a little help from one of the nurses, Jerodene opened the door. It was a very sad and mournful day at Rashaun's funeral but I was happy that I had gotten the chance to attend.

Although it was a bit early, we were already making plans for all four of us to be present at the Jodian Pantry and Friends' in Tenacity concert. Jodian wanted Jerodene to do a video inviting people to the concert. Jodian told us exactly what she wanted in the video and even though Jerodene was still admitted I was her videographer so I had to make sure that the video was done properly.

*Jerodene's Pleasant Surprise*

Around that same time, all the cancer patients on the Paediatric ward had gotten the chance to go to the circus which was close by in Kingston, and all of us as parents were asked to accompany them. Around the same time we were in the car park waiting to leave for the circus and Jerodene was seated beside me in a car. There we saw Kevin Downswell, Jerodene's other favourite Gospel artiste. When Jerodene saw him she screamed and shouted in excitement, ***"Kevin Downsweelll!"*** By the time Kevin turned around Jerodene leaped into his arms and they both hugged. Jerodene then introduced herself to him since Kevin did not know her personally. She then told him that she was one of his biggest fans and that she was diagnosed with stage 4 muscle cancer and that she was a patient at that same hospital. It was obvious that Kevin was happy to have met her. So he told her that he would be praying for her and that she should continue to think positively. He then hugged her again then rushed to his car where he handed her one of his latest CDs entitled, 'ALL THE WAY'. I was then able to take a photograph of both of them. That was a priceless moment and Jerodene left feeling elated. She then told all her friends about her meeting Kevin Downswell. She was also elated to show them the picture that both of them took together as proof.

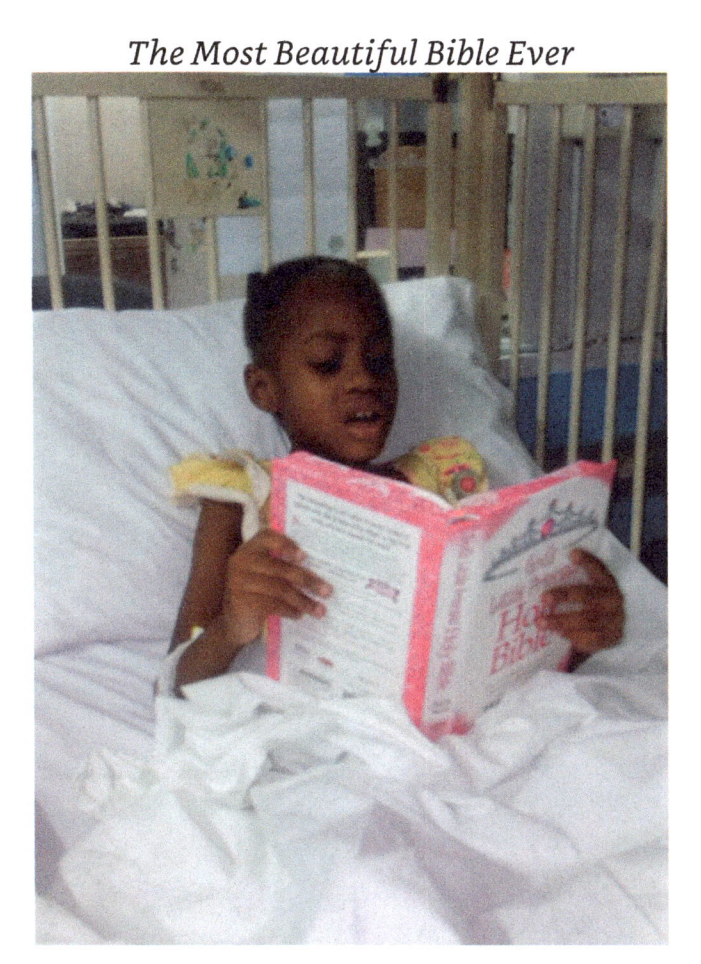

*The Most Beautiful Bible Ever*

Did I mention that our baby girl had one of the most beautiful bibles ever made? The history behind it was that I had a video on my phone of Jerodene while she was at church encouraging and praying for the congregation. I had shown it to one of Jerodene's favourite nurses, Nurse Mitchell, she was so thrilled watching the video and learning that we shared the same faith. When she was through watching the video she looked at Jerodene then uttered, *"Jerodene I am going to purchase a Bible for you to go preach the Word of God."* A few days later, Nurse Mitchell kept her promise and came back with the prettiest pink and white, princess Bible that I had ever seen. On the front of the bible was a beautiful white crown and the writing, 'GOD'S LITTLE PRINCESS HOLY BIBLE'. It was just so beautiful and Jerodene fell in love with it at the first glance. From time to time, one could see Jerodene, even on her hospital bed, reading each night before heading off to bed. Even while going to church Jerodene had it in her possession. She told Nurse Mitchell that she loved and appreciated it and it was in one of her favourite colours - pink.

*Jerodene Invented The 1st Pink Day*

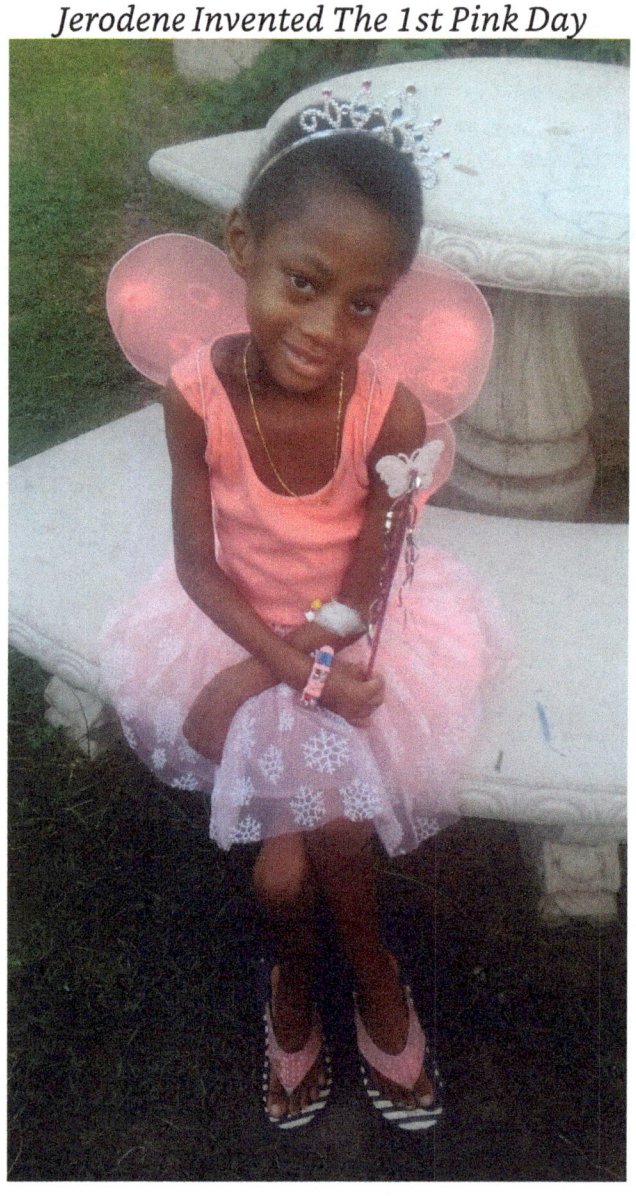

While Jerodene was a patient on Ward 16, she came up with the idea of inventing 'Pink Day'. She had told the doctors, nurses and even the PCAs that the following day they should all wear something pink because pink was one of her favourite colours and she wanted them to share that day with her. That they did and all who had something pink wore it. Jerodene was dressed in her full pink outfit, which included her pink fairy wings and wand. Pink Day was well spent and everyone enjoyed it, and for sure that day had gone into the history books.

## *Jerodene's Family Support*

Jerodene had a very strong and powerful family support behind her, with lots of prayers, love and support. Jerodene did not lack love or affection. She was loved by all, even by those who had not met her face to face, and she gave that love back in return. She was very kind, fun-loving, smart and energetic. She would give her last and left herself without, just to make someone else happy and comfortable. She loved her brother, Rasheed, endlessly and spoke very highly of him. At times, whilst at home, she would place him to lay down in the chair against his will, and would perform on him all the procedures that the student doctors had performed on her at the hospital. I felt so sorry for him at times but overall Jerodene was very determined.

After the deaths of Amielle and Rashaun, the ward was getting back to normality, somewhat. I prayed to God telling him that we did not need to hear of anymore deaths among our children. It had become too unbearable and based on Jerodene's last reaction to Rashaun's death I had to pray that prayer. I had no doubt that God had heard and answered my prayer.

## *Michelle's Visit*

A friend of mine named Michelle who lived in Canada came to visit us at the hospital. She loved Jerodene dearly and decided that she had to pay us a visit before she headed back home, which was the following day. A while before she came I noticed that Jerodene's abdomen was distended. I brought it to the doctors' attention but there was no good explanation as to what might have caused it. They had also administered some medications to Jerodene and within a short while I realised that she was having an allergic reaction. She was having severe pain and as usual they gave her the morphine injection. She never had any allergic reaction to it so I was a bit baffled. I showed it to the nurses and they gave her some DPH to counteract the allergic reaction. After a while, Jerodene felt some sense of relief and there she was with Michelle singing one of our Jamaican Old Folk songs. We were all having fun, Michelle stayed for a while but then she had to leave because she was due to travel back home the next day. Before she left, Jerodene told her that she did not want her to leave and that Jamaica was the best place to be. Michelle agreed and they both prayed before her departure. We really appreciated her visit and even though it was in the hospital setting, it was a visit well spent and Michelle left smiling.

*The Father of a Lifetime*

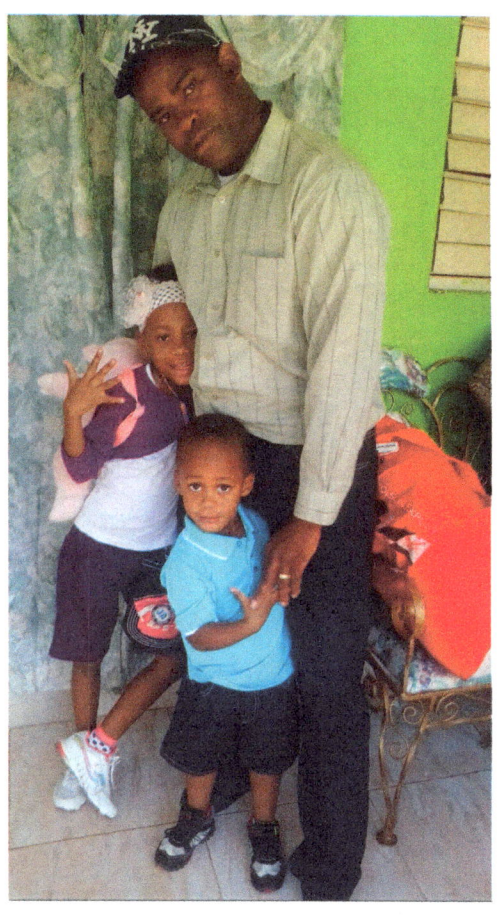

Due to Jerodene's constant stay in the hospital, Jermaine was the one who made sure that all of Rasheed's back to school shopping was done. Jermaine also was the one who had to make sure that Rasheed was on time for school and then at times he had to pick him up from school. He would get a taxi to take him to daycare or sometimes to Ms. Green, a past-teacher from his basic school. She would keep him until Jermaine finished working. It was a bit challenging for Jermaine but he balanced Rasheed and his work duties very well. I can recall a few weeks after Rasheed began his very first day at basic school, Jerodene was still admitted at the Hospital, so I had asked one of the nurses to watch Jerodene for me because I wanted to go visit Rasheed at his school, which was about two hours away. When I got there, I stood outside of his classroom and watched him for a while just to see how he interacted with his peers and his teacher. When he looked up and saw me it was as if he did not recognize me until after a while. As he came to hug me with a bright smile on his face, tears fell from my eyes. We were so elated to see each other, because we have missed out on so much for the past couple of months. I watched him as he ate his lunch and for a short while played with his friends and he would not take his eyes off me. I knew that he was aware that I might have to leave him again. It really pained my heart that I had to leave him so soon but I had to go back to the hospital to be with his sister. What could we do? As I turned my back he cried loudly, *"Mommy, Mommy don't go! Don't go!"* His teacher came to get him and tried to comfort him. I could not even look back. I literally cried because things should not have to be like that. I had taken a few pictures and videos because I had to show them to Jerodene. I got back to the hospital at a reasonable time and Jerodene was overjoyed to see the pictures and videos of her little brother. It was a day of mixed emotions but I gave God thanks, nonetheless.

## Jerodene And Akayden Bid Farewell

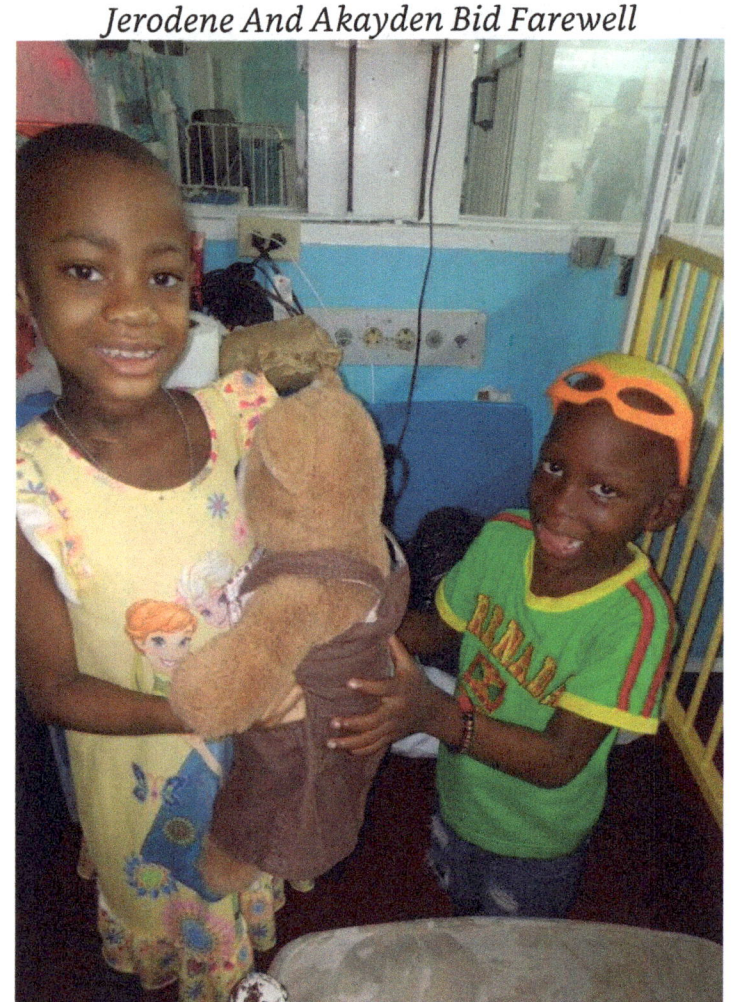

The time came for Jerodene's best friend, Akayden Wilson and his mom, Akili to make preparations to go back to their hometown, Grenada for follow-up treatment. The night before their departure, they came to bid us goodbye. Akayden had taken a brown teddy bear to give to Jerodene as a gift. He presented it to her as I got my phone to take a few pictures, because moments like those I did not want to miss out on. Jerodene then kissed him on his cheek and then they both smiled. I knew for sure that they would surely miss each other. They were playmates for quite a number of months; they had their disagreements at times but they just could not stay away from each other. They played and laughed together ever so often, for sure they would miss each other's company. As all four of us gave our final hugs, Akili and I got real emotional because we had no idea when all four of us would see each other again. We all grew as a family and it was so hard to separate. I knew for sure that Jerodene would treasure that gift and hold it close to her heart. For sure, one day in the future, we would certainly meet again and by that time both Akayden and Jerodene would have gotten over that dreaded disease and would be among those who kicked cancer's butt.

Jerodene's favourite cake was Black Forest cake, and every now and then we would treat ourselves to one whenever Jerodene was not in the hospital. Jerodene, for one, always looked forward to it more than anything else. After her best friend, Akayden and his mom left for Grenada, we got discharged that same weekend. Jerodene was extremely happy to reunite with her family and also to be sleeping in her own bed. It felt good for me to be in my own bed. She and her brother woke up early the following day and started to play because she knew that she would only be home for the weekend. They both could not get enough of each other.

*Church Time*

Jerodene's favourite part of the weekend was when she went to church. Everyone always looked forward to hearing her testimonies and that time was no different. When it was the preacher's time, our then pastor, Pastor Watson, asked her to share her testimony. You know that our baby girl did not back down because she had so much to share with God's wonderful people. She took the microphone while the congregation stood up and cheered her on. This was her testimony, ***"Praise the Lord church, I haven't been in church for a very long time and a few weeks ago my good friend, Rashaun passed off, and when I found out I was so sad and I didn't want to talk, and I was frustrated and didn't know what to do. But God cover us today. God bless me today because I wasn't*** *here for so long but today I am here and I am feeling better now. Satan back off because there's no space here for you. God says that we shall not die but live and declare the works of the Lord. We shall live, we shall live. God cover us in the name of Jesus. When I was at the hospital they gave me a lot of sticks, sometimes 8 and 10 times. But now I'm here, I want to thank God that I am here today at church cause it's been a while since I haven't been to church. But where am I at? I'm at church now. I want to tell God thank You for everything because if it wasn't for You we wouldn't be here, we don't know where we would be and we wouldn't want to know either. All we should know is that we should always believe in God. He is the One who made us. He is the One who covers you. He is the One who heals you. Some persons woke up and some persons didn't wake up. They died in their sleep. We are right here. You need to thank Him one more time. God cover us Lord, cause if it wasn't for You we don't know who we'd be, so we need to thank Him."*

After that testimony, she then paused and sang one of her favourite songs, "Whose side are you leaning on?" One could see her dressed in her red and black glitter dress with her black jacket that her Aunty Romayne/ Anto bought for her. As she sang and rocked to the song, the musicians joined with her. When she was through singing she continued her testimony by saying, *"We have to praise the Lord morning, evening and day. If it wasn't for Him, we would not have been here at church today. We would have been in our beds dead. But God didn't let us die. God chose you, He chose you. You are God's daughters and sons. Thank Him one more time because if it wasn't for Him, we don't know where we would have been. Thank Him one more time. Jesus, Jesus, Jesus!"* She shouted as she jumped and worshipped the Almighty God. *"Cover us Lord."* she uttered then she prayed, *"Oh Lord, we are Your children dear Lord, cover us under Your blood, Lord because if it wasn't for You we wouldn't be here. Back off Satan, back off, go away, go away. You don't belong here and you never will. Amen."* The church immediately stood up and worshipped, lost in the sweet sweet Holy Ghost. When she was through, she then handed back the microphone to the pastor. They all prayed a special prayer for her and it was a day well spent in the house of the Lord.

### *"I Don't Want To Go Back"*

By the time we got home from church, the reality had hit Jerodene forcefully that she would have to go back to the hospital the following day. Knowing that she had a stress free, fun-filled weekend with her family, especially with her little brother, Rasheed who was just three years old at the time, Jerodene started crying openly. It really broke our hearts. Our hearts shattered like broken glass. Even though we knew the reason for her crying we still asked her. She told us that she did not want to go back to the hospital and she wished that she never had to go back there. With tears falling from her swollen eyes, she then went into her drawer and reached for her princess diary and pencil and drew a sad little girl with tears rolling down the little girl's face and beside the little girl she drew a broken heart. As we looked at it tears rolled down my eyes and it was evident on her dad's face that he was torn. The pain was obvious in his eyes. This was painful for all four of us, and we could not even imagine how broken Jerodene's heart was. The picture that she drew needed no interpretation. She was the sad little girl with a broken heart. It was very painful knowing that there was nothing we could have said to comfort her. We tried to encourage her and let her know that it would all be over soon and that she would soon be able to live a normal life just like an ordinary child. Her question to her dad and I was, *"What do you call very soon?"* To that question we had no answer, we just had to look to God for answers because He was our only source. We trusted God that He would let it all happen soon. The main thing was that we were happy that she was not experiencing any more seizure attacks because if she was still having them then they would not have granted us the discharge. The seizure episodes were devastating and I wished no other child or even an adult would have to encounter such a terrible ordeal. Even though Jerodene had requested her baptism, she still was not granted her wish as yet because of the fact that she was still undergoing radiation treatment but we knew that very soon she would get her heart's desire.

### *He Thought That His Gun Was His Only Protection Until…*

A few days after we got back to the hospital, I checked my Facebook messages as usual and there were a few awaiting me. One was from a schoolmate of mine, we were very happy to have gotten back in touch with each other after nearly 20 years. He told me that he had been living overseas ever since he left high school. He also told me that he really wanted to talk to me. He said that he and his friends had been following Jerodene's story and had been watching all her videos on Facebook for quite some time. All that time, he had no idea that Jerodene was my daughter. He eventually called me and went further to say that all his life he thought that his gun was his only protection, but it was Jerodene that caused him to know otherwise, that Jesus was his only protection. He confessed that all his life he never owned a Bible because he did not see the need to. However, because of Jerodene, he walked into a bookstore and purchased a Bible for himself. Since becoming a father, he never had a relationship with his daughters, but he thanked God that Jerodene caused him to have a relationship with them. He advised that he was watching two famous American preachers who spoke highly of the 'little girl from Jamaica'.

He met in an accident and doctors told him that he would not be able to walk again due to how severe the situation was. He said that after he watched one of Jerodene's videos, he looked himself in the mirror and said that if Jerodene can do it, so can he. He built up his faith and with the help of God he was able to walk again. He claimed that Jerodene touched his life in many ways, and that he was very anxious to meet her when he returned to Jamaica. He said that he would visit the United States from time to time. He went to visit a church while there and they were all talking about the little fighting hero from Jamaica and the love that she had for God. They spoke of the faith that she had in Him, and even in her lowest times one would ask her how she was doing and she would say in a still small voice, **"I am okay."** He said when he told the members that he never knew Jerodene personally but he knew her mom because we went to school together, they were in awe and disbelief. They immediately sent their love and sympathy to Jerodene and said that they were praying that she would get better soon. From time to time, whenever he got the chance, he would video call her. On some occasions, instead of him encouraging Jerodene, it was Jerodene who was encouraging him. I remember Jerodene telling him to continue believing in God and He would come through for him.

### *Meeting Sister Eunice Beckford*

Another lady who also reached out to me via Facebook messenger was Eunice Beckford. She told me that even though she had not met Jerodene personally she saw Jerodene's story on Inspire Jamaica and videos on Facebook and they had really touched her life in a positive way. She told me of the love that she had for Jerodene, that she had a donation to help with Jerodene's medical expenses. She asked for permission to come pay us a visit at the hospital. Normally I would not do that but we connected in the first instance. She appeared genuine and since she claimed to be a child of God, I took the chance and told her that she would be welcomed. Days went by and Sister Eunice gave us encouraging words continually, which were well needed at the time. The time that she chose to visit us, we were back in the side room and we had arranged for her to come and visit. I was anxious to meet Sister Eunice and to tell Jerodene and Jermaine about her. At that time, visiting hours ended at 8pm, and the hospital's security was strict in upholding the regulations regarding visiting hours. Sister Beckford lived about two hours away from the hospital and at that time, the traffic would have already been at peak hour. She reached the hospital at approximately 8pm, and the security officer was understanding and let her through. I went to the gate to meet someone whom I was seeing for the first time. We both hugged each other and laughed as if we had known each other for years; the love and warmth was evident. She was a bit nervous because she had no idea if Jerodene would have accepted or welcomed her. Jerodene did welcome her with open arms and became fond of her. Sister Beckford told us that she drove as fast as she could to get to us on time.

We chatted for a while and I was able to share a few of Jerodene's testimonies with her that we experienced. Sister Beckford recalled during our conversation that while we sat in the side room, I called Eunice Sister Beckford, but Jerodene jumped up and pointed her finger at me then uttered, *"Mommy don't call her Sister Beckford, it's Aunty for you."* We both laughed at what Jerodene said. Each time I was about to say Sister Beckford, I remembered that I should call her Aunty. We had so much to talk about. We spoke about the goodness of God and His mercies towards us. I had always loved to videotape and take pictures. I always loved to make memories so I took out my camera phone. Jerodene was the photographer that time around. She aimed the camera at us then told us to say, *"Scooby Dooby cheese."* Jerodene then thought that she was taking a picture but instead of taking a picture, we were actually being videoed. She then took the picture. I wanted her to pose with Sis. Beckford and to have their picture taken but Jerodene was not up to it. Sister Beckford tickled Jerodene's neck and that was when she gave in. Jerodene gave the biggest smile ever. Sister Beckford recalled Jerodene singing one of her favourite songs, "Jesus on the telephone, tell Him what you need." Jerodene did the actions to the song with her hands and when she was finished she hung up the phone. Sister Beckford wanted to laugh out loud but had to hold it back then she asked where we got this 'old woman' wrapped up in a child's body from.

    Time really flies when one's having fun. When we checked the time, it was past midnight. The time came for Sister Beckford to journey back home to her family. Jerodene hugged her and her last words to her was, **"Thank you Aunty Eunice for coming and get home safely."** We hugged and bid each other goodbye and I told her to advise me when she got home. She told me that she left feeling excited, encouraged and joyful. She said that she felt as light as a feather. When she got home she was very anxious to share the testimonies with her mother who was also a strong woman of God. She could not remember all of them at once because there were so many. However, each time she went into her room and remembered another one, she would rushed into her mother's room saying, *"Mom, I remember another one."* Her mom was not tired of hearing them. Sister Beckford was also anxious to tell her church family about her personal encounter with Jerodene. Her entire visit was just overwhelming and we gave God thanks that she was able to come. She visited a few more times after that and God showed us favour each time with the staff and security officer. She was unable to meet Jermaine at that time because he came a few days prior to that but we knew that at some point they both would be able to meet.

    At that time Jerodene was doing radiation on her pelvis but she was also on other medications as well. She still was not able to have a proper shower but we hoped that it would not be for much longer. By then, she had already gone through the radiation treatments on her brain, shoulder and abdomen. We were optimistic and we gave God thanks for taking us thus far. If it was not for Him things would have been worse.

## *Secret Hiding Place*

    On a particular day I had gone to buy something to eat because I was feeling hungry. I went to a restaurant on the same property. By the time I got back, Jerodene was nowhere in sight. The doctors told me that they had gone to the side room and they noticed that her IV was infiltrated. They told Jero that they would be going to the treatment room to get the medical supplies in order for her to get the rest of her medication. Upon reaching her room they realised that she was not there. I went in search of her, I went to the ward but she was not there. I then went on the other two wards to see if she was there but she was not there either. I asked the nurses if they had seen her, they said that they saw her a few minutes earlier but had no idea where she went. *"Where could she have gone?"* I asked myself. I knew that she could not have passed the Security Post. Where was she? When I remembered what the doctors told me I figured that Jerodene must have gone hiding because she was afraid of getting a new IV. I looked all over but just could not find her. I looked everywhere she normally hung out, but no Jerodene. *"Where could Jerodene be hiding?"* I thought to myself.

After about 20 minutes of searching, I eventually found Jerodene hiding under a table in the passageway of Ward 15. Finally the search was over. When she realised that I found her, she started crying loudly and said that she was frustrated with all those pricks. She wanted to go home to her family. It was painful listening to her crying and explaining herself in such a manner. I might be empathising with her but she knows exactly what she was going through. She was the one feeling all the pain and torture. I always wished that there was something that I could have done. I tried to tell her that she would be going home soon, and I also told her how worried I was when I could not find her. The most important question I had for her was to ask her how she knew to find that particular hiding spot. That was when she said, **"Mommy the hiding spot is for me and my best friend, Akayden's, it's a secret."** So I told her not to have me worry like that ever again. She eventually had to get the new IV because she was behind on her medications. I told the doctor that the next time around when she had to change her IV, she should not mention it to Jerodene but to me instead. If they did that, she might have gone into hiding again.

## *Rehearsal Over The Phone*

November came and Jerodene was still admitted. At the time she and my sister, Romayne, rehearsed over the phone because both of them had planned to share the stage at the Jodian Pantry and Friends in Tenacity Concert. It was a concert that we were all looking forward to, especially our little princess, Jerodene. The plan was that my sister would have flown in from overseas because her visit to us was overdue and she promised Jerodene that she would come to visit her. She planned to take Jerodene to the beach and they would have a fun filled time together on her next trip here. Who would not be looking forward to that? Jerodene was overly excited and anxious for such quality family time. Additionally, Jerodene knew by then she should have already finished all her radiation treatments, and she would be able to have a blast.

## *Akayden's Passing*

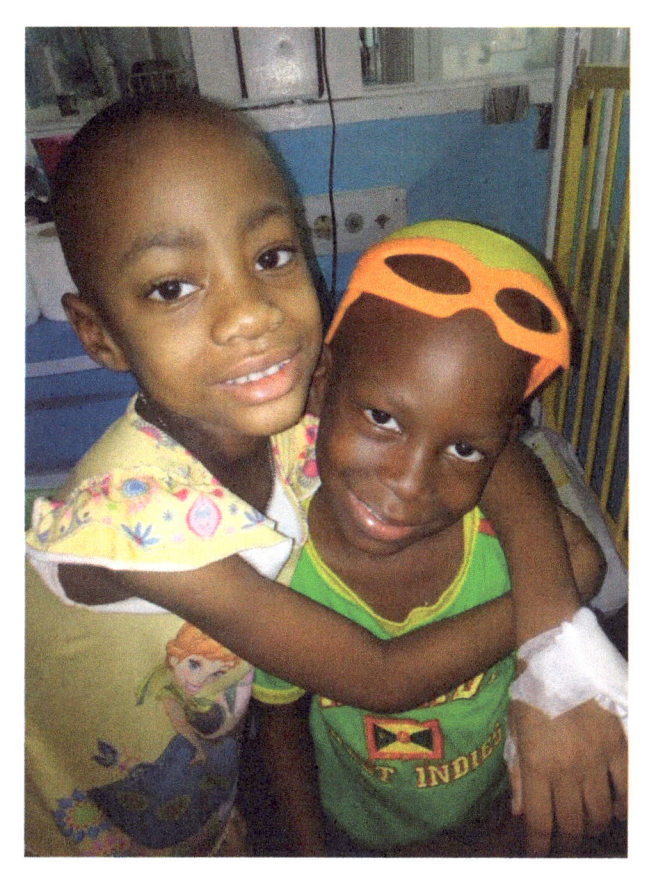

A few days later, while I was in the side room with Jerodene, I received a phone call one that I was not expecting. The news that hit me like a ton of bricks. On the other end of the line was Akayden's mom, Akili. I then waited patiently to hear of Akayden's status, only to hear Akili say, *"Rash! Akayden gone to join Rashaun a few minutes ago!"* Immediately I cried out when she told me but I tried to hold back the tears. Jerodene looked at me and said, **"Mommy, it seems as if you just heard some bad news."** I could not tell her what I just heard because this was Jerodene's best friend, whom she loved and got very attached to over the months. My heart ached badly, I could not even think straight. How? What? Why? I did not even know what to say or think. Deep inside I was so angry. Angry at whom? I did not even know. I honestly thought that he would have made it because of all the prayers that had gone up on his behalf. How could all this happen? He left Jamaica in good spirits, so what happened? Oh Akayden, why, why, why? My heart broke into a million pieces. How could he have died? I could not see through it all. Too many children were dying from that dreaded disease and there was still no cure. Those children were so innocent and promising. They had such bright futures ahead of them. One thing I knew for certain was that I could not mention it to Jerodene because of past experience. She would have taken it very hard. Only God knows. The whole situation was just too sad and I could not begin to imagine the pain that the parents must have been going through. I had rushed to the ward to inform the doctors and nurses because they all knew Akayden and to inform them not to mention it to Jerodene. My reasons were not personal anymore because the staff on Ward 16 already knew how sensitive Jerodene was. Things might have gotten worse, based on the experience during Rashaun's death. It was very hard not to tell her but I had to use wisdom. My heart went out to his parents because he was an only child for his mom, and if I felt so broken and in despair, I could not imagine the agony that she must have been going through. I wished that I could have hugged her or even given her a shoulder to lean on. It would not have healed her pain but a hug could do wonders to help someone hurting. I felt so helpless and that there was nothing I could say to ease her pain. Jermaine and I decided that when the right time came we would tell Jerodene, but it had to remain a secret for a while.

I was unable to go to pay my final respects to Superhero, Akayden Wilson because they were in another country. His mom kept me informed and she sent some photos. Despite the outcome, we were grateful that we crossed paths. A few days after Akayden's death, Jerodene was scheduled to go home for a few days. I was so happy because that would lessen the chances of her hearing of Akayden's death.

### *"Help, Help!"*

Overall Jerodene was excited to be home again with her family and friends, especially her little brother. All four of us were not able to attend church when we just got home because Jerodene was not feeling well. Her dad went and left the three of us at home. After a while, Jerodene's belly started to hurt her and she began to cry. I rubbed it with the consecrated olive oil but she got no ease. She started bawling out to God, ***"Help, help, help, God help me please! It's just one thing I am asking You to do and is to stop what You are doing and help me God, help me!"*** with tears rolling down her face. Upon hearing her say that to God, I literally broke down and bawled out to God because of how helpless I was. I just wished that there was something that I could have done to help her. She bawled so loud that even people at the end of our lane could hear her. I was so concerned but all I could do was sit and rub her belly until she felt some relief.

*Responsible Big Sister*

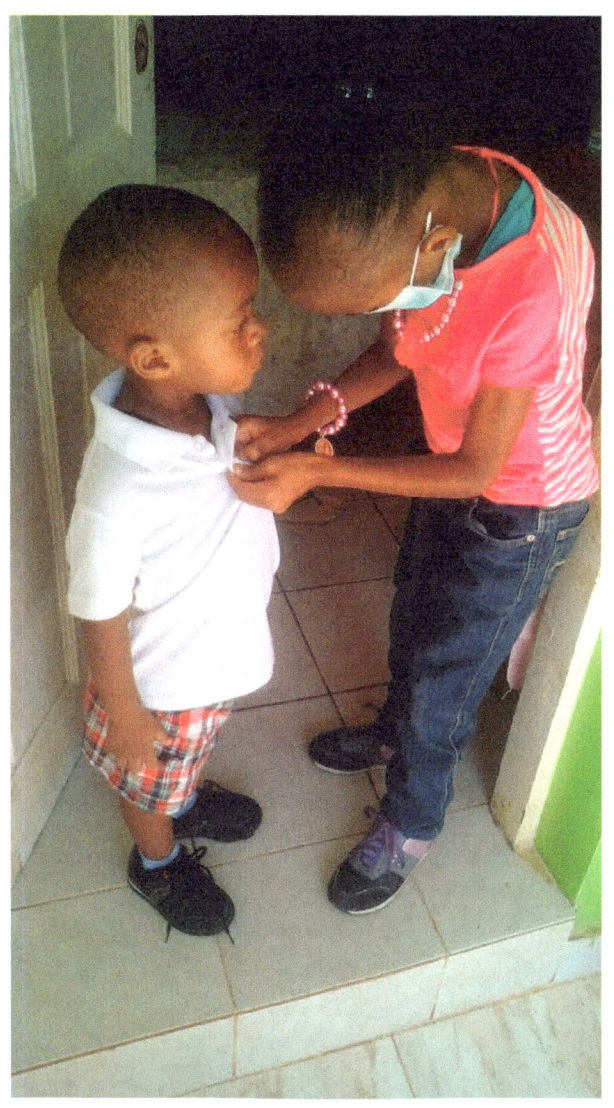

Even though Jerodene was not able to attend school, she went all out to make sure that Rasheed completed all his homework. If there was something that he did not understand then Jerodene would explain it to him in the simplest form. Sometimes, Rasheed would be reluctant to do his homework, but Jerodene sat down with him and held his hand and made sure that he completed his homework before they went playing. She made it easy for him. Jerodene would show love and affection to her little brother in so many ways. Being at home, it was a joy whenever Jerodene saw Rasheed getting out of the taxi. Jerodene would go to the gate to meet him. They both always had smiles on their faces, and one could see Jerodene leading Rasheed along the path as he held on to her hand. We live at the top of a hill and they would make a few stops on the way up. Whenever they came up on a little bump in the road, Jerodene would lead the way over it then pull her brother over it by his hand. It showed that Jerodene was such a responsible and loving big sister. I would use my phone to videotape both of them as they climbed the hill. They enjoyed every moment of each other's company. Rasheed could not have asked for a better sister and vice versa. They were compatible siblings. They really loved and cared for each other and enjoyed each other's company. Jermaine and I expected nothing less because we taught them the love of God.

*Beautiful Flowers*

Jerodene loved watering the flowers that she and I planted. I normally let her get a bucket and then she would begin the process of watering them. Rasheed would render assistance. If he was not doing it the way that pleased Jerodene then she would shout, ***"Rasheed, you are not doing it well!"*** That was usually when they both would start a quarrel. One could hear Jerodene on a sunny afternoon humming a tune that she knew or one she made up as she watered the plants and danced. They both had fun doing it, and I started videoing them making precious memories. The happiest moment for Jermaine and I was to see the children happy and none of that could have been possible without the Almighty God. To Him be all the glory and honour and all the praise.

The following day, as Jermaine left for work and Rasheed had left for school, Jerodene and I decided to journey to Mandeville to her cousin, Rashelle's workplace. At that time she worked at a KFC restaurant and we decided to go surprise her because Jerodene loved her so much and they had not seen each other for a while since Jerodene was admitted. It was indeed a surprise. They hugged and laughed so much. Rashelle was Jerodene's favourite cousin on her dad's side of the family. They loved each other dearly and had special places in each other's hearts, and no one could ever get between them. Before our visit ended, Rashelle gave Jerodene her favourite, hot and spicy chicken. She vowed to take it home so that her brother and dad could enjoy it too. The short visit was well spent and we all enjoyed every moment of it. Jerodene left smiling and Rashelle promised her that on her next discharge she would come home to visit her.

## *Staff Members Saying Bad Things About Me*

A few days after her admission, I left her at her bedside because I had to go to the wash area to do our laundry. While I was washing our clothes, I heard three staff members from another ward talking some bad things about me. All three of them were in a room, and the window was right at the wash area. I literally heard one of them say, *"Jerodene's mother is wicked."* I stopped washing and stood for a while and listened to most of what they had to say until I got angry. They had no idea that I was outside listening to them, so they just spilled their guts without fear. I wished that I could have confronted the main individual that was prolonging the conversation. Instead of doing so, I went to another staff member that was in charge and lodged my complaint who in turn went to them. The staff member who was the ringleader admitted that she said what she said without any apology. I guess the matter reached to the person in charge and she confronted her, and that was when she came back to me with a lame apology. I made up my mind that I was going to take the issue further because all that they said was false and I was not guilty of anything that was said. However, I remembered that I had more important things to focus on and at the moment Jerodene was my main focus.

## *Another Powerful Prayer*

During that period of admission on December 2, 2017, my brother, Randal called me saying that he was not feeling well and that he was on his way to the same hospital that we were at. I explained to one of the nurses about the situation and asked them to supervise Jerodene for me for a while. By the time he got to the hospital, I was already at the Accident and Emergency department. His wife and daughter came after a while. My family is very important to me and if it was another family member who was in that situation, I would have done the very same thing. Unfortunately, he had to do an emergency surgery and so he was admitted for a few days. That same weekend our mom was at his house because she had a convention in a neighbouring community where she was asked to be the speaker for the first night. Because of my brother's admission, she had planned on staying a while longer. We knew it was a pleasure for her to have been there. The surgery was scheduled for the following morning. With Jerodene being admitted on the Paediatric ward and Randal on the surgical ward, I had to go back and forth. I did not mind it at all, it was just that the entire situation was extremely sad. However, it was a successful surgery and we gave God thanks. They had him there under observation for a day.

The following day, before he was due for discharge, his wife and daughter, also my mom and Aunt Sandra along with his wife's cousin and two friends came to visit both Jerodene and my brother. They stopped to see Randal first then heard that he was scheduled for discharge. We were happy that his admission was not for a long time. We were still in the side room and they were all happy to see the happy spirit that Jerodene had. During that time, Jerodene was scarcely in a happy mood. Jerodene's visit was not a long one but it was well spent. Before they left they had a prayer meeting and as usual Jerodene volunteered to pray, and this was her prayer,

*"Oh Holy Father, we are your children Oh Lord. You said you love us, Lord. You know me before my mother even conceived me. God, You know even the hairs on my head are numbered Oh Father. You said to me that God I shall not die but live and declare the holy word God. But I shall live God, not die God because You said that You will never turn Your back on me God, because you said I shall live. I shall live and declare because you are Lord God and Lord forever, and you will be Lord forever. Nobody can't say that you can't be Lord, God, because You said to me that You love me, You love me oh Father God. So cover me God, cover me God. Cover my family, cover my grandma, cover my grandpa, cover my uncles, cover my cousins make them know that You are the best God. Make them know that they should not tell lies God. Make them not tell lies oh Father because if they tell lies they will be going to hell oh God, and I know that they don't want to go to hell Lord. So cover them God, cover them under Your blood Lord. Because You say You will never turn your back on us. You said You love us. You know me before my mommy even conceived me. So cover me God cover me under Your blood. Make me not tell lies. Make my friends not tell lies and make my mommy and daddy not tell lies. You said I am your daughter and I will be your daughter forever. So seeing as I am right here Lord, cover me under Your blood Lord cause You said You love me God, so cover me under Your blood oh Father God, when I am sleeping God cover me. Watch me everyday when I am sleeping and even when I am not sleeping. Cover the poor people out there God. The bad people are doing the things to the good persons God, let them be nice to each other God, don't let them do bad things to each other oh Father because you said that we should be nice to each other. Oh Holy Father, please let those bad people be nice to each other. Cover them under Your blood because if it wasn't for You we don't know how it would be Lord, and we don't want to know to know Lord. We don't know and we do not want to know. We should be nice to each other. So Holy Father as I speak to You this morning cover us and bless us Lord. Cover us under Your blood oh Lord cause You say You hold us up in Your hands. You said You love us and You care about us because we are Your daughters and Your sons oh Holy Father so cover us and bless us and forgive our trespasses oh God. In Your name Lord I am healed, I am healed in Your name God because You said so, and I am not sick in Jesus' name. You said that I should believe in You, and when I believe in You I will go to heaven and not hell. So cover my family in Jesus' name oh Lord, cover them oh Lord and I know that I will be fine in Jesus' name. I am not sick in Jesus' name, no cancer can back me down oh Father, cause you said I am not sick because I don't have any cancer. I am strong enough to handle satan. Satan back off! God said that you don't belong here and you never will. There's no space for you and there never will be any space for you. God cover me under Your blood, cover my father, cover my family cause satan you don't belong here, you are a liar from the pit of hell, my grandma always say satan you don't belong here, you never belong here before. Just go away, Jesus hold us in His arms, because He said He's going to protect us. Oh Father cover us under Your blood oh Jesus because we know that You can cover us. We believe in You God, and You are the only one who we believe in because if it wasn't for You we don't know who we would be and we don't want to know. So Holy Father today just cover my family, my friends in Your name. Amen."*

It was another powerful prayer from our little prayer warrior, Jerodene. All who were present were very touched and left teary eyed. Jerodene's hobby was praying and she also knew the power of praying. She told her dad and me that she wanted to become an Evangelist or a Nurse because she would love to preach the Word of the Lord. We told her that whatever her choices were in life that we were with her a hundred percent.

December came and the Christmas holiday was right around the corner. We really hoped that they would give us the chance to go home because Jerodene was more stable at that time. There was a possibility but the doctors would have the final say, so we had no other choice but to wait. From time to time, one could see Jerodene walking with the IV stand in one hand and her tablet in the other hand. At times when she was not allowed to go on the ward, she could be seated on a chair right outside her room. Another friend of hers, Aliyah, used to go there to play with her and keep her company, which she appreciated.

*"Mommy, Something Bad Is About To Happen".*

The following Tuesday, after my brother was discharged, Jerodene was still admitted in the side room. I went to get some food to eat and before I left Jerodene was fairly well and was in high spirits. At that time it was a few minutes after 9 p.m. I went to take a shower and planned to go to bed a bit earlier than usual because it was a hectic day. Before I went to lie down I turned the ringer on my phone to silent because I really wanted a good night's rest. Jerodene and I then went straight to bed after she had got her night's medication.

I actually dosed off for a while then I opened my eyes and to my surprise Jerodene was seated in her bed. I then asked her what was the problem and she told me that she was unable to sleep. I assured her that everything was going to be okay then told her to go back to bed. She still refused to go back to bed. She then told me that the reason that she could not go back to sleep was because ***"something bad was about to happen"***. I had asked her what did she mean by that and her response to me was, ***"Because I can feel it Mommy."*** I was extremely tired and it was very late so I prayed a short prayer with her then I anointed her with our bottle of consecrated olive oil and told her that we are fully covered by the blood of Jesus and that He would not let anything bad happen to us.

I was too tired to sit up with her so she started using her tablet then told me that I should go back to bed but she would not because she still could not sleep. The little folded bed that I had was almost a wreck because it was so worn out. I could barely turn on either of my sides because of the squeaky sounds that it made. By the time I was about to go back to lie down it dawned on me to check the time on my cell phone. Instead of seeing the time I instead saw 12 missed calls from my brother, Randal. I thought to myself what could have possibly gone wrong? When I returned his call, he told me that there was an emergency and that our mom and his wife were on their way to the same hospital where we were because his daughter, Xariah was not well. My heart skipped a beat when I realised that was what Jerodene was referring to. She actually knew that something bad was about to happen but could not have specified what it was. Jerodene then asked me what was wrong and I told her that Xariah was not well, tears rolled down her cheeks. They both loved and cared for each other and Xariah was Jerodene's youngest cousin. Immediately, I told the nurses who were on duty and they told me that they would watch Jerodene until I got back from the Accident and Emergency Department. I left one of my cell phones with Jerodene so that she could call me from time to time to get updates on Xariah.

The doctors who attended to Xariah said that she would have to be admitted for a few days. That night the ward that Jerodene was on was not accepting any new patients so she was placed on Ward 15. I had never seen anything like that before. Our mom was still at my brother's house because my brother was recuperating from the surgery while my sister-in-law, Venieca, would have to be at the hospital with Xariah. Our dad, on the other hand, would have to journey on a bus from the countryside, which was nearly two hours away on the Friday morning to bring us breakfast. However, instead of visiting one grandchild as he normally did, he was visiting two. It was a devastating situation. Aunt Sandra came to visit two nieces instead of one. Oh how unfortunate it was. We still gave thanks to God because it could have been worse.

Jermaine came to visit us as usual with Jerodene's favourite hot and spicy KFC chicken. She had a brilliant smile as she licked her fingers in delight. Her favourite piece was the drumstick and she would not change it for anything else. At that time Jerodene had the IV in her right foot, close to her ankle. The other foot was swollen because they had just removed it from that foot earlier that day, because of that, she was unable to walk so I had to be lifting her to and from the bathroom. She was very happy, nevertheless, and really enjoyed the day spent with her dad. She really wanted her dad to stay with us but we knew that was impossible. We were very anxious that Christmas was right around the corner, and we were all hoping for the same thing - for all four of us to spend the Christmas holidays at home as a family.

*Christmas Celebrations On The Ward*

Over the years at Christmas time, unfortunately, a lot of children had to spend their holidays in the hospital. Normally, groups from all over Jamaica made it as their point of duty, out of the kindness of their hearts, to have Christmas treats on a yearly basis, and 2017 was no different. Even though the children were very sad being away from their family and friends during the festive season, they were happy for the fun time that they could look forward to. The news came that Jerodene was scheduled to be discharged. That was great news for us and Jerodene was so excited to tell her dad and brother. We were happy because that would have been our first Christmas together at our home as a family since Jerodene's diagnosis in 2015.

The day before we got our discharge, a group of people came to the hospital to visit and to treat the children who were there. Both Jerodene and Xariah were there having fun. Jerodene was dressed in her pink top and her multi-coloured pants that she loved. The group had a lot of food, games and gifts for all. They also had a singing competition where Jerodene and one of her favourite nurses sang one of Jerodene's favourite Christmas carols 'Jingle Bells' as everyone looked on. Jerodene only knew a part of the song and so she only sang the line that says 'with a one horse open slay.' Everyone laughed and joined in singing with her, almost everyone took part - nurses, doctors, parents, and other staff members from different departments near and far. We all sang Christmas songs, ate and took part in most of the activities that were prepared. All the children had fun, especially Jerodene knowing that she was scheduled to go home in a few hours. The host of the event was one of our very own Television and Radio personalities, Jennifer "Jenny Jenny" Small. She had another engagement so she left before the event was over. On her way out I had asked her to pose for a picture with Jerodene, which she gladly did. Jerodene hardly slept that night because she was so excited to go home. She had mixed feelings because she was happy that she was going home but was sad that her cousin would have been left there. Nonetheless, we knew that Xariah was not going to be there for much longer because she was recuperating.

*Home Sweet Home For Christmas 2017*

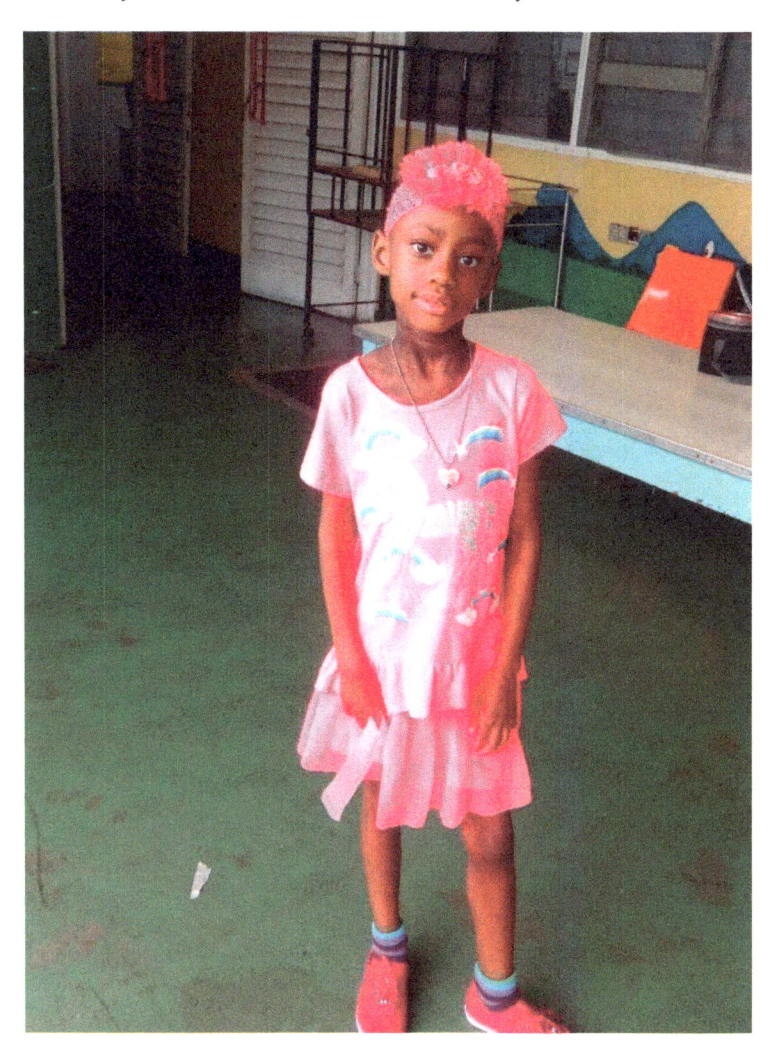

So the day finally came, Sunday, December 10, 2017, and there we were in bright colours ready to go home. I remember that day as if it were yesterday. Jerodene had chosen her outfit to go home and it was in one of her favourite colours - pink. As a matter of fact, her entire outfit was pink, in addition she had on her pink headband that I purchased recently along with her pink shoes. She was all 'pinked' out and most of all she had on her Frozen necklace that her dear friend, Danique Williams had bought her as a gift. Her beautiful outfit was courtesy of Portia, the same lady who helped us to fund the $1.8 million via a foundation overseas to stand the cost for the radiation. She was helpful and very considerate. We told her that her help did not go unnoticed.

As we finished packing our bags, Jerodene went to all her doctor and a few of her nurse friends to bid them goodbye. Jerodene was a friend to everyone. She had a few friends in her age group who were admitted at the time and she went to say goodbye to them too and most of all to her cousin, Xariah. Jerodene told the nurses that she was very happy that she had gotten the chance to go home because my birthday was coming up and that she, her dad and Rasheed were looking forward to treating me like a queen. I was also looking forward to my big day because since Jerodene's diagnosis that would have been my first birthday at home with my family.

Jerodene smiled as she waved goodbye to the staff members on Ward 16 and a few on Ward 15. You all should have seen her with her discharge slip in her hand as she happily modelled down the corridor. It was as if she was waiting for that day for ever so long. We were all happy and I was looking forward to sleeping in my proper bed without any squeaking or any disturbance whatsoever. We were looking forward to a fun-filled holiday, a well deserved one at that. Unfortunately for my brother and his family, they had to stay in the hospital a while longer. We hoped that they would have been out before Christmas.

It was raining heavily and it would have been difficult for me to go on public transportation to head Downtown, Kingston with Jerodene so my brother decided to take us there in order for us to get a bus. We were grateful for the ride and we knew that if his daughter was not admitted, chances are that he would have taken us home, which was two hours away. We got home a little before 6pm and thanked God for a safe journey home. It was a very happy and exciting feeling being home with my family. Rasheed's school was not yet on break for the holidays but was due to close the following day. The staff at his school had a Christmas party and Rasheed went with mixed feelings. He was happy that he was a part of the party but then he was sad because he figured that by the time he got home then Jerodene and I would have gone back to the hospital. We reassured him that Jerodene would be home for a few days, and that was when he felt better. Jermaine and I had so many plans for both Jerodene and Rasheed because that was our first Christmas at home as a family in three years, and we planned to go all out for both of them to have some fun-filled time together. We started off our celebrations by purchasing her favourite black forest cake. We waited so long for that moment to arrive and we would not let it slip away. They both sang and danced as I increased the volume on the radio. We all danced together just having some crazy fun, which we all enjoyed. After a while, they left to watch their favourite cartoon and play games on their tablets. It just felt great being home and one could have seen that the children were really enjoying each other's company.

*Granddad Time*

The following day was a bit better than the day before. Their granddad, Anthony, had promised them that he would have taken them to KFC and he kept his promise. Jerodene got her favourite hot and spicy chicken and was boasting to her brother that she was old enough to eat the hot and spicy chicken while he had to settle with the original because he was a baby. They really loved their granddad and always looked forward to receiving his phone calls. I remember during Jerodene's earlier years of diagnosis, I was feeling very tired and exhausted and my dad volunteered to stay two days at the hospital with Jerodene. She enjoyed that time with him. Also, previously, whenever their granddad would often visit us, Jerodene would give him a list of the things that she wanted him to take for her. Her granddad would go the extra mile to make sure that both Rasheed's and Jerodene's demands were met. They really enjoyed their day out with granddad. Jerodene had lost a few pounds and we hoped that she would have gained it all back before it was time for her to go back for admission. Her other grandad, Jermaine's father, Stanford, visited Jerodene while she was admitted at the University Hospital because his home was closer to the hospital.

## *The Day That Turned Out To Be 'Not So Good'*

My mom's sister, Estrinetta, affectionately called Estri, was visiting from overseas. She always spoke to Jerodene over the phone but had not met her in person. So her being here in Jamaica would have been the perfect time for them to meet each other. We had planned to meet her at my Aunty Sandra's house, which was an hour away from our home. When we got there we all greeted each other in love and unity. After a short while Jerodene told her dad and I that she wanted to go to sleep, which she did, so during that time we were there catching up on old times. I was so excited because my birthday was in two days and I was really looking forward to spending it with my immediate family. Can you imagine spending two consecutive birthdays in the hospital and now getting the chance to spend it at home with family? I could not have asked for anything else. After a while, we checked on Jerodene and she was still sleeping while Rasheed was watching cartoons. Within an hour or so, we heard a strange sound coming from the bedroom where Jerodene was. We hurriedly rushed to see what had caused that sound. Upon reaching the room, Jerodene was vomiting. There was vomit all over. Her dad jumped on the bed as we were all in shock. My knees immediately got weak, Jermaine grabbed her up in his arms in disbelief as Jerodene was just waking up out of her sleep. Jermaine then asked her how she was feeling and she told him that she was feeling fine. But I asked myself, *"How could Jerodene say that she was fine and she was just vomiting?"* I just could not see through it all but God was on the job. We then decided that we would observe her for a while and see if it would recur.

We knew that she must have felt nauseous due to past chemotherapy and radiation treatments. The reason it hit us so hard was because it has been quite a few months since Jerodene had vomited, and we gave God thanks that it was not the worst. Jerodene slept for the rest of the afternoon and that was unlike her, the good thing she was not in any pain neither was she having a temperature. Nonetheless we watched her keenly and figured if she had gotten worse we might have to take her to the nearest hospital. Aunt Estri and Jerodene were not able to spend as much time because Jerodene was not feeling well, but Aunt Estri understood it all.

The members at my mother's church had previously planned an Appreciation Service for our mom, which was planned for the following day and we were all invited. Within an hour we left my Aunt's house to go home in order to make preparations for the function. Her dad had to lift her up on our way home because by then, Jerodene was already complaining that her legs were tired. Her dad had no issue lifting her throughout the long walking distances.

By the time we got home it was a little before night. Jerodene had refused to eat because she told us that she was not feeling hungry. We knew that she barely had any appetite sometimes but it has never gotten to the point where she had hardly eaten in a day. It came to our minds that she might have wanted something to eat but was scared to because she feared that she might have vomited again. As the night progressed, Rasheed wanted to play with her but she just went mute. Jovial, talkative and outspoken Jerodene was just mute. We were not used to her in that state. She looked weak but was not complaining of any pain whatsoever. When we saw what happened throughout the day we were then having second thoughts about my mom's Appreciation Service. We planned on taking her to the hospital in the event that she got worse. She told her dad that she did not want to sleep on her bed but instead wanted to sleep with me. Knowing her dad, he did not have a problem with sleeping on Jerodene's bed because that had been going on ever since she got back home from the hospital. She had gotten her wish and since she was not feeling well, I hugged and comforted her as best as possible as both Jermaine and Rasheed looked on. That night was not one of our best nights because Jermaine and I had to take turns watching our baby girl and prayed for her to feel better.

## *Emergency*

The following day was December 29, 2017 just a day before my birthday. That was when the realisation hit us that Jerodene was not feeling any better. Jermaine was outside while the children and I were inside our bedroom. Jerodene was lying on the bed and suddenly she just blocked out. I was so frightened that I screamed out loudly and called Jermaine to our assistance. He rushed in, jumped on the bed and grabbed her up in his arms shouting, *"Jerodene! Jerodene! Jerodene!"* but she was not responding. We could not pray at the time because we all were in shock, so I hurried outside to call my mom for her and her team to pray for Jerodene; there was no cellular reception inside our house. Our hearts leaped as we both were confused and tried to consider our next move. After a few seconds, Jerodene became conscious but she looked wild as if she was in a strange place. Her eyes were just glaring, something that we have never seen before. The look that she had on her face was similar to that of the seizure episode. As all that unfolded before our eyes, Jermaine ran outside to call our taxi driver, Shawn, for him to take us to the hospital. We figured it was best for us to take her to the University Hospital instead of the one in our parish. We hurriedly grabbed a few things for her and packed them in a bag. Rasheed stood there crying because he was too young to understand what was going on.

Within a few minutes the taxi arrived and we all rushed out because we had no one at the time who we could have left Rasheed with. By then Jermaine had already told the driver about the situation and he knew that he had to drive speedily but carefully to get to hospital as soon as possible. As we journeyed into Kingston, two hours away, Jerodene was still not talking so we had no idea what was going through her mind. As she sat in her dad's lap in the back of the car, Rasheed was seated beside them while I was seated on the front seat. Ever so often I looked behind me to see if her eyes were still opened. At that time, Rasheed was playing on his tablet while the taxi drove at full speed on the highway. We prayed in our minds that we would reach the hospital in time. We prayed that God would work an instant miracle just as he did with the blind man or the woman with the issue of blood as referenced in the Bible. Our hearts kept pounding faster and faster. We had no idea what to think or say, but only to look to God, Who was our only source. Each time that we came upon another car in front of ours I would shout in my mind, *"get out of the way, get out of the way!"* The next time I looked to see if Jerodene was awake, I heard Jermaine shout and by the time I looked Rasheed was vomiting all over in the car. Immediately, the driver pulled over and Jermaine was helpless because he had Jerodene in his hand. I then took Rasheed out of the car and tried to use a rag to wipe off his clothes. We left hastily and forgot to take a change of clothes for Rasheed. The driver had to use another rag to wipe off the seat so that Rasheed had somewhere to sit. Eventually, I had to take off Rasheed's pants and spread it on the dashboard while we continued our journey so that the sun could dry it somewhat.

As we continued our journey it came to my mind that I should make a call to the Paediatric Ward that Jerodene was always admitted on. But then I figured that I should make a call to her oncologist first to let her know that we had an emergency and that we were on our way to the hospital. The doctor's number went unanswered. I tried it again and the same thing happened. I then decided to make a call to the Paediatric Ward. After explaining to one of the senior nurses about everything that transpired, she told me that when we got to the hospital, we should take Jerodene to the Accident and Emergency (A and E) Department. I got livid because how could that nurse be telling us that we should take Jerodene to A and E instead of the ward? Jerodene's situation was an emergency and Jerodene was no stranger. She was a long term patient on that same ward for the past three years. Jermaine and I decided to do the total opposite of what she said, and by the time we reached the hospital gate, my phone rang and on the other line was Jerodene's doctor. I then gave her a synopsis of what was happening to Jerodene and she told me that she was going to call the doctor team that was on the ward and tell them to make preparations for Jerodene. She told us not to go to A and E but instead go straight to the Ward. We did as we were told. By then, Jerodene was helpless, she was unable to walk, and her dad had to lift her. When we got to the Security Post and looked ahead, we saw Dr. O and another doctor awaiting us. Bed three was already prepared for Jerodene so we were asked to place her there. Even at that moment Jerodene was barely talking. The doctors examined her for a while while another sought to find a vein to place an IV. Upon examination, they told us that Jerodene was badly dehydrated and that they would have to give her some fluids.

The team then took a history from Jermaine and I of what transpired during her time at home and the reason we brought her in. We told them everything that took place and they told us that they would have to do further examination on Jerodene. It was so hard for Jermaine and I to process all that was going on at that moment. Only God knew what was happening. It took a while for the doctors to do a full examination and by then it was getting very late, so Jermaine decided to stay with Jerodene while I took Rasheed to my parents' house. I stayed by her bedside until she was fully settled in, and that was when I told her that her dad would be staying with her because I had to take Rasheed to my parents' house. As Jerodene laid on the bed and stretched out her hand to Rasheed, they both smiled but one could have seen the pain in Jerodene's eyes as she barely waved goodbye to us. Her last words to me were, *"Be safe Mommy, be safe."* My heart pained me to the core as tears slowly rolled down my face. It was hard that I had to leave her, I just wanted to stay by her bedside.

I remembered, a few weeks before, while her dad was at work she told me that she had a question for us. When I asked her what it was, her response was, *"Mommy, do you and Daddy promise to be with me to the end?"* I looked at her in shock and asked her what she meant by that. She looked at me and smiled and told me, *"Mommy, you and Daddy already know what I am talking about."* That thing had not left our minds, we told her that yes, and we promised to be by her side to the end no matter what. We had no idea where 'the end' might take us but we vowed and we knew that with God's help we could keep our promise.

Rasheed and I ended up leaving after Jerodene was fully examined and told her dad to keep me posted as much as possible. We both went back home in the same car that we arrived in. The plan was for us to go back to our home first to get some clothes to take to my parents' house because I had no idea how long Jerodene would be admitted for. I had no idea how long Rasheed would be at my parents' house. My mom's church was a little distance from her home so I had stopped at her church instead. We got there by 8 p.m. Her Appreciation Service was in full swing. My sister, Romayne, had arrived on the island the day before. She and my other sibling along with my other two aunts were also present. I honestly tried to put the best outside but deep down I was screaming for help; I was actually dying. My heart was so heavy laden. My body was there but all along my mind was at the hospital on Jerodene. I felt as if I was about to explode because of how down I was. I just wished that someone could have grabbed me and given me a hug then I would have just fallen to the ground and bawled. Only God knew how I felt. His Word says that we should cast all our cares upon him because He cares for us. With so many things going on in my mind and in my heart, I had to ask the question, *"Where was God in all our circumstances and tribulations that were present before our eyes."* Since Jerodene's diagnosis, we cried ever so often and throughout it all Jerodene had given us so much hope that everything would be okay. *"But would it be okay?"* I asked myself. Jermaine and I prayed so hard for God to show up in our situation, but sometimes we felt alone and forsaken on our journey. Through it all we had not lost our faith and trust in God.

As my mom's Appreciation Service continued, I called Jermaine a few times to find out how things were with Jerodene. He told me that she was doing a little better than she was before. He also told me that some changes were made but that he would have to tell me in the morning. He said that if he told me then, it would have been too much for me to bear. My heart skipped a beat and I wondered what could have been. I then agreed and told him that we would talk in the morning.

## *Uncontrollable Tears*

Prophet Alexis Brown was the guest speaker at the Appreciation Service. My mom had already told him about Jerodene's situation from the first time she was diagnosed, so he was aware of it. My mom had also shared some of Jerodene's videos with him and he had also seen some on Facebook. He saw me seated in the congregation, he then called me to the altar and prophesied over my life. As I stood and listened attentively to every word that God had given to him to deliver to me, before I knew it, I burst out bawling. I cried as a weeping mother who was in travail. My heart felt as if it was going to burst open as I wept. I had all that pain and agony within me and it seemed as if it was the time for me to just let it all out. After I was through crying I felt a bit better and even felt lighter. It felt as if a thousand pounds had been lifted off my shoulder. Despite the fact that Jermaine and Jerodene were not there I thanked God that I had gone because I felt the urge to continue our journey with our warrior princess Jerodene. To God be all the glory. It was a wonderful Appreciation Service and everyone felt satisfied.

## *Back To Back Seizures*

After the service had ended, I called Jermaine and he told me all that happened after I left the hospital. Jerodene had several seizure attacks. He also said that the doctors put her on oxygen because at one point in time she was gasping for air. He continued to say that Jerodene was complaining that she was hungry and she asked for some soup. He then asked one of the nurses to stay at Jerodene's bedside and watch her while he went to a nearby restaurant to purchase the soup. He left to go get the soup but upon return the nurse was not there and he found Jerodene in the midst of another seizure attack. He was so shocked and frightened he called out to the doctors for help. The doctors rushed to her bedside and literally had to work on her in order to revive her. He said that was one of the most terrifying moments that he had ever experienced. I could relate to exactly what he was talking about. I felt the same way when she had the first seizure attack. So I could just imagine how frightened he must have been. He told me that he was very upset when he noticed that the nurse was not present and had she been there then things might not have gotten that bad. He also told me that they had to attach the vitals machine onto Jerodene because her blood pressure was fluctuating and they had to monitor her closely. He continued to say that she had another seizure episode and that time was the longest that he had ever seen. After a while, he left to get a bottle of water and by the time he got back he was told that chemotherapy drug was administered to her without his knowledge. He said that he was upset because he was not informed about her getting any chemotherapy drug. He said even if he was notified, he would not have agreed due to the multiple seizures attacks that Jerodene was experiencing. I too agreed with Jermaine because I thought that was wrong.

He went on to say at one point, when things got real bad, the doctors drew screen while they tried to resuscitate her. By then she was also getting some medications to help with the seizure and after a while the seizures decreased. Just listening to him explaining it all was so devastating, so one could just imagine him being there and experiencing it all. How hard that must have been to stand and watch as the doctors try their endeavour best to save Jerodene's life. He said it took a while for her breathing to go back to normality, but after a while it did. He said he sat up in the wooden chair for the entire night because he was so scared of her having another seizure attack. It was very terrifying, listening to all of what had happened during my absence. It felt as if I was watching a movie but even then we still believed God that Jerodene would be okay. Her favourite bible verse, Psalm 118 verse 17 says "I shall not die but live and declare the works of the Lord". Each time the pressure came on, where Jerodene was concerned, that bible always gave us reassurance.

## *Another Birthday*

It was finally December 30, 2017 - my birthday. After hearing all that Jermaine had told me the night before, along with everything that was going on around us with Jerodene, I woke up giving God thanks for another year but I was totally out of it. It was a day that we were all looking forward to but when it came I had no idea what to think or say. There was nothing much to say with Jerodene being in the hospital. It was just too hard for us to process. I woke up feeling very tired because it was too difficult for me to sleep throughout that Friday night. The first phone call that I received was from my precious gem, Jerodene wishing me a Happy Birthday, in her weakest state. She then asked me, **"Mommy, are you okay?"** I was not expecting her to ask me if I was okay due to the fact that she was so very ill. I told her how much I missed her and that I would be coming to see her soon. Her voice sounded very weak but went lively when she heard my sister, Romayne's voice. My entire day was spent at my parents' house but there was no happiness within, no celebration whatsoever. It was just another day, one that I really wanted to be over and gone. We were looking forward to a splendid day the same day that Jerodene had said that she would make sure that all three of them would treat me as a 'queen'. But with Jerodene in the hospital, my entire day was just dull. Rasheed had been asking for his sister ever so often but I guaranteed him that she would be okay. Throughout that day there was not much improvement but we were still hoping for the best.

## *New Year's Day - Jodian Pantry And Friends In Tenacity Concert*

The Jodian Pantry and Friends in Tenacity Concert was scheduled for January 1, 2018 and that was just two days away. Obviously, things were not working out according to plan but nonetheless, Jermaine and I had agreed that I should go to the event to represent Jerodene. We all knew how much we were all looking forward to such a great event, especially Jerodene. In addition, Jerodene and her Aunty Romayne had had a few rehearsals together over the phone. It was a very well attended event and other relatives of mine were present - my dad, my brothers and their families, my aunt Sandra, but unfortunately for my mom she had to babysit Rasheed so she was unable to attend. Throughout the entire concert my mind was on Jermaine and Jerodene. I had to be checking my phone from time to time to see if Jermaine was calling me. The Concert went well and a lot of people came out to support. People were disappointed when they heard that Jerodene was not there, because they were looking forward to seeing and hearing her encouraging words, but they understood the circumstances. A special prayer was made for her and everyone hoped that she would get better very soon. Jodian kept her promise to give part proceeds towards Jerodene's medical expenses, for which we were grateful.

## *Life Back At The University Hospital*

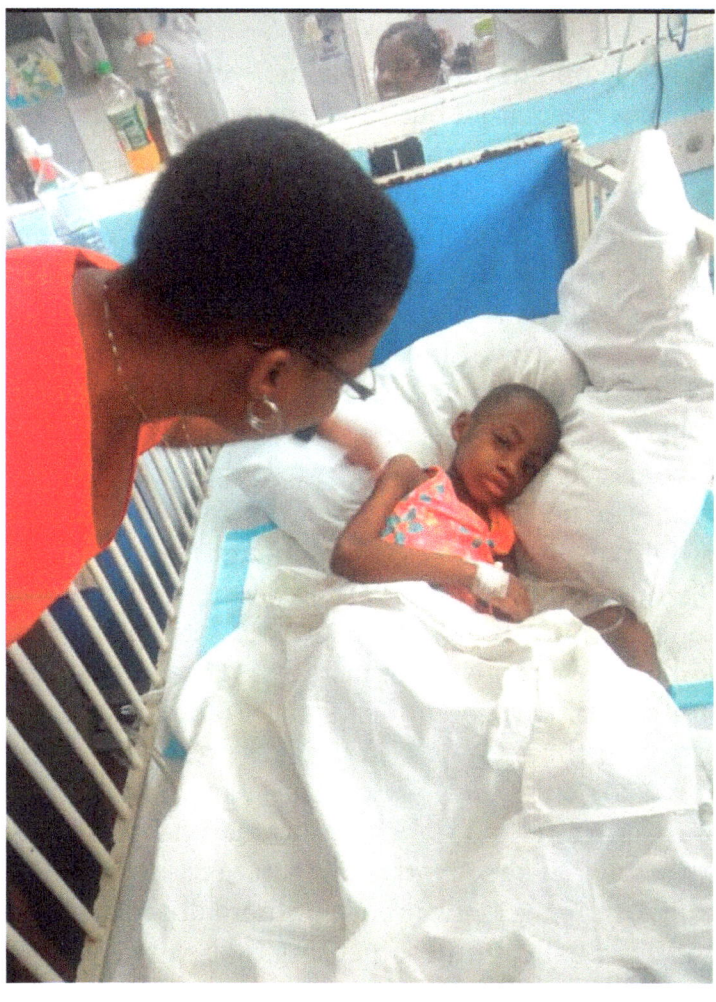

The following day I had to go back to the hospital to release Jermaine because he had to resume work. The good thing was that Rasheed would be staying with my parents so we were not worried about him. When I got back to the hospital Jermaine told me that the nurses had to remove Jerodene from bed three and place her back at bed one, because she was not stable and that they had her on close monitoring. I was very happy to see her but seeing her in that position was very difficult, because she had not been that sick before. She was very weak, and was just lying down because she was unable to sit up on her own. That was unlike her. My sister, Romayne came to visit her and even though Jerodene was not talking much we could see the smile on her face that told that she was happy to see her aunt. We just wished that Jerodene was alert like before. All Jerodene did was smile and squeeze her aunt's finger. Romayne carried a portable karaoke microphone for Jerodene. Even though she was unable to use it, I would normally attach it to her tablet and sing some of her favourite songs from time to time. A few days after the concert was aired, Jodian Pantry and her husband came to pay us a visit. They laughed and took a few pictures then unfortunately the doctors had to find a site for Jerodene's IV again. She told Jodian that she wanted them both to hold hands during that painful experience. Jodian never hesitated. She then prayed for Jerodene and told her that she would come to visit her again soon.

## *Another Visit From Kerlyn Brown*

Jerodene would have gotten a lot of visitors and on one particular day Kerlyn came to visit us. She took Jerodene's favourite fast food for her but Jerodene was unable to eat any of her hot and spicy chicken but she ate the fries. Aunty Kerlyn was making fun of her just for her to eat something. As I took up my phone to take some shots, you would not want to see the look on Jerodene's face. She was not pleased at all but I had to take those photos because I wanted them for our family collection and also to show them to her when she was cancer free. Even though she was not that talkative as before, Kerlyn told her that they both would sing a song. Kerlyn used the portable microphone that Romayne had gotten Jerodene. They started singing 'You Deserve It' but in the midst of it all Jerodene fell asleep because she had recently gotten some pain medication and those caused her to be drowsy. She was so determined to sing to the end, in a drowsy and weak voice Jerodene then said, **"Aunty Kerlyn, I would love to pray."** She then started off by saying, **"Oh Holy Father"**. She then fell asleep and that was when Kerlyn finished Jerodene's prayer. We all knew that was unlike Jerodene because she always finished her prayers.

A few days went by and Jerodene was not improving and Kerlyn and a doctor friend of hers came to visit Jerodene. The doctor wanted to meet Jerodene because she had heard so much about her through Aunty Kerlyn. She was concerned about the types of medications that Jerodene was on. She had asked Jerodene what her favourite colour was and Jerodene told her pink and purple. That same day, one of my brothers, Randal, and his family came to visit us and the slow release morphine that Jerodene was on was almost done. The doctors gave me a prescription but unfortunately the hospital's pharmacy had none in stock. I mentioned it to Kerlyn and her doctor friend and the doctor gave me the money to go fill the prescription and to buy a nice gift for Jerodene in her favourite colours on my way back to the hospital. My brother offered me a ride. The doctor also told me to purchase a few cupcakes because Jerodene loved them and had requested them. Jerodene told the doctor that she wanted to sit in her lap, which the doctor honoured her request without hesitation. Before we knew it both of them dozed off together. At the pharmacy I looked for a long time and eventually found something that suited Jerodene. I purchased a purple teddy bear along with a pink princess ball. It was not an ordinary ball, it had her favourite cartoon character from Frozen on it. Even though she loved it, she was not as excited as she would have been at other times because she was not well. Aunty Kerlyn and her friend left shortly afterwards because her friend had another engagement. She told Kerlyn that she would love to visit Jerodene on her next visit to Jamaica.

*"I Love My Family"*

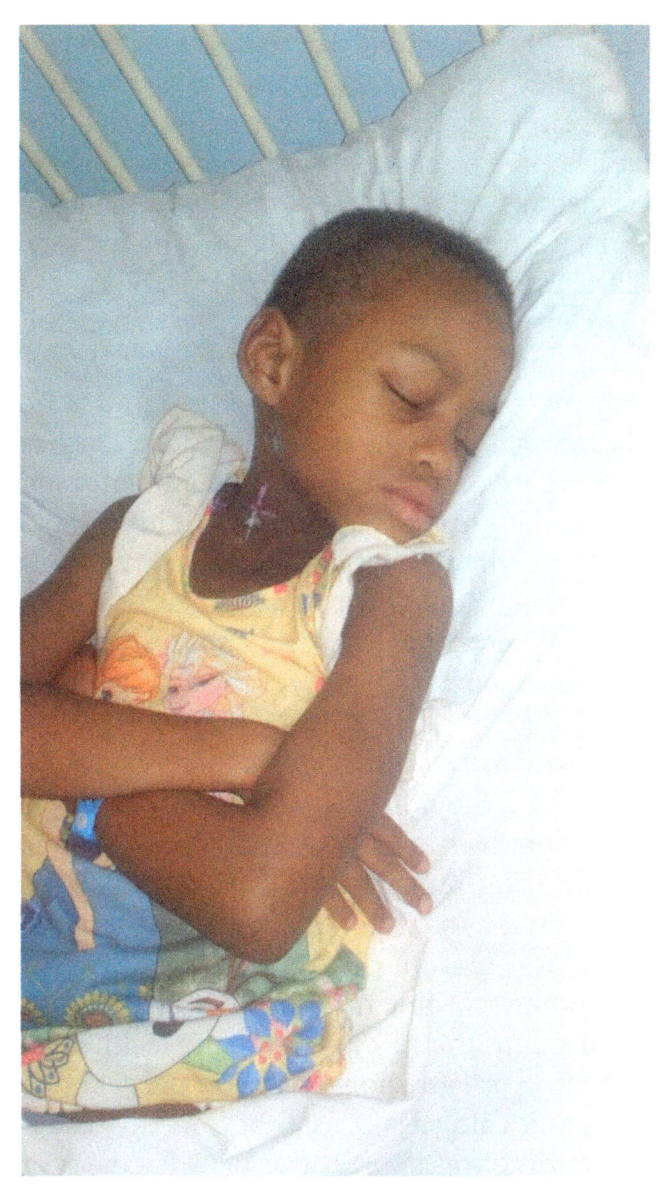

Shortly after they left, I did a short video of Jerodene while one of my sisters-in-law, Venieca, was there. These were Jerodene's exact words, *"I love my family and I don't want to make them give up on me, so I have to keep fighting. I want everybody to stop telling lies, my family is depending on me, so I, myself, have to keep on fighting."* She then fell asleep but our belief was that she said what was on her mind. The things that she said always brought us to tears. She was just too mature for her age.

## *Jerodene Getting An IV In Her Neck*

Days went by and there was no improvement. At that time Jerodene was very weak and helpless and she still was not able to sit up on her own, so we had to brace her with the pillow in order to support her back. The veins in her hands and feet had got more difficult to locate. I remember on a particular Sunday morning, the previous IV had gone bad and they had to replace it because Jerodene was behind on her medications. I stood at her bedside and watched a few doctors take turns and pricked her over 20 times. I watched with my eyes filled with tears because I knew that Jerodene was in pain, but she was too weak to cry or even scream as she normally did. Oh how I wished that there was something that I could have done. She just laid helpless on her bed without making a sound. I wished that I could at least hear her cry even once more, but she just laid still and her veins were still nowhere in sight. They gave her a break and then another doctor came a while later. When they realised that they were out of options they told me that the only place left for them to try was her neck. My entire body was filled with chills. It seemed as if my brain was frozen. That was the last thing that I wanted to hear because I have seen children who had IVs placed in their necks. It had never crossed my mind that one day Jerodene would have been in that same situation. Oh no, not our Jerodene, not our Jerodene at all. The reality of her getting the IV in her neck was staring me in the face. I still did not tell the doctor if they should proceed. It then dawned on me that I had no choice. My entire body went numb when the doctor asked me, *"Mommy, which side of her neck do you want me to try first?"* She asked as if it was an award being issued. Oh God, give us the strength that we need. My heart leaped while I stood and watched. As they inserted the needle into her neck, I could see that Jerodene was in so much discomfort even though she was unable to speak. By then she was back on oxygen because her breathing pattern had decreased. She had to be in one position for hours due to the IV in her neck. It just broke my heart seeing all of that. Words were not sufficient to explain how I felt inside. Only parents or other relatives who had been through what we were going through could have related to our situation. God knows it was not a good one. Having received all the encouraging words that we did was much appreciated. We received a lot of prayers, love and support from all over the world.

## *Fluid Surrounding Jerodene's Lung*

After a while Jermaine and I thought that Jerodene was improving because she smiled randomly with us so we knew that was a good sign. Until one day when her dad came to visit us we noticed that Jerodene was breathing irregularly. We brought it to the doctors' and nurses' attention. After doing some scans, they told us that she had a lot of fluid surrounding one of her lungs and that the way forward was that they had to pull the fluid. They told us that they would pull as much as possible and in doing so would have lessened all of what was happening. Let me add that, that was the second or third time that they had to remove fluid from her lungs. The first time was in 2016 when they took her to a private room on the property and did the procedure. I thought that they would have done the same thing again but that time they did it right at her bedside. I was able to see exactly how the procedure was done. It was hard for me to stand and watch, especially seeing the size needle that they had to insert into her back. I asked God for the strength for Jerodene to endure. She still was not able to sit up on her own even though the procedure required that. So I had to brace her for the entire procedure.

## *Signs of Hope*

The following day Jerodene had a host of visitors - her dad, Mr. and Mrs. Oliver and their daughter, Jestina. They had a great time while Jerodene and Jestina played on their tablet for a short while. Jestina even read her stories. They really loved and cared for each other and Jestina had made a promise that whenever Jerodene got discharged from the hospital they would spend more time together. Jermaine and I stooped over her bed and posed for the camera. We then took turns with the Olivers and we all were happy that Jerodene was having a great day as opposed to previous days. To God be the glory! Before Jermaine left for home, he promised Jerodene that he was going to repaint our room and Jerodene told him that he should paint it in pink. Jermaine also told her that on her next discharge she would be able to see it. We knew how excited she would be.

With the IV still in her neck I would normally still attach her portable microphone to her tablet and would play her favourite songs just to cheer her up. Some days she would not talk at all so we had no idea what was going through her mind. We were praying for a miracle and other people were praying too, and we knew that there was nothing too hard for God to do. As the days went by she was still on oxygen because she was not able to breathe properly on her own. Beside her always was her favourite teddy bear whom she named Lamie. She loved it dearly. During that time, Rasheed was going to school and Jermaine had to balance caring for him and also going to work. He dropped by the hospital from time to time.

## *Uncontrollable Seizures*

Jerodene was on 24 hour 7 days a week monitoring. I noticed at one point that she was interfering with the IV line that was attached to her neck. Remembering the torture that she had gone through for them to find a proper vein, I had to ask the nurse to put a knit on her hands because I really wanted to secure that one. I had also asked the nurses to have her screened around because we needed our privacy. They respected and granted our request. On that same day, her friend, Mr. Chance came to pay her a visit, but was unable to stay because he was not accustomed to seeing Jerodene in that state.

The seizure episodes seemed as if they came back with a vengeance because they became uncontrollable. At times when it was time for her bed linen to be changed the nurses and the Patient Care Assistant would place Jerodene in my lap while they changed the linen as swiftly as possible. On a particular day, while she was seated in my lap, the seizure came on suddenly. For people who can relate to having seizure attacks or have relatives who experienced them, they would know that it was very hard to witness. For me, to have her seated in my lap, I really needed extra strength, so I braced myself because I did not want her falling out of my arms. It was difficult seeing her experiencing such a terrible thing. At times when the nurses and I were by her bedside and the episodes came on, I fought hard to hold back my tears. When I did not want her to see me crying, I went behind the screen to wipe my tears then return to her bedside.

## *Jerodene's Spiritual Request Granted*

When we realised that Jerodene would not be going home anytime soon, Jermaine and I organised with our then pastor to have Jerodene baptised. He explained Jerodene's situation to our Island Overseer and had explained to him that Jerodene had requested her water baptism before. However, she was not able to receive it because she was in the hospital for most of the time and she was also doing the radiation at the time of her request. He told him that we really wanted to grant her request. The Island Overseer, Bishop W. A. Blair had told our then pastor, Pastor Watson, another way of doing it. He and his wife came to the hospital on January 13, 2018 and gave Jerodene her wish. Jermaine and Rasheed were present too and we gave God thanks that Jerodene's wish was granted. She got her baptism indeed. She was not responding to us for a few days so we had no idea if she knew what was taking place. Rasheed was overly excited to see her but he was very disappointed that she was not playing, laughing, or even touching him the way she always did. He was not accustomed to her just lying there without any response. That same day, her friend, Danique, came to visit her. Danique was a volunteer at the hospital and that was how they both met. They had not seen each other for a while because she had gone overseas. So upon her return to the island, the first person she wanted to see besides her family was Jerodene. She was very happy to see Jerodene. We knew that Jerodene had sensed her presence even though she did not utter a word.

I had asked the doctors what could be done since Jerodene's veins had become invisible. They told us that they would have to place a picc line in her chest area. We were happy that they had considered doing so because it would have lessened her discomfort and it would have been less stress for her. They did the procedure and it was a sigh of relief for us. The unfortunate thing was that within two days the line was totally blocked. That made me angry. I questioned how that could be? It was not even a week since it was placed there. It reminded me of the port that they placed in her a few months before even though the port was not blocked within such a short time span. Having the picc line blocked in such a short time span had me worried. They eventually had to remove it after. God must have answered our prayers because they found a vein and we were grateful.

*Jerodene's Wish Came Through*

On January 18, 2018, we were graced with the presence of Jerodene's favourite athlete: the World's fastest man, Usain Bolt. As he stood by her bedside and looked at her, Jerodene was semi-conscious because she had recently got some pain medications that had caused her to be extremely drowsy. Because thousands of people had seen Jerodene's video to Usain, by the time he reached the Paediatric Ward, the entire place was jammed. Jermaine and I stood and watched as Usain held on to Jerodene's hand as helpless as she was. We told her that Usain Bolt was right there but she just looked at him then closed her eyes. The good thing was that I was able to take some photos of us together for future reference. Majority of the staff members, upon hearing that Usain was there, left their departments and came to see him. We basically had no privacy. By then, those who were present, drew the curtains that surrounded Jerodene and the cameras were rolling. Some had gone live on Facebook, while others were videoing and taking pictures. We were sorry that Usain not able to come see her before because we knew that she would have requested a race with him. We said to ourselves, and other people were saying that they hoped that he would come and pay her a second visit whenever she was feeling better. Nonetheless, we were happy that he honoured Jerodene's wish and that he kept his promise. A few days went by and Jerodene had improved a little. I then told her that Usain Bolt came to visit her the day before, but she shook her head telling me no. I then showed her the pictures that we took at her bedside. When she saw it her entire countenance was changed from sad to her being happy. That was when she believed that I was telling the truth. Seeing the expression on her face, I then knew that she had no idea that he was there.

### *Jerodene's Fight Continues. Lord Where Are You?*

The following Saturday night while Jerodene was still admitted, her blood pressure skyrocketed. She was just unstable, her pulse rate was very high as well. Her limbs were getting cold while her torso was very hot. The seizure attacks came on ever so rapidly that she had roughly 10-20 seizures for the night. She was barely out of one episode before another one started. That topped the chart because she had never had so many back to back. As I watched the vitals machine, which was attached to her at the time, the numbers were just fluctuating. I remember crying so much seeing Jerodene struggling to survive. It was just too much to bear and I doubted I had more tears to cry. The doctors and nurses worked extremely hard to bring her back to stability. They did not let us feel as if we were in it alone, they were there with us throughout the entire ordeal. Jerodene went through so much. That was the longest night that I had ever seen. The medications that she was getting to prevent the seizures did not seem to be working. I just wished that I could have grabbed and run with her screaming for help. I felt as if I was in a dream. I stood there and wished that someone could have shaken me and woke me up but I just had to face that reality. After such a long, hectic and sleepless night, day had dawned and Jerodene and I were able to see another day. A new day to make things right with the Creator. I remember, after I had tidied Jerodene, I went to the car park where I picked the most beautiful flowers and used her white bath towel to make a beautiful swan on a table that we had at her bedside, I then decorated it like all the love her dad and I had for her. I did it because Jerodene always loved it when I did it at home, and after such a long night I thought doing so would have brightened her day. It was difficult for me to tell her dad about her ordeal but I had to.

While the doctors were having their ward round, they told me that they needed to have an urgent meeting with Jermaine and I. So the following day Jermaine came to the hospital. It really pained his heart when he saw the state that Jerodene was in. Looking at our daughter who was once an active, vibrant, energetic, talkative and athletic child having been bedridden for days, we had no idea when she would be better. It was very hard watching her knowing that there would have been a lot of things that she would have wanted to say to us and places that she would have wanted to have gone, but sickness crept in and stole it all. Through it all, Jerodene was a fighter and that she would have pulled through.

### *"There's Nothing Else That We Can Do"*

Shortly after Jermaine arrived, the meeting was called to order in one of the doctor's offices. We had an idea what to expect, and Jermaine and I decided that no matter what the outcome was we would stick together as a family and remain positive as we continued praying for Jerodene's healing. The doctor then asked us how we felt about Jerodene. I told her that we still had faith in God that she would pull through and that we did not know what God's plans were but in the meantime we were still hoping for the best. Jermaine then told her that Jerodene was going to be okay and that he agreed with what I said. The doctor then told us that from their point of view, there did not seem to be any other treatment option for Jerodene for the cancer. They said day by day it was affecting Jerodene more and more. They also said that she had a lot of fluid accumulating in her right lung and also in her abdomen. They went further to tell us that she had been having uncontrollable seizure attacks and that there were signs that the fluid around her brain was compromising her brain function. The doctor said that she knew that we were believers and that they were focusing on making Jerodene as comfortable as possible. She said that she meant that the team would be supplying Jerodene with oxygen, taking care of her pain and nourishing her body. They were treating her for an infection in her urine and that on the ward round they decided to focus on Jerodene's comfort and not sticking her too often. She also said, as the cancer progressed, which it would, unless God intervened, Jerodene was not on any treatment and that would cause other parts of her body to malfunction. Without a cure or anything holding off the progression of the cancer, if they were not careful, they would just keep injecting her to try and manage problems and so on. That might give some comfort but at the end of the day it really would not change Jerodene's quality of life. It was not curing her and probably it was causing more pain to her.

The doctor then made mention of the palliative care team, which was sent to have a discussion with us. She then continued to say palliative was the term used for care for end of life. She said that it was hard to sit and talk about it, but that was where they were at, and how to make her life as comfortable for her as possible. They would do the necessary things to take away her pain, give her oxygen etc and also reduce the dehydration. We should bring her family members to see her, and we should spend a lot of time with her. She said that if they had a well established place, with well functioning service at that point, they would prepare her to be at home with her family. She would get all the love and support, even if we needed a nurse to come in daily and that she would have been in a loving and caring environment.

After all that was said, the doctor then asked us how we felt about all that she said. To be honest, I was not able to answer, because for us to sit and listen to all that was said about our only daughter, it was all bitter and hurtful. I took a deep sigh, while Jermaine proceeded to answer the doctor's question. Jermaine drew an illustration telling the doctor that in construction if there was an issue he would have gone the extra mile to get the issue resolved. He went on to say that the doctor's job was to work on humans, but there were some things that the doctors could not do because they, themselves, are human. He also told them that whenever he was cornered and could not help himself, he called on Jesus to help him. That was where Jerodene was at that moment. He realised that there was nothing much that they could do and that we understood. The doctor then continued to say that they would love to cure but they also love to care and that they have not stopped caring for Jerodene but they have shifted the focus.

Jermaine then said that all we had to do was to ask God for help because there was something about Jerodene that made him believe that it was not her time to die. He said if God said that it was her time then fine, but deep down within he just did not believe that it was her time to go. The doctor then said that she believed that God was in control, and that all was in His hands. She said there comes a time when we have to recognize that sticking Jerodene ever so often would not benefit her in the long run. She said that the neurosurgeon could not intervene in the event her condition continued to worsen. She said that they pulled some fluid from her lung just to make her breathe comfortably but the fluid would reaccumulate because of the cancer that could not be treated. She then said that she did not have the final say, but what she was trying to do was to tell us clearly that we could probably think about it and then we would come to a decision.

She said that the entire situation was not black and white to which we agreed. She then inquired about Rasheed and if he and Jerodene had spoken on the phone in recent times. I then told her that due to the fact that Jerodene was not talking, I would just do video calls so that they could see each other. She said that she saw my parents come to visit Jerodene quite a few times. Then she asked when they would be visiting her again? We told her that they were there the day before and that they were praying endlessly for Jerodene's healing. She then said that all prayers were important and that we should also pray for them so that they would make the right decisions.

I then shared the experience that happened back in August 2017 a few days after Jerodene had the out of body experience when she was praying for Amielle, she had also prayed asking God to give the doctors wisdom, knowledge and understanding. The doctor then told us that Jerodene was a special child and that she was an angel. I then told her that whatever plan that God had it was not a case where we could be presumptuous before God and whatever He did was well done. Jermaine told the doctor that he knew that they tried their best with the help of God and that was the reason Jerodene was still with us up to that time, and it was not Jerodene's time to go. Jermaine went on to say that Jerodene had a bright future ahead of her and she had so much fight left, so much to accomplish in life, and that Jerodene had so much to say, so many places to go and it was just not her time to go.

Jermaine went as far as to remind me and to also brought it to the doctors' attention that over a year ago when we were all home, and Jerodene was crying for a terrible headache. By then we had to rush with her to the closest hospital to us, which was the Mandeville Regional Hospital. Jermaine sat with her in his hand while I had gone to do the lengthy registration. Jerodene started vomiting and during that time she was still crying for her head. Her dad eyes were filled with tears rolling down his face. Jerodene stopped crying immediately then looked at his dad and said, **"Daddy why are you crying? Leave it and God will do it."** Jermaine then told the doctors that he had not cried since. He continued to tell them that it was not Jerodene's time to go. He told them that the good thing was that throughout it all he and I stuck together with the help of God. He told them that it is a rough situation but we stuck together. He also said that he had no idea that things would have gotten that bad. His dream was to be happily married and have two children but for us to be facing all that was going on, it was just too difficult. Our only baby girl. We believed that Jerodene was going to be okay.

He mentioned to the doctors that they would be surprised to know the number of lives that Jerodene had touched. When we went to church and testified, a lot of people were left in tears and cried out to God in adoration. He said that Jerodene was just seven years old, and if seven years was what God had planned for her, well he was begging and pleading to God for more time on Jerodene's behalf. As I sat and listened, I fought hard to hold back the tears. He proceeded to tell the doctors that Jerodene had partially touched the entire world. The doctor then said that Jerodene was like the glue that holds things together, and even among the rest of the children that were facing the dreaded disease as well, and that Jerodene was special. The doctor then asked if we understood what had been said, and it was hard to agree. She then asked if we accepted what she had said. *"But how could we accept all that devastating news?"* we thought to ourselves. I then told her that was a tough question, but we understood but as to the acceptance part, no one could accept that.

She said if Jerodene had a fever or anything external that was causing her illness that they would treat it, or if any infection occurred. On the other hand, the day to day pulling of blood measurement was a little futile because if they did not arrest the process things would just continue to deteriorate. At that time they would not be doing anything to arrest the process. We told her that we heard everything that was said but we just could not accept it. The doctor wanted us to think about all that she said. She understood that we were expressing ourselves but they needed to clearly understand where we were as parents. She said that she knew that we had a lot of faith. She then asked if we were accepting what she said in terms of how they would approach the situation meaning no intensive monitoring but would certainly respond to any new illness that seemed to be separate from Jerodene's underlying condition. She told us that accepting would be different from giving up because she knew that we would not be giving up on Jerodene. For sure, in our point of view, giving up was not an option. Jermaine stepped in and told her that we would love for Jerodene to go home with us. The doctor said that would be ideal but we would have to have oxygen at home, nursing care and that she did not see that happening. She said that it had always hurt her to see children who were sick spend their last days in the hospital, knowing that only a few family members would be able to visit them in the hospital as opposed to if they were home. All of those requirements they were looking into, she even mentioned that even Rasheed would have felt better having Jerodene home in her loving surroundings. They said that an organisation might be able to help so that was something that they were working towards.

She said that they would still examine her on a daily basis as usual, do her vitals as well and keep abreast of what was going on with Jerodene. She advised that we keep up the communication and if there was anything that was bothering us, we should feel free to come to her.

Jermaine and I sat in that meeting for nearly an hour. It was as if we were dumbstruck when we heard all that they had to say about our princess, Jerodene. To break the silence, Jermaine shared the scenario with the team of doctors that were present in the meeting about the day when Jerodene was born and he came to visit us at the hospital, Jerodene was crying on top of her lungs uncontrollably and we both were hurrying to change her diaper so that I could feed her. By the time we were through putting it on it was then we realised that we had put on the diaper backways. That actually put a smile on our faces, and that memory would be with us forever until Jerodene got old.

Jermaine told the team that Jerodene was born as a healthy child, and by the time she was four years old, she suddenly became sick. He then shook his head and told them that the entire situation hit us like a ton of bricks. He went on to say that Jerodene was an active child, and that she would have gone to school and took part in her Sports Day activities and came first in almost all of the races, and that Jerodene had all her certificate as proof. He told them that Jerodene also received a prize for best attendance when she was in K1. The following year everything went down a steep hill. He also told the doctors that even through the three years of tribulation that we have been through, that Jerodene made us so happy. He said that us, as a family, did not see all this coming. He saw Jerodene all grown up and attending college, of course that was our plan. We did everything right but that was just the way it was. Jermaine thanked the entire team for all that they were doing and that we really appreciated all that has been done. As the meeting came to an end we told them that we would have a discussion with close family members then we would get in touch with them.

After such a lengthy meeting with the team of doctors, it was difficult for us to come to grips with the situation. It was difficult to swallow our own saliva because it all left a very bitter taste in our mouths. I had to let Jermaine go by Jerodene's bedside without me while I went to the bathroom. I literally broke down in tears wishing all that they had said was a hoax, a dream and none of it was true. Despite it all, we would still be fighting with our princess, Jerodene Bailey. Even though they had told us that there was nothing much that they could have done for Jerodene we told ourselves that what men gave over, God took over. It really puzzled us that our talkative, smart, loving and energetic daughter had not spoken for days but we still knew that miracles could still happen.

### "We Have To Place An NG Tube In"

After a few days, Jerodene stopped eating completely. I had brought it to the nurses' attention and they told me that they would have to put a Nasogastric intubation (NG) tube in. I heard that name before but had no idea what it was until a nurse explained the term to me. To the sound of things, we knew that it would have been very uncomfortable for our Jerodene. When I called Jermaine and told him about their plan for Jerodene, we both agreed to anything that would make Jerodene comfortable and get something into her stomach, because she had not had anything substantial for days. They started feeding her some nourishment but they were not able to tell me the duration of time that she would endure it for.

### A Cheque From The Optimist Club

Remember Mrs. Hanson? She and another member of her team came by the hospital to visit us. Jermaine was not there on that day because he was there the day before. Mrs. Hanson was shocked when she saw Jerodene, she had never seen Jerodene in such a condition before. You could see her sad countenance knowing that the once active and energetic child was now bedridden. She knew that if Jerodene was up and about like before, they both would be having their little conversation. Mrs. Hanson was elated that she had gotten the chance to come pay Jerodene a visit. Before she left, she handed me a cheque on behalf of the Optimist Club of Manchester, Jamaica, to aid with Jerodene's medical expenses, for which we were very grateful.

Jerodene was stringed left, right and centre. She also had on the pulse oximeter, NG tube, blood pressure machine and IV lines were also attached. At times we wondered how she managed all those things and because she was not talking we had no idea what was going on in her mind. That was the only time in my life I wished that I was a mind reader. Jerodene spent most of her days sleeping, and even if she was not sleeping she would just be looking all over without a word. The issue with her veins was not getting any better. At one point the IV again was infiltrated and the only suitable vein that they found was one over her right eye directly above her eyebrow and unfortunately that was where they had to place it. I was not happy with the decision but then I thought that if it was to make her able to get her pain medication, then okay, whatever it took to make her feel better. I asked God to take full control. We had been so gentle with her because we did not want that IV to become infiltrated like the previous ones. The unfortunate thing was that within a day or two her right eye was terribly swollen and the entire area was very red. I was furious because I was not comfortable with it in the first place and then that happened. She struggled for a few days to look out of that eye. It broke my heart seeing her in the state that she was in. The last thing that we wanted for Jerodene was added stress. That was not acceptable and there was no explanation as to what might have caused it. The situation was that they had to remove the picc line that they had placed because within three days it was blocked. So I knew that I had to brace myself because they would be sticking her all over again. That was one of the most difficult things that Jerodene had to face and the hardest thing that any parent could have stood and witnessed, but I knew God would grant us the strength.

### God Sent

I met this loving, caring, genuine and understanding soul, Nordia Vassell. She is the godmother of my niece, Xariah. I had met her on the day when my brother, Randal, was scheduled for discharge. Nordia came to the hospital on a daily basis during January 2018. She came to visit and stayed with us for the entire day. She was a stranger who became family, she would sit with me at Jerodene's bedside for hours and whenever it was time for Jerodene to have her bedbath, Nordia was always there to help me along with the nurses. Things were not as before when I could have given her a quick bath. Those days were sort of difficult and hectic when it was time for bathing and change of clothes due to all the attachments that Jerodene had on.

I remember one day when the pressure came down on me. I felt as if I had 1000lbs on my head and I was about to explode. I felt as if I could just bawl out and did not care what others thought. Only God knew the feeling. It was only Him that I could have cried to. Nordia stayed with Jerodene while I ran to go seek a church, and for a pastor to pray for Jerodene, because the burden was too much. A pastor prayed for her and us as the parents that God would have given us the strength to cope. I must confess that I felt better afterward, we really appreciated all that Nordia did. One could hardly find those types of people in recent times.

When we realised the intensity of Jerodene's situation, we told the doctors not to administer anymore chemotherapy to Jerodene until she was strong enough, to manage, to which they agreed. Obviously, Jerodene's body was not in any shape to receive such treatment.

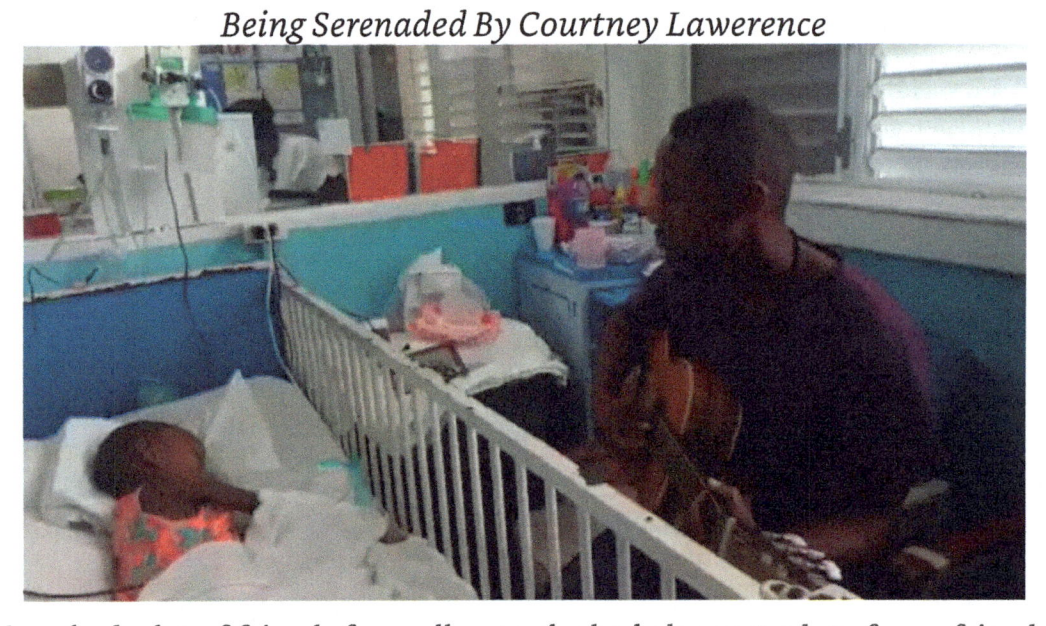

*Being Serenaded By Courtney Lawerence*

Jerodene had a lot of friends from all over, she had also met a lot of new friends that were staff at the University Hospital of the West Indies. For most people, I would have just passed on the hospital corridors and would maybe have given them a smile but because of Jerodene I would have to stop and exchange a word or two. That was what happened with a young man named Courtney Lawerence. He and Jerodene had become friends from quite a few months back. He knew of Jerodene's diagnosis and was shocked when he heard. He had left his department on a particular day in January 2018. He had no idea that Jerodene was not doing too well but he took his guitar and sat by her bedside and sang her a song entitled, 'Wrap me in your arms.' As I stood videoing them both, he sang from his heart and I could see that he was passionate about what he did. I asked him what had prompted him to come and render such a powerful song for Jerodene. He told me that Jerodene had told him the love that she had for guitars and that she wanted him to come and do a musical piece for her. He said that she had also told him that she wanted him to teach her how to play the guitar as well. Courtney told me that he was seated in his lunchroom worshipping, and while he was doing so Jerodene flashed across his mind. He said that even though he was so shy to come and sing for her, the Holy Spirit was bidding him to come and do so. He said that he obeyed and even before Jerodene had gotten worse she really wanted him to come and play the guitar for her. He continued to tell me that he did not want anything to happen to her and he did not get the chance to do so. He said that he had put shyness and pride aside and came and sang for her. He said that he was happy that he was obedient, and I was too.

## *Still No Word From Jerodene*

Weeks had gone by and Jerodene still was not talking. Her lips had gotten so white and dry that we had to use lip balm to keep them moist. I could not use her toothbrush in her mouth any more so the nurses had to use gauze wrapped on a tongue depressor and cleaned her mouth with chlorhexidine mouthwash. We could only assume that she was having pain or having a seizure attack when the digits on the blood pressure machine had increased. The seizures had gotten out of control and even though the doctors had increased the seizure medication, they still were not helping. But we knew that there was still a God somewhere who cared even if we thought that he did not. He sits high and beholds all things. We still held on to our faith that Jerodene would be made whole again. On that same day my other brother, Melbourne and his wife Kemarie came to visit her. My other brother, Ryan was not able to make it but his wife, Keysha, came as well. Ryan and Keysha came to visit previously because they said that they had to fulfil their promise to Jerodene. Unfortunately, the visit was not the same as before. Knowing Jerodene, she would have been having her little conversations with them. For them to see her laying on the bed helpless and motionless and not saying anything at all, they knew that it was unlike her. My cousin, Lorraine, who was living abroad was not able to visit us but she asked one of her friends, Lorraine, who came to Jamaica to come pay us a visit, which she did. She prayed before she left, and wished for Jerodene to get well soon.

## *Excessive Swelling*

Unfortunately, the nurses had to insert the catheter into Jerodene because her urine was not flowing as before. Even though she was wearing diapers all over again for weeks now, she always hated the catheter. After a while, she was not able to control her bladder movement. Her abdomen was swollen and so were her hands and feet. The swelling was excessive and because she was not able to walk for about a month now, her feet started dropping. Even though Jerodene was bedridden at the moment, I had to put on her sneakers just to keep her feet in place. That had helped somewhat, I thought. All the time for the past month I just wished I could just lift her off the bed and hug her, that mother to daughter hug, that warm embrace. Just to feel her warmth again, but all that was made impossible because of the several strings that were attached. I was scared of her falling out of my hand when the seizure episodes came along. We had very hectic days. I always stayed by her bedside every second of every minute. If I wanted to use the bathroom and Nordia was not there, I asked one of the nurses to stay by her bedside until I got back. Jermaine called sometimes three or more times during the day to ask how Jerodene was doing. I sat up for hours during the nights watching Jerodene, just being by her side made me feel extra special. At times during the nights the nurses would see me seated in the hard wooden chair nodding due to how tired and exhausted I was. Jermaine came to visit one evening and due to the state that Jerodene was in, he had to stay overnight, so we had to take turns sleeping and watching her. The nurses who would have been on duty around that time helped us watch her on and off while I took a short nap. There was also a staff member there who was a Christian, Cherriel Passley, she spent time at Jerodene's bedside praying numerous times, may God continue to bless her.

It got to a point where some dark brown fluid was coming from the NG tube. I was so naïve to all that was going on. I had asked them what it was and that was when I was told that the correct name for it was coffee grounds, and that they would be watching it for a while to see when it would clear up. They also told me that they were not allowed to feed her with her nourishment until it was all cleared up.

### *O What A Positive Improvement! Thank God.*

On the bright, sunny morning of January 22, 2018, with the help of the nurses, we had given Jerodene her usual bed bath. Immediately afterwards, I sat in the chair and tried starting a conversation with her. I knew that she was always hearing me even though she was not responding. So there I was, videoing her. I called her name and she then looked at me and responded by giving me a little smile. I told her to wave her hand and she gave me just a tiny wave. I smiled because even if she did not do anything else, I felt as if I was over the moon. No one could have even imagined how happy I was. I laughed, I cried and I immediately told God thanks for such an improvement for Jerodene. I told myself that better days were ahead, I was overly excited to share such great news with Jermaine and the rest of close family members and friends. I called Jermaine and told him and he could not contain himself. He shouted on top of his voice giving God thanks and praise for the healing process. If someone had given us an award, we would not have been that happy.

### *Can You Believe It? She Said, "I Love You More"*

The following day was the happiest day of our lives. After almost a month of not hearing a word from Jerodene, she eventually spoke and when I heard her talking to me I grabbed my phone and started videoing her and this was our conversation.

*Me : Jerodene, give Mommy a kiss.*
*Jerodene: Blew me a kiss.*
*Me: I love you Jero.*
*Jerodene: **I love you mommy.***
*Me: I love you darling, so much.*
*Jerodene: **I love you more.***
*Me: What else do you want to tell mommy?*
*Jerodene: **I kiss you** - she then blew me a kiss*
*Me: Give me a bigger kiss.*

Indeed she blew me a bigger kiss with all her might. I asked her if she wanted to say anything else and she then shook her head telling me no. One of the Patient Care Assistants, Euphand Prince, came along at the same time while I was videoing Jerodene, she then started talking to Jerodene but Jerodene was not saying much by then. Jerodene then said, *"I love you."* The PCA then asked Jerodene who she loved. Then Jerodene uttered, *"I love my Mommy."* Jerodene had an issue remembering who the PCA was even though both were very close friends. Jerodene made my day, my week, my month and my year. I was actually on cloud nine as some people would say. Her dad was excited, we were at a loss for words to describe how we felt. We thanked God for his continuous healing upon Jerodene's life. All the staff, especially the nurses who were friends with Jerodene were elated for that 'moment.' We all waited patiently for that moment to arrive and finally she talked. God really answered our prayers. She still had that beautiful and unforgettable smile. I then told her that I was going to do a video of her and send it to Rasheed but by then she went on mute. I then asked her if she remembered who Rasheed was and she nodded her head signifying yes. I did not bother to stress her anymore because I realised that she must have been exhausted. She then went back to sleep because the pain medication had started to work.

It was difficult for me to know when Jerodene was in pain, so I assumed that whenever her blood pressure increased maybe that was when she was in pain. At another time, her blood pressure skyrocketed because she was having or going into another seizure that would have lasted for quite a few minutes at a time. It was easy for us to know whenever her blood pressure would go up because that was one out of the several machines that was attached to her.

## *High Temperatures*

Jerodene started having very high temperatures, and those figures were even higher than in previous times, and to be honest I had never seen such high figures before. With the help of the nurses, Nordia and I took off all her clothes and had to keep sponging her down with some water and prayed that the fever would go away soon. Unfortunately, each time that it went away then it came back shortly afterwards so, we had to keep monitoring her. Jerodene had lost so much weight, more than we could possibly imagine. Her breathing pattern became irregular all over again and I had to bring it to the doctors' and nurses' attention. The doctors also noticed it while they were doing their daily examinations as well. Each time I would see a change with Jerodene, I would always inform the team, but that time around I noticed she took a deep breath and it would take a few seconds before she took another breath. After a while, her breathing pattern went back to normal. At times, I would have placed her tablet close by her in order for her to watch her favourite cartoons. Another time when her dad was there, I had used the microphone that her Aunty Romayne had given to her. I attached it to her tablet and I sang the song 'Overcomer' by Mandisa and Jerodene would look on and smile because she loved the entertainment. I had asked Jermaine to video us, while some of the nurses stood and smiled as they watched us.

## *Stajaun's Prayer*

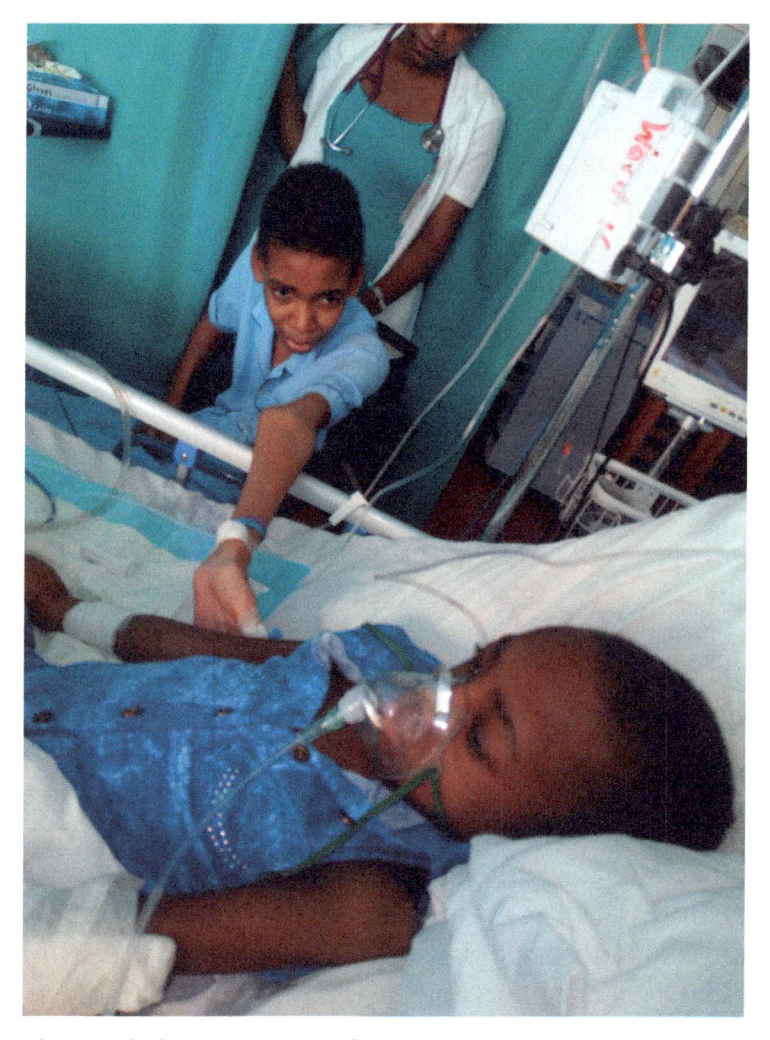

A few days went by, and there was another patient whose bed was opposite Jerodene's. He had told me that his name was Stajaun. He was a very humble and quiet young man and seemed to be in his mid-teens. Stajaun barely talked but as I passed his bedside on a daily basis, we would smile at each other. On that particular day, the nurses had placed him in a wheelchair because his feet were not strong enough for him to walk. He told one of the nurses that he wanted her to take him to Jerodene's bedside because he wanted to go and pray for Jerodene.

Upon reaching Jerodene's bedside I saw him lean forward, stretch out his left hand and he held onto Jerodene's right hand. A doctor and a few nurses stood there anxiously waiting to hear Stajaun's prayer. He looked at Jerodene with tears rolling down his cheeks, then I heard him utter, "*Save her.*" One of the nurses then turned to him asking, "*What did you say, Stajaun?*" He then responded, "*I am begging God to save her.*" That was the end of the prayer. As I stood and watched, my eyes were filled with tears, I just could not hold back the tears; nurses and doctors who were present wiped their eyes too. It was just an emotional moment for all who watched. I knew that God had heard and answered Stajaun's prayer. That reminded me of the time when Amielle was very ill and Jerodene had told me that she wanted to go pray for her. Each time I remember Stajaun's prayer for Jerodene I tend to get very emotional. You should have seen the look on his face as he desperately asked God to heal Jerodene.

### Prayer Time

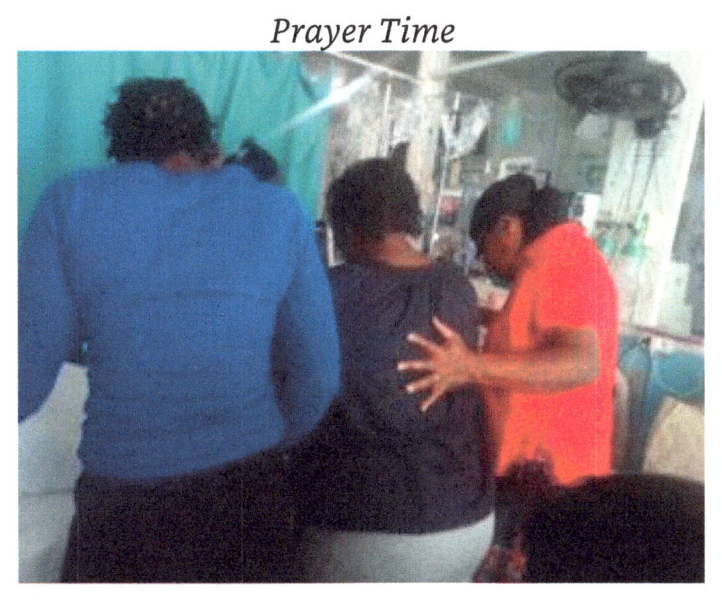

That same day, my mom and a few of her church members had journeyed to the hospital to visit and pray for Jerodene. They stayed a while with us and we really enjoyed the company. Even to that moment, Jerodene had not said a word since our last conversation the day before. Jerodene still had the NG tube in, but by then they had switched it from one nostril to the other. She was still on oxygen, and the coffee ground cleared up, so happily Jerodene was able to be fed. I was very happy that it had all cleared up because she had not gotten anything to eat for a while up to that time. The unfortunate thing was that the scar and swelling were still over her right eye from the previous IV access. I really prayed that it would disappear soon.

### Neiko's Visit

Before the day was over, Neiko Brown came to see us; his visit was long overdue. He had just gotten the chance to come visit. It was a pleasure meeting the concerned young man who really helped us to have got some financial help to assist with Jerodene's medical expenses. We were very grateful. I had told him that Jerodene was not able to eat solid food at the moment and so he had taken some Pediasure for her. He stayed with us for a while. He also told me the things to look out for because he had recently lost his wife to that dreaded sickness. He told me the things that we should expect, and before he left, he had encouraged me to continue praying and that God was always listening. He also told me that giving up was not an option. He noticed that Jerodene's feet were swollen, and so he told me to keep a close eye on them and that if it worsens, I should let the doctors know. Those encouraging words meant a lot because it had now reached a point where I could not even pray: the burden had gotten so heavy and I did not know what else to tell God. I had poured it all out.

### "I Shall Not Die, But Live And Declare..."

Days had passed and I had no appetite whatsoever; nothing had any taste. Just by looking at the meal, my stomach felt full. I did not want to leave her bedside, not even for a second, not even to go to the bathroom even though Nordia was there. At times my limbs would get very weak, and sometimes my mind would go blank. All that was because I was worried and concerned about our princess. As I sat, I remembered all that the doctor had said to us in the last meeting. A lot started flashing across my mind, even though we sat and heard all that was said. What if they were telling the truth? I thought to myself. But then I remembered Jerodene's favourite scripture: 'I shall not die but live and declare the works of the Lord.' Those were the words that I used to encourage myself.

### The Situation God Worse

The situation was barely got better. On numerous occasions, her torso was hot and her limbs were very cold and after a while her pupils had stopped reacting to light upon examination by the doctors or the nurses. Her blood pressure was fluctuating but it was mainly on the high side, her pulse rate was also high. I was also told that there was bleeding in her stomach. When I thought of all that was going on in Jerodene's life, I asked myself, what more could she bear? I wished that I could just take all those away from her in order for her to be better – just as any parent would have thought. The pressure was just overwhelming and became unbearable for Jerodene and by then we thought that the swelling in her feet would have gone down but unfortunately it had got worse. Even then we still had faith in God and believed that He would work things out on our behalf. Almost the entire universe was praying for Jerodene's healing, and as much as things were not getting better at the time, we knew that God still worked miracles.

It came back to my mind when Jerodene was admitted at the Mandeville Regional Hospital in 2016. My mom and one of Jermaine's aunts, sister Charmaine, came to visit Jerodene. Before they left, Jerodene told them that she wanted to pray, and in the midst of her prayer I remember her saying, **"God, Lazarus was dead for 4 days until he started to stink, but I am not dead."** My understanding was that she was still alive, and she knew that God had raised Lazarus from the dead and that the same God then was still the same God in her situation and He never changes. When I remembered all that she had said in her prayer, I had the reassurance that Jerodene would be well again, through Jesus Christ.

### Her Dad's Visit

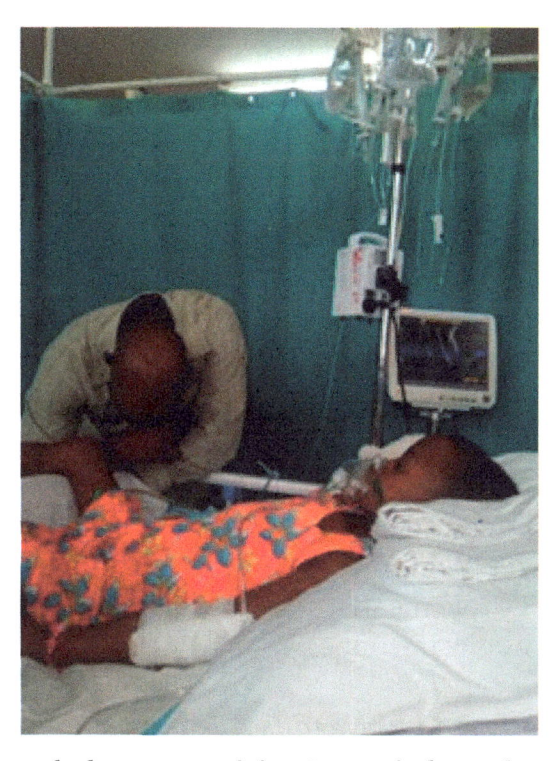

On January 31, 2018, her dad came to visit. He carried Jerodene's favourite KFC and because she was not able to eat, he and I went on the outside and took turns to eat because we felt really bad that she was not able to partake of any. It pained our hearts to see how Jerodene laid helpless and motionless on the bed; her eyes were open and we knew that she heard her dad's voice and sensed his presence. Even though she was not talking, we knew for a fact that she was hearing every word that we said. Therefore, we continued speaking positive words to her as we always did. We would read her bible, which one of her favourite nurses had given to her, and some of her favourite books to her. Her dad stayed with us for a while and told us not to worry ourselves because Jerodene was going to be fine with the help of God and the doctors. Before he left for home he laid his hand on her as we both agreed in prayer. We knew that our lives had been built on prayer and there was nothing too hard for God to do. Jermaine told Jerodene to always believe that God is our healer and she should not stop believing in Him. We knew that she heard every single word that we uttered.

## *That Warm Hug*

The following day I had the chance to hold her in my arms. Oh, how her warm, soft skin felt great against mine. I made full use of that moment because I had not had her that close for quite a while; it felt really good. I just sat there staring at her sleeping so peacefully. I just did not want to let her go. I had no idea if she was uncomfortable so within 15 minutes I placed her back on the bed. The nurses had to put the pillows behind her as we normally did. Because Jerodene was not able to move on her own, the nurses had to change her position every two hours in order for her not to develop any bed sores. Whatever side she was on, the pillows had to be placed behind her just to keep her in place. I told the nurses that anything to make her comfortable was okay with us. That same day, my brother's pastor, Pastor Monroe Wisdom, and another church member had come to visit and prayed for our Jerodene. We were grateful.

## *Another Day To Be Grateful For*

February 2, 2018 started off to be a great day. We gave God thanks for another day to be on top of the ground. Things might not have been the way we all wanted it to be; nevertheless, we were grateful. No matter how our situation had seemed dull, as if there was no way out, it still could have been worse. We knew that people were experiencing worse situations than us. Nordia had come to visit and she stayed the entire day with us; she helped out as usual. She left in the evening to go pick up her children from school but had promised Jerodene and I that she would be back the following day and that she would be taking a few of her church members with her so that they would come and pray for Jerodene's healing.

### *We Never Lost Hope*

Further during the day I received a telephone number from a friend whose husband was recently diagnosed with a particular cancer. She told me that there was a hospital in Mexico that specialised in cancer treatment other than using chemotherapy. I was so happy to hear such news, so I jumped on it immediately and called them. The doctor who I spoke to had asked me about Jerodene's well-being. But when I told him that Jerodene was on oxygen and everything else that she was facing, that was when he told me that they would not be able to assist her. Even though he had told me that, we still were not losing hope.

### *A Friend In Need Is A Friend Indeed*

I remember in 2015, when Jerodene was diagnosed at that same hospital, just as the doctors then had given me the unfortunate news, and I started crying, Stacey came on the ward at that same time and we both cried together. A good friend indeed and in need. Just as Nordia had left the IV became infiltrated again, I stood and watched the doctors stick Jerodene 16 times just to find a suitable vein. Seeing all that made me want to push to find out from them when they wOULD be able to put another picc line in, just to lessen all the torturing. Jerodene would normally cry when she got one stick but now she just laid there without a sound. That was not Jerodene. In the late evening, my very good friend Stacey came to visit us. She told me that she wanted to pay us a visit before but she had just gotten the chance to do so. She stayed for a few hours and I had updated her on Jerodene's well being. When I told her the latest update she agreed with me that no matter the look of the situation, God was still in the healing business. We also had a good chat about back in the days when we were children and the fun things that we did together along with her identical twin sister, Tracey. I had not laughed so much in a long time. We had a few hours of laughter that was well needed because our days of late had been on the down side. Before she left, she told me that she had other plans the following day, which would have been the third of February. But instead she changed her mind and told me that she would be coming to spend the day with us.

### *Breathing Pattern Changed*

Saturday, February 3, 2018 started out very well. Plus, it was another day among the living, for which we gave God thanks. The night staff had helped me to give Jerodene her early morning bed bath, helped change the sheets before they handed over the shift to the day staff. I had let her wear her pink and white sleeveless top with her matching shorts, and of course I had placed her favourite stuffed toy that she named Lamie right beside her. We laid her on her back and braced her with two pillows to start her day. It was a beautiful morning indeed. The sun came out in all its glory, the sky was blue and overall it was just another beautiful day. Jerodene seemed well rested after such a long night, I prayed with her afterwards then read her bible for her. Stacey told me that she would have taken some home cooked meal for me. I told her that I would be grateful because it had been a while since I had a home cooked meal.

A lady had journeyed from another parish to come visit Jerodene. At Jerodene's bedside, she held on to Jerodene's hand for a short while and as she started asking me how Jerodene was doing, her eyes were filled with tears because she remembered the last time that she came to visit Jerodene. Jerodene was all up and about giving her encouraging words. She could not hold back the tears so she decided to go outside for a while. She told me that she had to leave because she was not able to manage seeing Jerodene in such a manner. About 15 minutes afterwards as I stood by Jerodene's bedside I noticed that Jerodene's breathing pattern had changed again. I realised that after she took one breath then it took her 15 seconds before she took another breath. It was something that I had seen already so I was not too alarmed because I knew that it would go back to normal after a while. Even though I had seen it all happen before I went to inform the nurse who was very close by. She then came by Jerodene's bedside and timed her breathing on her watch by then it took Jerodene 12 seconds before she took another breath. The nurse hurriedly ran from behind the screen and told me that she was going to call the doctors that were on the neighbouring ward 15. While the nurse left to call the doctors, it took Jerodene 21 seconds before she took another breath.

## *I Never Saw Death*

By the time I looked I saw a few doctors running speedily towards Jerodene's bed just to hear one of them say to me, *"lower the bed."* I did just that and they hurriedly removed the pillows from behind her back. As I looked on, they started resuscitating her. By then a lot more doctors and nurses were already behind the screen. They asked me to step on the outside because they said that I would not be able to manage. I told them that I would not be going anywhere and I wanted to be by Jerodene's bedside. We all knew Jerodene was a brave fighter and we knew with the help of God, that she would have pulled through. As I stood there watching them resuscitating her, I prayed. I prayed quietly as I have never prayed before. I told myself that it was another out of body experience similar to what Jerodene had had the year before. That was all that could have comforted me, because death was not in my book. As the doctors took turns in resuscitating her, I stood watching helplessly with my heart pounding. I looked at Jerodene laying on the bed motionless and helpless with her eyes closed as they had been most of the time. I then called my mom and aunt; they were roughly about an hour away. I told them that I had never seen things get that bad before, I told them to call Jermaine and let him know that Jerodene was not doing well, because I was not able to. They called Jermaine and told him that he had to make it to the hospital immediately because Jerodene was not doing well. By then, my mom and aunt were already on their way to the hospital. My brother and his wife along with Kerlyn Brown were on their way too.

The situation was not improving, and I still did not see death. As they continued to resuscitate her, PCA Prince was the time keeper. By then, the other parents who were on the ward were already aware of all that was going on, and they were all praying quietly. I knew that Jerodene was going to be okay, so there was no need for me to cry or scream. In the midst of resuscitating the consultant came to me and told me to go tell Jerodene that I love her. I honestly did not tell her at the time because I said to myself, *"It seems as if this doctor thinks that my daughter is going to die."* I took a walk outside a few times then came back and just stood there watching Jerodene just waiting for her to take another breath. The consultant then realised that I had not gone to tell Jerodene that I love her and told me again to go do so. I then said to myself, *"Since this doctor insists, let me go tell Jerodene that I love her because I knew that she was not going to die."* As I went by her bedside and stooped by her bed head, I looked at her motionless body. I just wished that she would just open her eyes and tell me that she was okay. I then whispered gently in her left ear, *"I love you, Jerodene. As a matter of fact, everyone loves you."* I then took a step back while the time keeper uttered loudly, "20 minutes." I was not scared or anything of the sort. I was just waiting patiently for Jerodene to take a deep breath. *"Prove them wrong, Jero, prove them wrong."* I said quietly. After that the doctors continued to resuscitate her and within a few minutes the consultant came to me saying, *"Mommy we've been trying with her for the past 25 minutes and if we go for another five minutes and hear nothing from her, I'm afraid we'll have to call it quits."* Even then I still did not see death.

Stacey had come but could barely keep up when she saw all that was happening. We hugged each other as we both stood and watched without being able to do anything. The doctors went for another five minutes and that was when the consultant gave me a sad look. When I realised that the five minutes were up and there was no movement from Jerodene whatsoever that was when I bawled out openly. *"Jerodene, Jerodene, Jerodene,"* I cried. *"Come back to me, come back!"* My heart felt as if it was going to burst wide open when I realised that Jerodene was really dead. I shook her, I tried feeling for her pulse, but there was none. It seemed like a dream - one that I wished someone would wake me from. It could not be true, I thought to myself. Jerodene just laid there helpless and motionless. To me she was just sleeping; she looked so peaceful. It seemed unbelievable. I cried knowing that all the dreams that we had for Jerodene had vanished. How could we move on without our princess, Jerodene?

We had so many plans for Jerodene: we envisioned her going to college and pursuing her career in nursing, because that was what she dreamt of being. We could not see our lives without Jerodene. What would we tell her little brother, Rasheed, whom she loved dearly?

By the time my parents, aunt and my brother and his wife had got to the hospital, Jerodene had already transitioned. They knew that the doctors were resuscitating her, but they had no idea that she had already passed. By the time they got to the ward Stacey and I stood by Jerodene's bedside crying. They saw the look on our faces and could tell that something was wrong. It was hard for someone to see her and not know that she died because she just laid there peacefully as if she was just sleeping. All could see the pain on my relatives' faces as tears rolled down their cheeks. My dad wept openly and uncontrollably. Kerlyn had come and just like everyone else it was just too hard for her to accept that Jerodene had really passed. She wished that she could have stayed longer but she was actually on her way to work, so she promised to keep in touch.

By that time Jermaine was in a bus already on his way to the hospital not knowing that Jerodene had died. How could I tell him over the phone that his first born had died? Sigh, that was not possible. I was scared that, on hearing the news over the phone, he would totally lose it. While he was on his way, I called to find out what his location was. Immediately when I called him his first question was, *"Rasheda, is Jerodene okay?"* I knew that she had died so there was no way possible for me to tell him that she was okay. So as soon as he asked me that question all I could do was to just hang up the phone. I had asked PCA Prince, who was the time keeper, what time Jerodene had transitioned and that was when she told me 2:10 pm. Randal called Nordia and she, not knowing what happened, had told my brother that she was at the church picking up a few church members to take them to the hospital for them to pray for Jerodene. She was then greeted with the sad news.

I still would not leave Jerodene's bedside. It had gotten to the point where the nurse had asked my relatives to step outside because it was time for her to change Jerodene's outfit and to wrap her in a white sheet. As hard and devastating as it was, I stood there and helped the nurse to change her outfit, and also to put her diaper on. I begged God for the strength to assist all the way until my husband came. When it was time to stuff her, the nurse had asked me to step outside, because she thought that I would not be able to manage. They had also asked my relatives to step outside while they started the procedure. I told the nurse that I would not be going outside because I wanted to see all that was happening no matter how painful it was.

People might ask how I did it. But my only answer to such a question would be that Jerodene had asked her dad and me to promise to be with her to the end. So even though Jermaine was not there as yet, we vowed to keep our promise. As we stood there with such dark clouds hanging over, a nurse then told me that the protocol was that a deceased individual can only stay on the ward for a short period of time and that was when they wanted to take Jerodene to the morgue. I got really angry and told them Jerodene's body would not be leaving the ward until her dad got there and viewed her body. They really understood. As I stood and watched the nurse remove all the IVs, the resuscitating machine, the oxygen, the NG tube from her nose, the catheter and all the other attachments I bawled out helplessly. That was when I was forced to face the harsh reality: that Jerodene was no more. My God, my God is this really true?

## *"Jerodene Wake Up, Wake Up"*

A while afterwards Jermaine had called and told me that he was in a taxi and that he was very close to the hospital gate. My aunt Sandra decided to go by the gate to meet him because Jerodene was well known and so we did not want anyone to meet him on the way and to tell him before he got to the ward. We all knew that the outcome would have been different. I was so scared because I did not know what to expect when he got to the ward. My heart raced, my feet got weak and my entire body felt numb. Other parents knew that Jerodene had passed - some stood with their hands on their head, others sat looking out of space because all of them knew Jerodene. When Jermaine got to the ward he came and drew the screen and saw the rest of family members surrounding Jerodene's bedside. He then looked at Jerodene covered under the white sheet with her face showing. As he looked he realised that he did not see any attachments on her, neither did he see that big red resuscitating machine. With tears filling his eyes he shook her quite a few times well and called, *"Jerodene, Jerodene, Jerodene!"* but heard no response. He shook her again saying, *"Jerodene wake up, wake up, wake up, I can't believe that you only gave us 7 years, just 7 years."* As he got really emotional, he held his head as tears rolled down his face.

We all looked on in disbelief knowing that Jerodene was no more. How do we tell Rasheed who was at that time by his Aunt Charmaine? I then called Mrs. Brown (Amielle's mom) and told her about Jerodene's passing. Mrs. Brown, her mom and her sister had come to the hospital. It was so hard for them because they all loved Jerodene plus they had recently lost a daughter, granddaughter and a niece but nonetheless they came to give us their support, which was well appreciated.

Jermaine and I had never faced anything so hard and devastating in our lives. Our little world literally turned upside down. Jerodene left without saying goodbye and it really pained our hearts, and even if she had gotten the chance to say goodbye, we doubted it would have made any difference. The fact still remained that Jerodene had gone on to that Heavenly playground that she spoke about in previous times. Oh how we wished that she did not have to go. We just could not see life without her, she always spoke of the Four-Bailey's family.

## *That Labour Pain*

Within a few minutes, the porters came to take Jerodene's body to the morgue as we stood there helpless and at a loss for words. The porters took her off the bed and placed her on the concealment trolley. I felt a sharp pain under my belly button, I felt as if I was in the labour room about to give birth. I often heard parents talking about that labour pain when they lose a child, but never thought that I would have experienced that myself. We remembered telling the porters to be extra careful with her because we did not want them to bump her head. We just wanted them to be careful. As they wheeled her out, we all walked behind her while Jermaine rested his hand on the container as the security on duty opened both sides of the gate. I cried out so loudly, *"Jerodene, Jerodene, Jerodene!"* I just could not hold back. I felt that I had to let it all out; I did not care what anyone wanted to say because that was our daughter going to the morgue not anybody else's and worst of all we knew that she would not be coming back.

### *"I'm Sorry Mr. Bailey But You Can't Come Any Further"*

When we got to the exit of the security post, my relatives along with the Browns stood there with me and watched Jermaine as he still had his hand on the concealment trolley, while he continued walking with the porters as they bent the corner and went out of sight. I bawled even more uncontrollably. I stood there waiting for him to come back and when he did, he told me that when he reached the elevator that was when the porter said to him, *"I'm sorry Mr. Bailey but you can't come any further."* And that was when he literally broke down and was forced to face the reality that that was the 'end' that Jerodene spoke of a few weeks ago. But honestly her end had come too soon, and we were not ready to let her go.

# Saying Goodbye

### *Leaving Without Jerodene*
Since Jerodene's diagnosis in 2015, I saw a lot of parents come to the hospital with their child for admission and in the long or short term their child died and the relatives were left to pack up their things and leave for home without their child. We had no idea that such a reality would have reached us; not even in our dreams did we see that coming. As a matter of fact, no parent would have seen that coming. Our thought was that children were to bury their parents, not the other way around. No parent should be going through what we were going through. Going home with only Jerodene's belongings was one of the most difficult tasks for us. As we moved Jerodene's belongings one by one to my brother's car, tears, tears, tears flowed nonstop. The only question that came to my mind was, how do we move forward without Jerodene? Only God knows. It was hard to accept after many sleepless nights and torturing of the children with so many needle pricks. Some parents stuck it out on hungry stomachs most of the time (because I had seen it all). Some children ended up suffering during the latter days and at the end, parents still ended up losing their child to cancer or other critical illnesses. It just was not fair.

My brother volunteered to take us home but then the rest of relatives thought that it was not wise for us to be home all by ourselves. So they took us to my parents' house. While we were on our way there, the word had gone out about Jerodene's passing. It was all over social media; it plunged the whole nation into mourning. Our phones rang off the hook because people were calling to find out if such news was true; they were all in disbelief.

### *The Harsh Reality*
The tributes started pouring in mainly on Facebook and Instagram because Jerodene had thousands of viewers and followers. All that was getting to us, so we decided to give social media a break. We could not sleep that night, we tossed and turned so much. When day dawned, my eyes were red and swollen. Jermaine did not say much about how he was feeling but it was evident that he was very hurt because it was impossible to have a restful night after such a devastating ordeal.

### *"Mommy And Daddy, Where Is Jerodene?"*
Our son, Rasheed had to sleep at his Aunt Charmaine's house, which was closer to our home but was an hour and a half from my parents' house. My dad left out early to go get Rasheed so that all of us would have been together. Jermaine and I decided that whenever Rasheed asked for Jerodene we would tell him that she was gone to heaven because in fact that was where she had gone. There was no other way that we could have explained it to him; he was just three years of age. He knew that Jerodene was mostly in the hospital and for us to break the sad news to him we knew that he would not really understand.

As he got to my parents' house and saw his dad and me, I tried hard to hide the tears because I knew that he would have asked me why I was crying. Jermaine and I were lying on the bed so he jumped on top of us all excited and happy to see us. He had not seen me for several weeks. It was hard for me and Jermaine because we laid there pretending that all was well. Each time Rasheed would smile I felt as if I would have just burst out crying. We smiled back but deep inside we were dying. After all the excitement on Rasheed's part, he then looked around in all the rooms then came back to us, only to hear him say, *"Mommy and Daddy, where is Jerodene?"* Our hearts broke into a million pieces. We were so broken that we had to pause before we could utter another word. His first question was just as we imagined. Jermaine then told him that Jerodene had gone to heaven. Then his response was, *"Daddy, I want to go to heaven too, because I want to be where Jerodene is, so that we can play."*

### *"I Saw The Boss"*

That same morning, I got a call from Kerlyn. She told me that Jerodene appeared to her in a dream before dawn that same morning. She said that Jerodene looked at her and said, *"Aunty Kerlyn I took the 2A you know, I took the 2A, and the A is for angel. I was hearing you know Aunty Kerlyn, I was hearing."* And just as Kerlyn was walking away, Jerodene then said to her, *"Guess what Aunty Kerlyn… I saw the boss."* And all of that she said in her sassy voice just as she would have talked had she been here. That was when it dawned on me that Jerodene did not pass at 2:10pm as the PCA told me. She passed away at 2pm based on the dream and the other thing that she mentioned in the dream that caught my attention was that when the doctor told me to go tell her that I loved her, in the dream she said that she actually heard when I told her. And her seeing the 'boss' meant that she saw Jesus Christ himself. That dream needed no interpretation; it was just clear. Our daughter had gone home to meet her Creator, but the void and emptiness that she left us with, only God knew. Only parents who have been through a situation like ours would be able to relate.

### *Homegoing Preparations*

The unfortunate realisation was that we would have to start planning our daughter's Homegoing Service. We wished that we could have dodged all that was going on, but the truth was that we had to face it all. The doctors told us that the following Monday after Jerodene's passing we should come by the hospital to sort out Jerodene's death certificate, etc and also for us to take her to a funeral parlour closer to our home. Jermaine and I had gone to a prominent funeral home in Mandeville, Jamaica and they journeyed with us to the hospital. By the time we got there, we first were instructed to go by the ward that Jerodene was on. Going back there brought back so many memories. It was an unfortunate situation knowing what some of the other parents were going through, it was just too sad. When we were through with the paperwork we were then sent to the morgue to collect Jerodene's body. But by the time we went there with a few of the nurses, we were told that her body was not there anymore but at another funeral home instead that was about 20 minutes away. We inquired why that was done without our consent and that was when they told us that the hospital morgue had limited space. One of the nurses volunteered to accompany us there, we had to identify her body as well. I was worried if Jermaine and I would be able to manage it all. But we knew that God that had granted us the strength for the past few years of Jerodene's illness, the same God would continue to sustain us. They had called us into a room where Jerodene's body was, and it was so hard seeing her lying on that cold iron stretcher without any blanket to keep her warm. Jermaine and I stood looking at her just laying there, we touched her and she was ice cold. I wiped her face with my bare hand then it became wet. Sighing, I thought oh Jerodene was no more with us physically. She looked so peaceful and her features and complexion were the same. We then drove back to the funeral parlour in Mandeville, then told them that we would be back on another day to make the final arrangements.

A few days had passed, and I decided to go see some of the outpouring tributes for Jerodene on Facebook. As I was scrolling through I saw rumours that Usain Bolt would be taking care of all Jerodene's funeral expenses. We were furious because we knew that all that was a hoax. By then, our phones started ringing off the hook, people from all over were calling us telling us how happy they were knowing that all of Jerodene's funeral expenses would be taken care of by Usain Bolt. All those daily phone calls, plus other people who did not have our numbers were then sharing it on their Facebook pages and also commenting. Everything was becoming overwhelming, and that was when I decided to do a video on Facebook just to make it clear that all that was a lie. That video was not shared as much as the rumour, but we were happy we did it.

Planning our daughter's Homegoing Service was no easy task. No parent should have to go through such an ordeal. Several times I made the attempt to ask God, *"why Jerodene?"* But ever so often I was told never to question our Creator. Jermaine and I decided to have Jerodene buried in my parents' yard. My parents agreed, others had concerns but at the end of the day, we were Jerodene's parents, and it was our decision.

A few days had gone by and Jermaine and I went back to the Funeral Parlour. They told us that they did not know Jerodene in person but they followed all her stories on Facebook and they even watched her on the Inspire Jamaica Program on more than one occasion with Kerlyn Brown. So they told us that Jerodene was no stranger to them. In the meeting we told them all that we needed in order for her Homegoing to be a memorable one. They then told us the cost for the package then handed us a piece of paper with all of the requirements. They took us to the section where they had all the caskets lined out. Right there and then we knew that we had to choose one. Every decision ever since Jerodene's passing was difficult for us as a family just as it would have been for other parents burying their child. But we realised that we had no choice. Our eyes were set on a beautiful white glass top casket, we really loved that one. We then told them that we would have wanted it in Jerodene's favourite colours - pink and purple. The director was saying that she did not see where those two colours would have blended in. But Jermaine and I insisted on having both colours with a touch of white. We had no doubt how beautiful it would look.

Days had gone by and there were more questions than answers. We all had prayed earnestly for Jerodene's healing. Partially the whole world was praying as well and we had had faith that she was going to be made whole. Not to mention the amount of faith that Jerodene had. But I constantly asked myself, *'Was it that we didn't have as much faith? Was it that more prayers were needed?'* It was just hard for us to wrap our minds around it all.

As the days progressed, I cried more and more. Men on a whole tend to hide their emotions. So my husband barely wanted to talk about Jerodene's death. We thought about Jerodene everyday - her laughs, her jokes, her smile, her sassiness, just about everything about her. It was hard for me to smile but despite our situation, I had to find time to, because God was still amazing. As difficult as it was, things still could have been worse.

We had gotten together and Jerodene's Homegoing was planned for March 10, 2018. We all had to put things together for that date. During the time of our preparation, we received a call from a marching band by the name of the Magnificent Troopers. They told us that they were following Jerodene's story on Facebook and also on the Inspire Jamaica program, and that they were saddened by her passing. They also made it known to us that Jerodene had really inspired them as a group and also as a family. They said they would love to show their appreciation at her Homegoing if the band could be allowed to do a musical piece. We gladly told them yes and that we were happy that Jerodene had touched and inspired them in such a positive way. We were not surprised at all because we knew that Jerodene had impacted thousands of lives. By then my Facebook messenger was flooded with messages from all over the world near and as far as Africa, the majority of whom we had never seen or knew existed. But they all wished that they met little Jerodene Bailey.

Things were not the same at home. We recalled the first Sunday that we went to church after Jerodene's passing. That was another hard thing for us to do because knowing that it had always been the four of us for a few years and Jerodene would have been there testifying, singing or doing something for the Lord. I really wanted the service to be over because I was hurting and nothing anyone said could have eased our pain. Losing a child is one of the most painful things on the face of this earth, and it was unfortunate that we had to move on without our first born, Jerodene.

With the help of Aunt Sandra and her friend, Mrs. Oliver, we were able to put the program together. They came up with a unique idea of how we could have done the book marker. Instead of us having the usual bible verse or quotes on it etc, we used some of Jerodene's own words to make it more personal. We went ahead and planned the grave digging for March 7, 2018, three days before her Homegoing Service. The deadline for us to bring the required things to the funeral parlour was getting closer and Jermaine and I had to go to the store to pick out a dress for Jerodene. We bought one of the most beautiful white dresses ever: it had some silver decorations on it. Had Jerodene been alive, she would have loved it. We also got her a beautiful white headband along with a white stocking. We knew that she would have looked beautiful in them. One of the hardest things was for me to be ironing Jerodene's outfit for her to be buried in. We honestly did not see that day coming, but we had to do what we had to. I literally cried while I was putting her stuff together. No parent should have to go through such pain and heartache. I oftentime thought of life being unfair. There were so many people out there doing all manner of evil and things were going well for them, it seemed, and Jerodene just wanted one chance to live and also to show us all that we could still have faith no matter the circumstances that we were in. Unfortunately, she did not get that chance to live but a gospel song declares, 'We will understand it better by and by' so we wait to understand.

## *Jerodene's Grave Digging*

On March 7, 2018, all three of us journeyed to the hills of Johnnies Hill in Clarendon to attend the grave digging of Jerodene's grave. Families and friends from all walks of life were present. We knew it would have been a rough day for all of us so we prayed that God would give us the strength for us to endure. We can say that it was well attended, and God had granted us a fair day that we all had prayed for. At one point, it got overwhelming and I had to go aside to shed some tears, because the reality hit so hard. My mom was there and was able to comfort me while Jermaine was by the grave helping out.

My sister, Romayne, and cousin, Lorraine, had flown to Jamaica from overseas because they wanted to pay their final respects to our little princess, Jerodene. Other relatives and friends would have wanted to attend the Homegoing Service but due to circumstances beyond their control they were unable to attend. When we were putting the program together, Jermaine and I knew that there would be no more suitable persons to have written Jerodene's remembrance but us, because we had so many fond memories of our Jerodene that would never fade. I told Kerlyn that she would be the one reading it on the day of Jerodene's Homegoing, because there was no way that Jermaine or I would have been strong enough to do so.

We knew without a shadow of a doubt that the Homegoing Service would have been massive so there was no way our home church would have been able to seat so many people. We had chosen a bigger church of the same denomination, Knowles Road New Testament Church of God, which would have been able to host 900 persons seated. Word had gone out from Jermaine and I that persons attending Jerodene's Homegoing Service would be requested to wear a touch of pink or purple, which were Jerodene's favourite colours. With the help of our then Pastor's wife, Sister Watson and Kerlyn Brown they had got some helium balloons in the same colours purple and pink, and we would have a section on the program where we would let them just disappear in the sky. Knowing that there were quite a few children that were diagnosed with cancer at the same hospital where Jerodene was a patient, Jermaine and I had decided that part proceeds of the offering that would have been collected at Jerodene's Homegoing Service, would go towards another child there that was in need of financial assistance and we kept our promise.

The funds and the outfit for Jerodene's burial were taken into the funeral parlour. Beforehand, we had told them that we wanted Jerodene's complexion to be the same, as when she was alive, and they guaranteed us that we would not be disappointed. Two nights before the service, we had a prayer meeting at our home. The norm in our country is that the family of the deceased would have a live band and people would come and enjoy themselves singing and dancing to gospel songs. We did ours differently because in Jerodene's seven years on earth all she knew and did was to go to church to testify of God's goodness and his grace and that was the reason we chose to have a prayer meeting a few nights before Jerodene's Homegoing Service. Our then Pastor and some of our church members came and took charge of it all for which we were grateful. The days were not getting any easier. At times, I felt as if I would just lock myself away from everyone and just try to process Jerodene's passing.

## Jerodene's Homegoing Celebration

The day had come when we had to lay a daughter, sister, granddaughter, niece and cousin to rest, a day that we were not expecting so soon. We knew for a fact that it would have been a mournful day. We had scheduled an 11am ceremony because the program was a bit lengthy and the journey from the church to the burial site was roughly an hour and a half drive. So we had to use wisdom where the timing was concerned. Jermaine and I along with Rasheed and my sister journeyed from our home to the church and the entire time we were just sad, and we had no idea what to expect. Jermaine and Rasheed were dressed in their purple shirts and pink vests along with their white pants and my sister and I were clad in our purple dresses.

When we got to the entrance of the street, the hearse was there waiting for us, along with the Magnificent Troopers Marching Band. Because Jermaine and I had told them that we wanted the band to march slowly behind the hearse leading to the church, by the time we got to the church it was already jam-packed. Families and friends came out in Jerodene's favourite colours, and those that did not have purple or pink, wore what they had in support of a life well-lived as others described her. It was hard for me to believe that a seven year old had lived a full life. Her dad said the same thing but I hoped someday I could agree. Her wreaths were of the same colours as we expected and oh what a beauty to behold. We got inside the church and beheld the beautiful decorations, all purple and pink with a touch of white, which was done by our then pastor's wife and a few other persons. There was an arch all wrapped in those same colours with balloons. A lady by the name of Mrs. Frazer had made the bows and decorated the arch with ribbons for us.

The atmosphere had mixed emotions as was expected. Jermaine and some other relatives had taken Jerodene's casket inside the church and it was placed underneath that beautiful well decorated arch. When we beheld the casket, it was the most beautiful thing we had ever seen. All three colours blended in so perfectly just as Jermaine and I anticipated. It was even more beautiful. Jermaine was already on the inside, so as I walked down the aisle towards Jerodene's casket there were a lot of wreaths placed on the ground all around Jerodene's casket. As Jermaine and I stood over Jerodene's body looking down on her, instead of crying we found ourselves smiling. We honestly did not know why there were no tears. I guessed God must have dried it all up. Jerodene laid there so peacefully, she was just sleeping. It was evident that she was at peace.

I have gone to several funerals in all my life and after viewing the deceased body, he or she does not look close to when they were alive. But when Jermaine and I viewed Jerodene's body, we had no doubt in the back of our minds that it was her. That was Jerodene, she looked relaxed and just so peaceful. We wished that she would just wake up. Jerodene loved dressing up and loved putting on her lip gloss, and there she had it all on. Her white dress looked well on her and she had on a purple and beige corsage. She looked like an angel, a princess; she was just too beautiful. Even though Jermaine and I were smiling, we were so hurt deep inside. We were broken, empty and distraught, but God had enabled us to smile despite our circumstances.

As we sat in the church and the program was in full swing I recalled telling Kerlyn that Jermaine and I would not be able to read the remembrance of Jerodene and she told me that she knew that we could do it. And with the help of God, Kerlyn and the Inspire Jamaica team, Jermaine and I were able to read it. When I started the remembrance I realised that it was not as hard as we imagined. We knew that Jerodene would not have wanted us to cry, instead she would have wanted us to be happy. As a result, we put on brave faces and read her memories with pride and dignity as she would have wanted and loved. All was going well until I got to the last part of the reading, when the reality hit me like a ton of bricks and that was when I broke down knowing that Jerodene would be no more. I could not hold back the tears and they freely flowed. It was hard for me to read it all. I had to take some deep breaths. Jerodene had told me once, that when and if I am nervous I should take some deep breaths, and that should do the trick. I did it and it really worked. The entire service went well with all the lovely items; it lasted for a little over four hours.

As the Homegoing Service for our first born came to a close and the casket was taken outside, we then had the helium balloon ceremony, which lasted for a few minutes. It was a sight to behold seeing the balloons in her favourite colours disappear in the thin blue sky. It was just a wonderful experience. It was not possible to supply everyone with balloons to release because of the large crowd. However, for those who participated, they will always cherish that moment. Rasheed had his for sure and was excited because he was too young to understand the solemn occasion. He will always remember that he had a brave, and protective sister named Jerodene.

## To The Burial Site

After the service, we all then journeyed to Clarendon where Jerodene would be laid to rest. It was a very long motorcade and we had no idea that so many people would have been there. I remembered a young man came and introduced himself to me telling me that he had never met us in person but that he had been following Jerodene's videos on Facebook. He said that she had touched his life in such a positive way that he had to come and pay his final respects to our little heroine.

By the time we got to my parents' house (Jerodene's burial spot) the motorcade stopped at the entrance of the street. They took the casket out of the hearse at that point and the pallbearers, relatives and friends marched with the casket along with the marching band as they blew their wind instruments and everyone danced to some gospel music. The graveside was less than 10 minutes away and when we got to the graveside there was hardly anywhere to walk because people from that community who were not able to travel to the church had just stayed there and waited for the burial. As we stood there looking at Jerodene's lifeless body cold as ice laying there in the casket, the majority of her friends had taken teddy bears and flowers to place in her casket. Jerodene's favourite stuffed toy was Lamby, and we thought of putting it in the casket with her but then we had second thoughts, and placed another one in. We really wanted to keep Lamby as one of our treasures.

## Our Last Goodbye to Our Warrior Princess

As they placed Jerodene's casket at the entrance of the sepulchre, people, both young and old were pushing and shoving because all wanted a glimpse of Jerodene's body. My dad did not cope well, he cried very much because they were very close. Everyone stood looking on and it was evident that all were very sad. The casket had a glass top and so there was no need for them to open it for viewing. By then, her casket was all filled with all different colours. One of Rasheed's uncles, Andrew, lifted him up in his arms as I showed Jerodene to Rasheed but he got restless just watching her lay there. Within another few minutes the pastor then committed Jerodene's body: *"ashes to ashes and dust to dust."* They then pushed her casket under and then they sealed her grave. I tried crying but I could not cry and I could not say why. It was a beautiful but very sad and emotional day. As we watched the workmen seal her grave, tears began to roll from my eyes as Jermaine was kept busy helping to put Jerodene under. The harsh reality had hit and sad to say that Jerodene was no longer with us physically. The outcome was not what anyone wanted but it was what it was. The sad thing was that there was nothing that we could have done to make the situation any better. The unfortunate thing was that we had to make up our minds that we had to move on without Jerodene. She was now pain free, no more torturing, no more needle sticks, no more headaches, no more swelling, no high blood pressure, no more stomach bleeding, no more seizures and the list went on and on. She was now soaring with the angels on that Heavenly playground that she always spoke of.

  We all agreed that Jerodene had got one of the best Homegoing Services one could have ever possibly thought of. Thanks to relatives, close friends and The New Testament Church Family who helped out financially to make Jerodene's send off a success. For those who were not able to help financially but were there for us, we say thanks too. Indeed Jerodene went down in fine style. People who were not able to make it to Jerodene's Homegoing Service were able to see a glimpse of it on social media and would have even seen pictures as well. If love could have kept Jerodene here, to date she would still be here with us but God did otherwise.

  Days went by after the service and I cried day and night, my tears had become my water. Each time that I would look at one of Jerodene's pictures all it did was bring back memories of Jerodene. At times, Jermaine would have to be the one comforting me because he seemed to be dealing with the situation better than I was. I gave God thanks for him every day, because he was and still is considered God sent. We knew that Jerodene was in a better place where there was no more heartache or pain but the emptiness and void was just too much for us to bear.

# After The Dust Settles

### Even In Her Tomb

I remember being in Mandeville a few days after Jerodene's burial. As I was walking, a lady had approached me asking if I was Jerodene's mother and when I told her yes, she embraced me and told me that my daughter was an angel. When I asked her the reason for her saying that she then told me that she and her husband had been married for a very long time. She said that they quarrelled and fought almost every day so that even persons who lived in the community would hear them. She went further to say that when things got heated they would toss anything that was present at each other. She said that after watching one of Jerodene's videos for the very first time, it literally changed her life for the better. She said when she watched and listened to it she then looked within herself saying, *"But if this little girl is diagnosed with stage 4 muscle cancer and she has such faith and has all those positive thoughts coming from her mouth, then what about me?"* She said that when she went home she then showed the video to her husband and from that day onward any disagreements that they had, both would sit down and work it out without other people knowing. She also told me that Jerodene had changed her married life from a miserable and unhappy one to a happy one. I was so happy that I had met her and for her to have shared her testimony with me. I really gave God thanks for the encounter and could not wait to go home and share it with my husband. When I told him he then smiled and told me that more people were going to come forward with more testimonies, and we both agreed.

### The Emptiness

Months went by and as Jermaine would leave for work during the days and Rasheed went to school it got worse for me. I was the only one at home, and because I had missed out so much on Rasheed due to circumstances beyond my control, I chose not to go seek for a job, but to stay home and spend some time with my family. People tend to see us smiling but they had no clue of how much hurt we had inside. I often told people never judge a book by its cover, and we could attest to that. We knew that God had brought us a mighty long way and that he would forever be leading and guiding us. We remembered His promise that He would never leave nor forsake us, but that He would be with us to the end.

### Trying To Move Forward

Within a few days of our grief, I felt as if I was going into depression, and things were not getting any better. Days without Jerodene had become more and more unbearable and that was when I decided that I wanted to go to driving school. I then met this wonderful lady on Facebook by the name of Stephanie Rowe who was a driving instructor. When I told Jermaine about my interest he gladly agreed and really pushed me to go. I told myself that I would do anything to get my mind off the situation. When I went to the Justice of the Peace office to get my pictures signed, he asked me the purpose for his signing my pictures. I explained to him and in doing so I could not hold back the tears and that was when he asked me if I was sure that was what I wanted to do at that time. In other words, he wanted to know if I was sure I could manage to concentrate on the road given my state of mind. I had already made my mind up, so I told him that I was ready. At first it was hard to grasp the driving lesson, but my instructor, Stephanie, was very patient and tolerant with me, and I became a proud drivers' licence holder. I could not have asked for a better instructor. Jermaine and I did not yet own a vehicle of our own, but everything would happen in time. It was not our timing but God's timing.

*HOME IS NOT THE SAME…*

We really miss Jerodene: home is not and would not ever be the same without Jerodene. Not one day has gone by that we have not thought about her. She was one of our sunbeams, she was all we wanted in a daughter and more. She was an angel, and we considered ourselves blessed that God saw it fit for Jermaine and I to produce such a beautiful angel. God loaned her to us for a reason and one of those reasons was to bring forth love and unity to the nation. That was what she did despite the challenges that she faced. She touched and impacted the hearts of many, many of whom we have not heard about as yet and many of whom would be coming forward, and some we probably may never hear about.

Despite the severe pains and the down times that Jerodene had, I had never heard her question God, she never gave up, and she never gave in. She taught us to have faith, she taught us all to be loving and also to be kind to each and everyone that we come across in this life. In all her speeches, if not all, she always said that she wanted the world to be nice. Jerodene knew exactly what it was to be nice and friendly. I recall listening to one of Sonny Badu's songs entitled, 'My soul says yes.' At one point, my sister and I were elaborating on it and we both loved it. I was telling her that it took a whole lot to say yes to God. Surrendering everything fully to God and telling Him that whatever His will is, that our soul says yes. Even hearing that song now I tend to get very emotional and tears would start to flow. At that time Jermaine had never heard that song and I think that song had helped us throughout and that might be the reason why I barely could have cried during Jerodene's Homegoing Service. God knew what we were about to face so He had set us up with that song. That song has now become my favourite of all time.

### "Heaven Does Have A Playground, And The Angels Came to Meet Me By The Gate"

A few months after Jerodene's burial, a lady who was acquainted with my parents reached out to my mom. She told my mom that Jerodene had appeared to her in a dream, she said that Jerodene was clothed in full white and stood with both hands by her side and this was what Jerodene said, *"Miss, I am asking you to pass on this message to my relatives, because for some reason they are a little bit off the wall that I had to leave so early. They wanted me to grow to become an adult, and I was not sent here to be an adult. My time is up I have done what I was supposed to do here. I tried to bring as much people to Christ and more people are going to be led to Christ even after my passing. Miss, please remember to give them this message and please have them play 'Heaven's Playground.' Tell them that I am alright and yes, Heaven does have a playground and the angels came to meet me by the gate. Tell them that I am happy and I don't want them to worry."* On hearing that dream my heart melted, and remembering the previous dreams that I had about Jerodene being an angel. As a matter of fact, I remembered my neighbour's dream and one of my mother's church member's dreams that happened in the past. We summed it all up, *Jerodene was truly an angel sent from God, no questions asked.*

### My First Dream Of Jerodene After Her Passing

I always asked myself, when would Jerodene appear to me or her dad in a dream? Seven months after her burial, she appeared to me in a dream. I dreamt that she and I along with her best friend's Akayden's mom, Akili, were in a room. Jerodene was so beautiful and peaceful and she did not appear sick whatsoever. Jerodene sat on the bed and then looked to the corner and saw Akili seated there with her hand at her jaw. Jerodene then said to her, *"Aunty Akili, why are you crying and being stressed? Akayden says to tell you that he's alright."* Within a few seconds I woke from my sleep, the interpretation of the dream dawned on me. I called Akili and gave her the message from Jerodene, and that was when Akili told me that she was feeling depressed since she lost her son and that she was happy for that dream from Jerodene and that she really needed to hear that message at that time. Something then came to me that Jerodene had no clue that Akayden had passed off, but that dream showed me that they both met up on that Heavenly playground. Oh what a beauty.

### Trying To Heal

Jerodene was a very kind and warm hearted angel born on the August 15 2010 at 7lbs 4oz. She would have given her last and do without. She cared so much for people no matter what their status or age was, and even though she is no more with us physically, we have to continue her legacy, and keep her memories alive. We knew that she would have been so happy that we did. There was a lady whom I had met in 2016 at that same hospital, her daughter was very ill and most times she was in and out of the hospital. She reached out to my husband and me for assistance. She had told me that it was hard to care for her child because she was unable to work because each time her daughter would go to school, her teacher would call telling her that she should come and take her to the hospital because she was not feeling well. She told me that if she had something to do at home she would have been grateful. That was when I mentioned it to my husband and we decided to seek help for both of them. I got her permission to make a post on Facebook about her situation without mentioning her or her child's name. Jermaine and I thought of asking my Facebook contacts for a contribution to purchase some chickens and a few bags of feeding that would have helped them until it was time for them to be killed then sold. We received enough money to help get the chicken coop fixed, so we were able to purchase zinc fencing, plyboard, nails, etc. We were grateful that with the help of the Almighty and others, we were able to assist her in the way we did. She was able to start a business at her home, which was close to her daughter's school. We were happy that our project was a success, and the lady was grateful, overjoyed and appreciative that things worked out well and that things were able to turn over. I then asked my husband what would be our next project? His response was, *"Well, let's wait and see,"* then we both smiled. We knew that even though Jerodene was no longer here with us in the flesh, she was indeed smiling with us, maybe giving us a pat on our shoulder and saying. *"Mommy and Daddy, well done."* Had she been here, she would have been very pleased with us.

# It Started With A Thought

We thought of writing this our first book in 2015, shortly after Jerodene was diagnosed. But shortly after we started putting pen to paper, we then paused because we had no clue where this book would go. A while after Jerodene had transitioned that was when the thought had come back to our minds that we should continue writing this book. When we thought about our ordeal, we knew the entire world needed to hear about the Baileys' life story. This book was first handwritten then typed. People had asked why I did not just type it up on my computer. But I told them that I did not want to miss anything. I wanted it all written down. That is the reason that you are currently reading our book. Writing this book was the best thing ever; it really helped our grieving process, and instead of me being home and crying on a daily basis. I just put it all into writing. Our life's journey was a bitter-sweet one but nonetheless God was and is still in the midst of it all.

Quite a few boys and girls passed away since Jerodene's death, and I have gone to just two homegoing services. I had to go give my final respects to those little brave fighters. Jermaine and I can no longer imagine the pain and heartache of losing a child felt like, like we did before Jerodene's passing. Unfortunately, we can say we are able to relate to everything they are going through. Jesus is the friend of a broken heart and we are depending on Him to put His plaster on our wounds where they hurt the most.

# Jerodene's First Birthday After She Transitioned

On August 15, 2018, a few months after Jerodene's passing, we went to her graveside. Our first born would have been all of eight years old. We ordered one of the most beautiful heart shaped wreaths in her favourite colours. Days prior to that the emotions started kicking in, but we asked God for added strength, and God granted our request. On her 8th birthday we reminisced on how she had a blast that said date the year before at her big seven, and instead of us crying, we found ourselves smiling. God granted us settled 'peace that passes all understanding' and knoweth no measure. Rasheed had so many questions to ask his dad and I, some that we were not able and would not be able to have an answer for. As the years go by, he will get the full understanding. As we stood there, staring at her grave, Rasheed then picked the dried leaves off the wreaths that were there before from her burial. We cleaned off her grave then added the new wreath to the collection. It was a day well spent, she deserved that much and more. We miss her everyday but especially on significant days and occasions. But we thank God for the healing process. We often thought that had Jerodene been here what she would be doing, or even what she would be saying to her little brother whom she loved dearly.

### *The Healing Process - A Rough One*

All that we are going through takes time to heal, and everybody's healing process has a different time frame. For us, we have no idea when we will be healed or if we will ever be healed. All that will not happen overnight, but stage by stage. We cannot say that we have learnt to let go but for sure we definitely learnt to move on.

### *Jerodene's Legacy Left Behind*

Jerodene left a legacy behind, her memories will always be in our hearts, especially in her brother's heart. I remember a few months after Jerodene's passing Rasheed got homework stating that he should draw the number of persons living in his household. I read the instructions to him then I left to do a chore, and when I got back and looked at his drawing, he drew all four of us, but this time Jerodene with hair on her head. Even though the last time he saw her, her head was bald due to the fact that the chemotherapy had taken it all off. We know for sure that he would never forget her even if it takes him 100 years. He tells his friends that he had a sister and that she is now in Heaven with Jesus and His angels. We give God thanks for allowing Rasheed to understand that no matter how old he gets, his sister, Jerodene will always be in his heart. With the help of Almighty God we vow to raise Rasheed the same way that He had helped us to raise Jerodene. He has to know that living for God is all that matters and everything else would just fall into place.

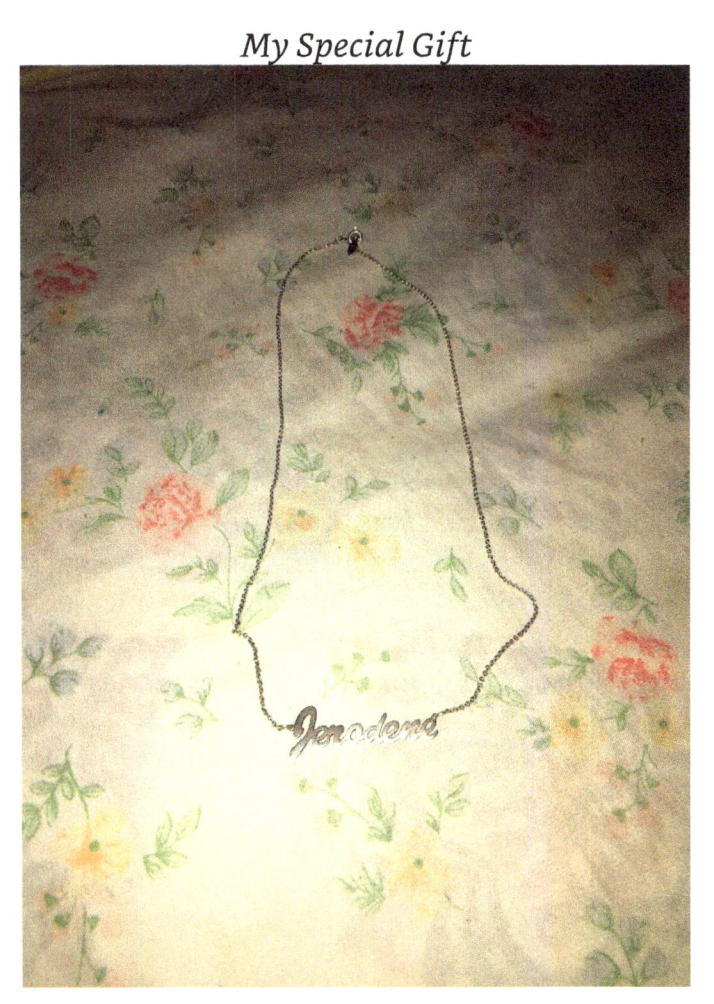

### *My Special Gift*

I had never been a fan of excess jewellery, but I was blessed with a necklace from my friend, Portia. That was the same lady who helped us to source the 1.5Million Jamaican dollars via a foundation overseas to pay the cost of the radiation that Jerodene had gotten. I received a necklace, one with Jerodene's name written on it. I fell in love with it at first glance. It was the most beautiful necklace that I had ever seen. Wearing it makes me feel as if Jerodene is with me always. I wear it with pride and dignity, and having that necklace means a lot to me, and will forever be a part of me, just as Jerodene will always be a part of us. I really thanked Portia for such a special gift and assured her that I would guard it with my life.

## *Our Beautiful Flowers*

We have some flowers at home in flower pots, some that I purchased and some that Jerodene and I would have walked the community on Saturday mornings and would have found them on the street side then we planted together. The last time that I paid quality attention to them was when Jerodene was here with us at our last Christmas. I remember both she and her brother watered them on a daily basis, and they had fun doing it but had little arguments as to who was supposed to water which ones. Jerodene being the eldest one would always put her point across then Rasheed had to listen.

Within the first nine months of Jerodene's passing, it was extremely hard for me to even look at them much, or even water them. I had no urge, no drive to continue to make them strive. I was so heartbroken and felt so empty. But on a particular Saturday in December 2018, I woke up and told myself that day was the day for me to turn a new page. God gave me the strength and the urge to pick up from where I started with our beautiful flowers. I even planted some more as well and oh how they are flourishing. I just kept planting and planting. I put all my love into them just as if Jerodene was here. I also realise that in doing so it helps my healing process while my husband would go out to work on a daily basis that would help his healing process. I bet Jerodene is smiling down on us and nodding her head in agreement. Oh what beauty those flowers brought our family.

## *Precious Memories, They Will Always Linger*

Our home would not be the same as when Jerodene was here with us. We give God thanks for both our children, and looking back now, if Rasheed was not in the picture, we honestly have no idea how we would have been able to cope. So God knew what He was doing, as matter of fact He always does. Rasheed is a replica of his sister, Jerodene. Each time that we look at him, we see Jerodene, and each time that he speaks, that was the same way that Jerodene would have brought her point across. Everything about Jerodene is Rasheed and vice versa. He talks about her almost every day and whenever he would come across an item that was once Jerodene's he would run with it to me or his dad with a smile telling us how much he remembered when Jerodene used to use it or play with it. Oh how those memories will forever linger in our hearts.

At the point I was writing, we were just a family of three, not knowing what God's plans were for us. We planned to welcome His plans with open arms. Whatever God does is well done, and even though He saw it fit to take Jerodene from us, we are still pushing forward with God. We are focusing fully on Him because He is our only source, and living for Him is all that matters. Our main focus is to live a life pleasing to God and that one day we would also be able to meet the 'boss' that Jerodene mentioned to Kerlyn in that dream.

## *Our New Blessing*

People who have been wondering if we gave birth to another child after Jerodene's passing. Oh yes! We gave birth to a healthy and energetic baby boy who we named Jhari Carlington Bailey. Jhari was born on the August 13, 2021, that was two days before Jerodene's birthday. We ended up getting discharged on Jerodene's birthday, which was August 15. It was a bitter-sweet moment.

Jhari's birthweight was just an ounce more than Jerodene's so they had a few things in common.

Rasheed was overly excited to meet his brother for the very first time. I recalled him telling me that he was happy that he finally has a sibling that will stay with him forever. Rasheed was seven years old when his brother, Jhari was born. He is not only a big brother but also a responsible one. I often hear Rasheed telling Jhari that he cannot wait for him to get older for him to tell him about his sister that he never knew.

With this year being four years since Jerodene's passing and Rasheed being eight years old now, it feels as if it was just yesterday. He still cries ever so often and tells us that he misses Jerodene dearly. He told us that even though he was only three years old when she passed, he remembers everything vividly. We try our best to comfort him the best way possible with the help of God. He went on to say that he made a promise to Jerodene that he would continue her legacy.

We give God thanks for blessing our family yet another time. We know that Jerodene would have been very happy seeing her family smile again. Rest Well Jerodene.

# For People Going Through A Similar Situation, Be Encouraged

1. Always remember that prayer is the key, and even though our daughter had transitioned, it is not that we did not pray. Oh yes we did, but God saw it fit to pick the prettiest rose from all the heartache and suffering that she underwent. That does not mean that the same thing will happen to your child. Our situation was an unfortunate one but guess what all is not lost.

2. Let your child know that he or she is loved dearly. Let your children enjoy life as much as possible.

3. You will need as much support as possible, especially from family or close friends, all positive support is very important. In some instances, you will need support from strangers who become family.

4. Be as gentle and supportive as possible.

5. Speak life over your child and let him or her know that God still loves them and cares for them, and that He knows their names.

I was often told never to question God, but don't be surprised if he or she asks God, "why me?" When frustration kicks in, chances are that they will ask. It is going to be a rough journey. My husband and I wish that we could have said it otherwise but if we did, we would be lying. Let us continue to pray that one day soon with the help of God and earthly physicians there will be a cure for cancer.

May your sweet sweet soul continue to rest in peace, our baby girl until we meet again.

# Reflections of The Heart

There are some fond memories of our little Warrior Princess Jerodene Jaiyana Bailey. Allow us to share a few:

1. Jerodene was a very kindhearted little girl. She would give and give expecting nothing in return. On one of her good days her dad gave her JM$100 to buy anything that she wanted. When we got to Mandeville, we were passing a blind man who was seated begging for money on one of the corners. Jerodene had taken out $50 from what she had got from her dad and attempted to give it to the blind man. She then looked at me saying, **"Mommy, if I give him all my money, would God bless me more?"** I then told her yes, she then took out the other $50 then smiled and gave the blind man everything that she had.

2. Our Jerodene was a little mischievous. Once she was misbehaving and I jokingly said to her, *"Jerodene, if I lick yu, yu sick in ya."* (Jerodene, if I hit you, you will get sick) To my surprise her response in a rough tone was, **"Mommy mi to, if I lick yu, yu sick in ya.** *(Mommy, if I hit you, you will get sick)* I scolded her immediately then I hurried to the bathroom to get a good laugh. That showed that as much as we loved her, we had to correct her.

3. One day, her uncle Melbourne and wife, Kemarie, came to visit us while we were at home. I remember Jerodene telling them that her daddy's pet name was 'Shebeh.' They then started making fun of her calling her 'Shebeh daughter.' She then uttered, *'a wey mi did tell unu fa Lord.' (Oh Lord, why did I tell you?)* We all laughed.

4. In her words, Jerodene was a genius, indeed she was very smart. One day we were home and at that time Barack Obama was the United States President. He was making a speech and we were watching it on our local television station. I then turned to her and was about to tell her what his name was. Only to hear her utter, **"Mommy, you don't have to tell me his name, because I already know his name, his name is. Back up!"** I did not have enough time to reach the bathroom with that laugh. It just came out right there and then.

5. Jerodene always spoke so much about her little loving family, and each time that her dad would arrive home from work her first question to him was, **"Daddy, what did you take home for me?"** Each time her dad would have spelled out LOVE, so one particular evening when her dad got home from work and she asked him what he carried home from work. Before her dad could answer, only to hear Jerodene shouted, **"and it better not be LOVE this time."** Thankfully, her dad had carried snacks for her and her brother, whom she loved dearly, she often called him her 'baby boo.'

6. Jerodene was a responsible big sister to her then three year old brother, Rasheed. Whenever they had any disagreement she would always reprimand him. If Rasheed was being naughty, Jerodene would shout, **"Rasheed you should always listen to your big sister."** Rasheed would then respond, **"and I am the big brother."** If someone jokingly

threatened Rasheed in Jerodene's presence, Jerodene would say, *"If you mess with my brother, then you mess with me."*

7. When Jerodene was changing teeth, there was that one tooth to the side of her mouth, that even though it was shaking, it just refused to fall out. So one day while she was admitted at the hospital, a nurse said to her, "Jerodene aren't you going to pull out that tooth?" I then told the nurse jokingly that I will be taking her to the dentist to have them take it out. Jerodene's response was, *"Mommy don't rush nature."* Well nature had its way because she had that tooth up to the day she went home to meet her maker.

8. There was never a dull moment with Jerodene. She loved dressing up and always had her little pink bag that her friend, Shauna had given to her packed with her girly stuff. Going out was a very big deal for her, she always took time out to put on her lip gloss and when hers was not enough she would go searching for mine. So because I stopped her from using my colourful nail polish, one day she said to me, *"Mommy, you are not allowing me to use the adult colours, so please allow me to use the clear one then, cause that one won't show."*

9. Our Jerodene was a prayer warrior, she loved to pray no matter what the circumstances were. She always knew right from wrong because she was taught from an early stage. She prayed even if the prayer was a repentance one. I remember clearly one Wednesday night while her dad left for Bible Studies, we were left home. At one point, I felt thirsty and had asked Jerodene for some water, she mumbled saying why is it that I can't go get it myself. She had no idea that I heard her, so I then asked her what she just said, she then answered saying, *"nothing mommy."* I then told her that she just lied to me, and that was when she started crying. In the midst of her crying she then said, "Mommy, what must I do?" I then told her that she had to pray. This was her prayer, *"oh God, here I come to you as a humble little child, God I just told mommy a little lie, and I am asking you to please forgive me, and as a matter of fact I had told another lie, a long time ago and I don't know if you had forgiven me for that one."* She cried during the entire prayer and after such a repentance prayer that was when she was able to go to sleep.

10. Jerodene knew exactly how to put persons into their place when it came to God, no matter who he or she may be. One day while a male doctor was in the process of flushing her port, Jerodene then looked at him asking him, *"Doctor, do you love God?"* The doctor then responded, *"Jerodene, of course I love God, as a matter of fact, everybody loves God."* Jerodene then stared at him in his eyes and responded boldly, *"Doctor, satan hates God and you know that I am telling the truth."* The doctor was in such shock that he just smiled and left.

11. When Jerodene was doing radiation at the facility in Kingston, she was just so happy and skipping in and out of the radiation room smiling as always. On a particular day she went into the room, as I waited for her in the waiting area. There was a lady seated beside me and she was telling me that day was her first day for radiation and she was so nervous and scared because she never knew what to expect. She also said that by the time she saw Jerodene skipping and smiling on her way in and out of the room she then thought to herself, *"but if this little girl is just 7 years old and can skip and smile during her radiation sessions, then why am I worried?"* She said that was when she got the courage and went in. She said that seven year old Jerodene really motivated her as an adult.

12. Jerodene was a very straightforward individual. I remember during the time of her

doing the radiation we were normally sent home on the weekends. So one particular Friday afternoon, we heard nothing about us going home. The Consultant, Dr. Olugbuyi, (whom we all called Dr. O), Dr. Swaby, other senior doctors and some medical students were doing their ward rounds. I was just in time to see them all at Jerodene's bedside discussing Jerodene's progress. Jerodene looked at Dr. Swaby then said, **"Dr. Swaby, when will I be going home?"** Dr. Swaby then responded, *"Jerodene, I'm unable to tell you when you're going home but you could ask Dr. O, he'll be able to tell you."* Jerodene then looked at both of them then blurted out, **"Dr. Swaby I'm not going to ask Dr. O when I'm going home, because Dr. O can't tell me when I'm going home and he is the head."** I was in shock hearing that from Jerodene. All the doctors stood there laughing while Jerodene had a straight face. In the end I was happy that Jerodene said that because with her boldness we were sent home for that weekend.

13. Jerodene was always a special child. At the age of three, I had left her in the care of her father because I had to go run some errands. By the time I returned I entered the verandah to go put some stuff in the kitchen that I had just purchased. On my way I saw drops all over the verandah, kitchen, bedroom and the bathroom. It really startled me, so I then asked Jerodene why she used the water to drip all over the house. Her response was, **"No Mommy, I did not use the water to drip all over the floor, I used the consecrated olive oil, because I am covering the house under the blood of Jesus."** Her dad was on the outside so I then called his attention to what had happened and it startled us both, because we were not expecting that from a three year old.

14. We remembered her telling her dad that if she had money she would have helped the poor and needy who were living on the street. She said that she would have gotten them a home and enough food to eat. That was how thoughtful our daughter, Jerodene was, and we knew that she meant every word.

15. At the age of three, I was getting Jerodene ready for school, she then said to me, **"Mommy, there are three people living in this house."** I then told her to name them. Her response was, *"Jerodene, Daddy and Mommy."* I then said to her, *"good girl."* She then gave me a frowning look then said, **"Mommy, but I didn't count Jesus, and He lives here too."** I smiled at her then told her, *"okay baby girl let's count again."*

16. One of Jerodene's favourite moments was when she would get discharged and one of her grandmothers (my mom) and her team would have journeyed to our home to have fasting and prayer meetings on more than one occasion.

17. During the early years of Jerodene's diagnosis, Jermaine and I were trying to source some funds to purchase some of Jerodene's medication. So Jerodene had a dress that she had outgrown, she then carried to us saying, **"Mommy and Daddy, seeing as I am not wearing this dress anymore then you could sell it and then you'll have enough money to purchase my medication."** We both looked at each other then smiled, and thought to ourselves how thoughtful of her. We told her not to worry because God would make a way.

18. Jerodene was very smart, and because she was so smart, if and when I was having a conversation with someone and I did not want her to understand, I would tend to spell the words. There I was one day talking to a lady friend, during the midst of our conversation Jerodene came on the spot, in talking to the lady I ended up spelling the word PARENT. Only to hear Jerodene uttered, **"Oh mommy, that word is parent."** I

immediately laughed out loudly then ended the conversation. Quite a few times after that if I am having a conversation and Jerodene would be present, then she would always say, *"Mommy, spell it out."*

19. Whenever Jermaine and I would talk, sometimes Jerodene would be present. If we were talking about a certain individual, then Jermaine and I would refer to him or her as 'such person.' So one day, Jerodene saw a lady with a similar handbag as mine, so when she got home, I heard her utter, *"Mommy, remember that we saw 'such person' with a bag like yours."* All I did was smile and could not wait to share it with her dad.

20. During the year 2016, during one of Jerodene's admissions at the University Hospital, they told us that they had to put a port into Jerodene because her veins were having issues due to the chemotherapy treatment. The porters, along with one of the nurses, had pushed her on a stretcher to the operating theatre. The doctors told me that the farthest I could go would have been the entrance of the theatre room. We prayed and left everything in God's hands. When we got there, one could have seen the sad countenance on Jerodene's face. I stood and watched her leaving as they closed the door in front of me. By the time I got back to the ward the nurses had told me that the doctors in the theatre had called and told them to tell me that I should come by there immediately because Jerodene was not cooperating. When I got there the doctors then gave me all the necessary gears for me to get dressed in because they wanted me to go talk Jerodene into doing the procedure. I went in and tried convincing her but she was not cooperating. They wanted to put the anaesthesia mask over her nose so that she would inhale then she would be sedated. Each time that they made an attempt to do so, Jerodene would utter, *"Mommy, tell them not to do it."* I honestly wished that I could have told them not to but we just wanted the best for our Jerodene. When the doctors realised that Jerodene was not having any of it, they then gave me one of the anaesthesia masks to put over my nose and assured her that it would not hurt. They then showed her that I had one too, Jerodene then boldly said, *"Yes doctor, Mommy has one too but hers doesn't have any attachments that are attached to her, so hers is very different from mine."* The doctors and I had to hold her down on the stretcher to place the anaesthesia mask over her nostrils, and within a few seconds she was fast asleep. Jerodene was just a smart little princess, and they all knew that. To God be the glory the procedure was a success.

21. Jerodene's first gift from Aunty Sandra was a very beautiful crib set. When Jerodene was not yet five months old, I had gone to work and Jermaine was the one who picked her up from the daycare. By the time I got home it was way past Jerodene's bedtime but she was not sleeping. That same crib sheet was on her bed at the time. It was well decorated with a lot of colourful flowers and ladybugs, to our surprise Jerodene spent the entire time trying to scrape off all the decorations that were on the sheet, she scraped the entire time. She just would not sleep. We had to place a blanket over the sheet in order for her to sleep, and within five minutes she fell asleep.

22. When Jerodene was in K1, she was three years old. I woke up one morning and we decided to give her some cerasee tea (that tea is often drunk as black tea, and it has a bitter taste). After giving it to her, she tasted it then uttered, *"Mommy I don't want it because it doesn't taste good."* I then took it from her and made her some milo tea. So the following morning, I made her the same cerasee tea but added some milk to it just

to change the colour. As she took the first sip, she then uttered, *"Mommy, but this is the same bitter tea that you gave me yesterday morning, but this one is white, and it tastes the same."* I then smiled because I could not hide the fact that I was trying to trick her.

# Paying Homage To A Lifechanger

Jerodene Bailey, my first daughter, wow. She was a unique and extraordinary child. Since her birth there was something special about her first, the way she slept. She slept with her hands clasped and on her knees. Oftentimes I wondered why she would sleep like that. And I came to realise that when we went to church there was an anointing revival service and the Holy Spirit ministered through her and she began to praise God and she marched around the church giving thanks to God, at that time she was not yet three years old. So I realise that Jerodene Bailey was a warrior for God.

Her attitude and behaviour towards people - she was not afraid to tell the world about Jesus. Her lifestyle was supernatural. Her faith in God was like Job. Despite the dreadful disease, Jerodene never gave up on God. She said that was healed and that she shall not die, but live and declare the work of the Lord, and that was her favourite scripture. Jerodene encouraged persons who were ill and told them about Jesus Christ. She loved to pray and her prayers were sincere, she was a prayer warrior. Jerodene Bailey did not believe in sympathy. The reason I said that is because one day Jerodene was crying because of severe pain, so we called the University Hospital and the Oncologist told us to take her to the nearest hospital which was in Mandeville.

By then she was still in pain, she then started to vomit and said, *"Daddy, please do something."* Then I realised that tears began to flow from my eyes. She then looked at me and said, *"Daddy, why are you crying?"* But I could not explain to her seeing that I could not take the pain away. Instantly she stopped crying and said to me, *"Daddy, leave it and God will fix it."* She then continued to cry. So then I knew that Jerodene only believed in the power of God.

Jerodene, Jerodene, Jerodene, warrior princess. She conquered cancer and lives with Christ forevermore. Why? Because of that dreadful disease Jerodene Bailey never gave up on God. Jerodene's testimonies, she brought broken marriages together, she made the gunman cease from using his gun, she caused the prostitute to stop prostituting, Jerodene brought broken families back together. Those are facts. Jerodene is a living testimony. My daughter, Jerodene Bailey, sleep well, beloved. Amen.

*Jermaine Bailey (Jamaica)*

∞∞∞

Jerodene, wow! What can I say about that special little angel? It has been said by everyone who knew her. She was beautiful, kind, loving, caring and smart. The warmest and brightest soul to warm and brighten the coldest and darkest heart. There is so much to say about her but not enough space. Even though she was going through rough times, Jerodene was always giving people hope and faith, she changed my life forever because of the love she had for all of us.

I have so much to say but I have to give others a chance to express their 'Jero' moment. She taught me that love is not only for family and loved ones, but to love each other. Love you my little ANGEL. Thanks Rasheda for letting me be a part of your family. May God bless you and your family. I hope one day we will meet face to face, the woman who made my hero.

*Adrian Cameron (USA)*

∞∞∞

A humble child of God, a daughter, a sister, an ambassador for children afflicted by sickness, a friend, an angel. How could we accurately describe such a remarkable young girl without using limitless descriptions? To say that Jerodene was special, extraordinary and unique is an understatement. Her resilience while she lived was so remarkable that she touched the lives of so many people she did not even know and with whom she would have never ever come in contact; such was the gift that Jerodene gave to people who thought that they had no hope.

Jerodene's legacy of determination, endurance and immense faith will never be forgotten. She's the light that cannot be hid, the light that shines and encourages us to be strong in spite of our struggles. Although we miss Jerodene, although she has gone before we were ready to let her go, we are grateful that God lent her to us so that our lives could be made better because Jerodene was in it.

*Natasha Thomas-Francis (England)*

∞∞∞

Sometimes in life you come across someone that you have never known in your life, and they touch your life with such love and emotion. That was what happened with this angel, Jerodene. I have never met her in person, but she has touched my heart with so much emotion. I know that you are in a better place and I will always remember you. Continue to rest in peace Jerodene.

*Yayi Aziz Khan (Africa)*

∞∞∞

My granddaughter, my angel, my flesh. You have gone too soon. But my spirit says no. When I remember how close you held on to your faith, I give God thanks that He blessed our family with you.

*Doreen Williams (USA)*

∞∞∞

Jj, Jero, sugar plum, a few of the names I called my angel, Jerodene. My mini me, she will forever be in my heart. I remember having a conversation with her. She was about three years old. I called and she refused to talk to me. Then she uttered, *"Aunty Yanto, I don't know where you are, I don't know if you're okay"*. She went on to say, *"you said that you'll come to my house and I don't see you"*. I never knew at her age that she would understand so much. I had to let her know that I was far away and I would have to take a plane to get to her. She then said, *"okay Aunty Yanto I understand"*. She was so mature for her age.

I will cherish every moment spent with her, she was sent from heaven and will always be in my heart. The last moment I spent with her was very special. She was excited to see me even though she was in pain. She opened her eyes for a few minutes, smiled at me then squeezed my hand. Jerodene was a little girl with a grown mentality, she would reason with you like a grown up. When she was younger and just started talking, I called her JJ, but then she said, *"Nana na JJ, nana na JJ"*. She was trying to tell me that her name was not JJ. I then explained to her that the first J is for Jerodene, and the second J is for Jaiyana, which was her middle name. She then said, *"oooohhhhhh"*, as if to say "now I get you". Even though in my eyes her time here with us was short, I came to realise that she left a lifetime of memories. Letting her go was the hardest thing that I ever had to go through. I know she's in Heaven resting in the arms of Jesus and playing on Heaven's playground. Sleep in peace my niece, Jerodene.

*Aunty Romayne Thomas (USA)*

∞∞∞

What can I say about this special princess? She was truly a gift from God, sent here to love her family and care for others. Even through her difficult and hard times, she was still reaching out to others, giving them encouragement and love. Jerodene was a very special angel and she loved her family. She lives on through them, especially her brother, Rasheed; who is just an amazing boy.

I miss her so much, but I know that she is looking down on us. She touched so many lives including myself and she has made me a better person of which I thank her. Continue to rest in peace my warrior princess and play in that Heavenly playground. Love you girl.

*Lorraine Colphon (England)*

Jerodene and I were friends from basic school. She always acted as if she was the bigger one. She would boss me around and tell me to put my shirt into my pants. She would share her snacks with me whenever I forgot to put mine in my bag pack. She was always there for me the same way that I was there for her. When I got bullied at school, Jerodene was there for me and she would always tell me that I should not fight or else my mom would have to pay the bill.

We were best friends, she would have helped me with my school work whenever I didn't understand. When Jerodene got sick it really made me cry. It pained my heart to see her cry. That time when I went to visit her at the hospital was a good day because we got the chance to play and see each other. Even though she could not play much because she had a catheter, it did not stop her. We were always happy to see each other. I miss you very much Jerodene.

*Love, Raheem Mitchell (Jamaica)*

∞∞∞

My grief, oh baby Jero has produced something remarkable inside of me. How can a baby teach an adult to take control even in pain? Jerodene was all I couldn't be, if it were you, if it were me. She'd smile through pain, even when it stained, even when it got to her brain. She would make me laugh, make me cry, she just left without a goodbye. She had to go, I was left with a low, but her kindness and compassion for God, that I did know.

*Jodian Pantry (Jamaica)*

∞∞∞

The bible says, the Lord giveth and the Lord taketh, blessed be the name of the Lord. Jerodene came into our lives and took a piece of our hearts that will remain with her. It was like a vow in life and in death. I felt afraid to ask Jerodene's mom how she was doing because I didn't want to hear anything sad, though I knew how sick she was. Jerodene was an inspiration to me and by extension the world.

I knew people who were not sick who Jerodene inspired instead of the other way around. I loved her faith in God, and she had taught me that no matter what situation I am in I can trust God and I can smile. Jerodene will forever be in my heart. I must say that Jerodene was blessed to have such amazing parents. Enjoy your new home in Heaven Jero.

*Sharna-Kay Christian (Jamaica)*

∞∞∞

When I approached that little princess, Jerodene, she inspired me in two sentiments - tenderness for who she was, and respect for who she may have become. You don't know what unconditional love is, you may say you do. But if you don't have a child, you don't know what that is. And when you experience it, it is the most fulfilling ever. One could have learned many things from Jerodene Bailey. How much patience do you have for instance?

The potential possibilities of any child are the most intriguing and stimulating in all creation. Jerodene was the most valuable source. Rasheda and Jermaine raised a great child, she made your life important. She was a beam of sunshine from the infinite and eternal, with possibilities of virtue and vice, but as yet unstained. She was a divine appointment. Thank you Kimoy for the opportunity to have such a connection with that beautiful lady-girl. I love you Jerodene Bailey.

*Love, Earon Benjamin (Jamaica)*

∞∞∞

Psalm 127: 3. Hearing about Jero first being ill, my heart was broken. As time moved on and Jerodene's illness progressively got worse, I prayed for healing from our great physician. But our God is in control of us. God is the giver of life and also the taker of it. Any illness that savages our body is not from God. Those of us who are followers of Jesus Christ, know that this world is not our home. Jerodene was a true child of God in her short life. The lessons she taught us as adults were truly memorable. Jerodene did what we should do as true believers of Christ, touch somebody as we go along daily. Then our 'living' would not be in vain. God allowed us to share Jerodene but for a short time, however the impression that Jero made will always be. St. John 3:16

*Iyonie Thomas (Jamaica)*

∞∞∞

My granddaughter, Jerodene was truly a chosen vessel of the Almighty God. She was an Evangelist, a preacher, prayer warrior, a rebuke, etc. She wasn't a coward, she was as bold as a lion. She would tell you the truth just as is. Her seven years that she spent here on earth was to the glory of God. I know God will say to her, *"Well done Jerodene."* I am just looking forward to meeting her again. I know that she is having a glorious time now on that playground in Heaven.

*Rose Thomas (Jamaica)*

∞∞∞

Isaiah 11:6: "a little child shall lead them." Jerodene has inspired me in many ways. She was a true manifestation of the Word of God. She was not just an ordinary human, she was a replica of Jesus. An angel wrapped in a human body. I remember vividly when I surrendered my life to the Lord Jesus Christ. My first visitors were Rasheda and Jerodene. They journeyed all the way from Manchester to Clarendon and spent the entire day with me.

When it was time to leave I heard Jerodene's little voice. She was about 2 years old at the time. She then said, **"Mommy let us pray before we leave."** I was so surprised, and that will always live in my memory. May her soul rest in peace in the arms of the Almighty.

*Nockisha Campbell (Cayman)*

∞∞∞

We made a bargain for a loan, only a pity the timespan was not known. Jerodene, during her time with us, was a bright light penetrating every avenue of souls of any life she touched.

The prayers, the conversations, wise counselling and kind deeds were beyond her age limit or even her state of illness sometimes. She was relentless.

Tears still flow freely as we hold our memories dear. Daily we hear her voice so sweet as her words of wisdom linger. The hope of the great reunion day is our best treat each day. Play on Jerodene! Celebrate Heaven's playground.

*Colleth Bloomfield (Jamaica)*

∞∞∞

Phenomenal, beautiful and perfect you are. An angel who touched hearts leaving, leaving your impactful footprints everywhere you go.

A fighter, strong and brave, who never gave up till the end. You did your job well changing minds and heart, God said you're too perfect for this world, gave you two wings to fly home.

You will be missed my dear and you are always loved Jerodene.

*Charles Cole (USA)*

∞∞∞

It is with great sadness that I am writing this tribute to Jerodene, a little angel, who I met in August 2017. I am a cancer survivor and we both had radiation sessions for a month, during which Jerodene and I always exchanged a smile and words of encouragement.

Jerodene I did not get a chance to tell you how much your smile, your strength and your encouragement helped me to gain the strength I never knew I had. In my heart you will always live on as a little angel. Love and miss you, Jero. Sleep on little angel.

*Geraldine Dowe (Jamaica)*

∞∞∞

My niece, Jerodene. Words cannot express how much I loved her. She was my world. I never had a dull moment with her. She always made me laugh. The things that she would say and do would just amazed me. The last stage of her life was the hardest for me. There were days when I wouldn't even talk about what she was going through. It really broke my heart to think about what she was going through.

My first niece, Jerodene will always be in my heart, even now I still don't want to talk about her passing because there are more questions than answers.

*Uncle Ryan Thomas (Jamaica)*

∞∞∞

Knowing and meeting Jerodene, I can't recall a dull moment with her. When I was getting married in 2013, Jerodene was our flower girl. Playing her part as our flower girl was something else (smile). She was such a loving little girl, she was an angel. In the last stages of her life it wasn't easy for me. I prayed and I cried.

What she taught me through it all, was how to fight, how to be strong and never to give up, fight to the end. She will always be remembered. My niece, Jerodene, I loved her so much.

*Aunty Keysha Logan-Thomas (Jamaica)*

∞∞∞

Journey on clouds my child with angels soaring high. The pain you felt was too real. So fly high my darling protected by wings of mighty angels to meet the one mightiest in power.

O beautiful soul, rest! No longer in pain and pieces. In perfect peace, take your eternal rest Princess Jerodene Bailey.

Good souls never die, they live in the hearts and minds of the ones they have touched. So Jerodene lives today in the minds and hearts of many.

*Errol Chevaughn Anderson (Jamaica)*

∞∞∞

How does one put into words the immense pain experienced during the loss of a friend? I'm still working on it. Jerodene Bailey cannot simply be discussed in passing. For me, Jerodene created such a lasting impression on my life, in such a short time, that she is no longer just a person; but has become a concept, an inspiration, a choice we make on how to live.

It feels like just yesterday that I walked onto the Paediatric Ward, feeling slightly overwhelmed at the patients' list, the new procedures, and for the first time hearing about the ominous "cancer ward.' There was no easy way to describe it. Life really isn't fair. How can God allow this to happen? How is innocence rewarded with such suffering? These were just a handful of inextinguishable thoughts running through my mind.

At about 10:00 am, we were preparing for ward rounds. I had to flush my first Paediatric port a-catheter on who I heard was a very outspoken young lady. I was apprehensive and nervous to say the least. She introduced herself with presidential confidence, assisted like an experienced resident, and was sure to highlight any shortcomings or imperfections in my technique. We did the entire procedure, the first of many, together. Acutely aware of the significance of the procedure, her sterile technique excellent, knowledge base impressive, and the fact that we were doing this relatively invasive procedure, on no other than her, herself, left me in awe.

I spent the rest of the day feeling humbled, grateful, enlightened, but (looking back now) most importantly I had an invigorating yet disconsolate feeling that 'the battle could be won,' that with enough determination, discipline and faith, mountains could be moved.

This was an aura of our friendship; both as doctor and patient as well as two human beings, who crossed paths but briefly, on our entirely different journeys.

Jerodene (Jero, Jero) truly exemplified what it means to have strength of heart and mind; she knew her time was limited, she experienced a range of suffering, forced maturity, and experiences that no one, let alone a child should have to go through. In spite of it all, she remained happy, hopeful, grateful, loving to her friends and family, and ready at all times to bear her burden unapologetically, and with 100% effort.

One day, she gifted me with a framed picture of us taken by her mother, to which I am greeted daily, serving not only as a reminder of her, but also to be fearless, give freely, don't be bitter be better, strive for excellence, and that our time here is brief so make the most of it.

In short, the greatest gift she has bestowed on me is the experience of being her doctor as well as her friend. For that I am eternally grateful.

Until our paths cross again Jero!

Thank you.

*Dr. Alex Barnett (Jamaica)*

∞∞∞

I paused here to acknowledge that all that has been written in this book by Rasheda Thomas-Bailey and husband, Jermaine Bailey is true.

It was at the age of three, one bright Sunday afternoon as Jerodene along with others marched around the church shouting and praising God. The Holy Spirit told me to put a mark on her. I did as I was told, hoping that she would have grown up and become some renowned person. But unfortunately it was not so.

The Lord saw it fit to allow her to go through great pain and sickness. She testified, evangelised, witnessed to thousands over the world via social media, and has now gone home to be with our Lord and Saviour. Rest Jerodene rest.

*Paulette Elliot (Jamaica)*

∞∞∞

Jerodene our friendship and sisterly love was more than spending time together. Our hearts matched. You have touched my life deeply.

*Love, Jestina Bryan (Jamaica)*

∞∞∞

A big heart in a tiny body I would say (A smile on my face). My time here with you might have been short lived but our memories live on in my heart forever. Jerodene you were more than a mere encounter, you were my friend. On February 3, 2018 a beautiful rose was picked from my garden and ever since that day gardening has never been the same. I still think of you every day, how I miss your cute smile, small talks, laughter and fun. You were the child despite the pain you'd do anything to brighten another person's world. Sleep in peace my baby girl, you were loved.

J – Joyful

E - Elegant

R - Real

O – Overcomer

D - Darling

E - Entertainer

N - Nice

E – Eager

Nurse Shakile Martin (University Hospital of the West Indies, Jamaica).

"And a child shall lead them" This line taken from Isaiah 11:6 is taken out of context but it fits my memories of Prophetess, Missionary, Nurse, Evangelist Jerodene Bailey, perfectly. A young lady with an adult mind who touched the life of this adult, in more ways than she could ever imagine.

*Eunice Beckford (Jamaica)*

∞∞∞

My sweet Jero, your smile always made my day brighter. When God made you, He made a smile brighter than the sun. You had a heart of gold and a soul as pure as snow. Your smile and the love that you gave will forever be engraved in my heart. Thank you for sharing the love of God with me and showing me what strength and love is.

As I sit here thinking of you, I wonder what you are doing in Heaven. I imagine you blowing bubbles, playing in a field of flowers while angels play music in the background. You brought so much joy into my life the short time that we knew each other. I wish you could be here with us just so I could hug you and tell you that I love you. But God has much bigger plans for you.

He knew that this world didn't deserve an angel like you, so he wrapped His loving arms around you and whispered your name, and took you to Heaven with Him. While my heart is heavy because I miss you, I have peace knowing that you are in Heaven looking down on me. But this isn't goodbye, because I will see you someday. Until then, in my heart you will stay.

*Love, Auntie Portia (USA)*

∞∞∞

A star went back to heaven too soon. October 2014, I started a new chapter in the education field. I started to volunteer at the Hope Demonstration Basic School. I came across more than 100 students of which Jerodene was a part. She would always have this smile on her face, so I would make sure to go over to her to have a little chat. I must tell you that she was at basic school, but talking with her was like you were talking to an adult. But while I was at school I realised that the beautiful smile that I used to see at school would not be seen. Only the tears you would see and you could hear her little voice, *"I am in pain,"* or *"my head hurt."*

But as the days went by, Jerodene started to be more absent from school because most times she was in the hospital due to her sickness. But that didn't stop me from reaching out to her. I remember going to work in the morning and then to classes in the evenings. Classes ended at 6:30 pm, I would then go home, put down my books and head over to the hospital to see my star girl. When I got to the hospital I would normally let her mom go home to get some rest and I would stay with Jero at the hospital until she went off to sleep. I would let her watch cartoons and bible stories on my tablet. While she was watching the tablet she would say to me, *"Miss, I want a new cartoon when you're coming tomorrow."* And I would make sure that she got a new cartoon to watch on my next hospital visit. But time passed and she was then moved to the University Hospital in Kingston to continue her treatment. I was not able to see her like how I used to see her when she was in Mandeville, but I would call and do my checks on her.

I remember one Christmas holiday when I was in Kingston on my holiday, I wanted to go look for her but wasn't able to make it, so I called her mom and was told that Jerodene was in Portmore spending the day with her family. I was in Portmore at the time so I had got the direction to where she was, and I got her a birthday gift and some other things and went in search for Jero, and yes I found her.

My dear baby girl, you went back home too soon. But I am not able to say what is too soon or too late when it comes on to God's child. You were here for a short time but your smile will be here forever. Love you and miss you, you are now in your Heavenly Father's hand and He will take care of you until I see you again.

*Ms. Kerry Ann Green (Jamaica)*

∞∞∞

Dear beloved warrior princess, Jerodene Bailey, beautiful soul that's gone to a better place. You have touched my heart in a massive way. Your words of strength moved everyone who surrounded you. Jerodene Bailey was an inspiration with her overwhelming spirit of joy. I strongly believe that God has a purpose for her in Heaven. We will forever have you in our hearts. Sleep in peace my love.

*Nadine Stacy Beneby (USA)*

∞∞∞

A bright promising princess you were, born to inspire, love and encourage anyone you met. We can't forget your melodious voice singing songs of zion, your testimonies and your exhortations. Oh how special, caring, smart and sweet you were, always looking out for others even when times were hard.

You were braver than we believed, you were stronger than we could have ever imagined. Proverbs 31:25, "you were clothed in strength and dignity and laugh without fear of the future". You are so wonderful to think of but so hard to be without.

*Stacy-Ann McLeod (Jamaica)*

∞∞∞

It is very easy for me to say you are so precious. It is uncomplicated for me to say you are a joy. It is unchangeable for me to say you are remarkable. It is effortless for me to say you are an angel. I understand you are resting peacefully now. But for some reason when I think about you, it is hard for me to say you were precious. It is difficult for me to say you were a joy. It is impossible for me to say you were remarkable. It is unthinkable for me to say you were an angel. It is amazing how easily we take for granted the time we are given with our loved ones.

Jerodene you taught me that every second counts and I shouldn't waste it for it never returns. If you can hear me though I'd like to just say I'll love you Jerodene always.

*Aunty Timmoy Whyte (USA)*

There was never a dull moment with you. You fought like a real girl and refused to be a victim. There's emptiness inside when I reminisce of the love and joy that you dispelled. A child of promise and purpose you were.

*Tracy-Ann McLeod-Robinson (Jamaica)*

∞∞∞

Jerodene – emergence of a warrior princess

"Angels walk among us. Sometimes the only thing we might not see are the wings on their back." Molly Friedenfeld.

Jerodene "Jero" was a special girl.

I met Jerodene in May 2015. She was four years old at the time and had been having fevers and bony pain. A lump had also been noted in her left leg. Her parents were given the devastating news that this was likely cancerous. After a few weeks, she was diagnosed with alveolar rhabdomyosarcoma, a cancer made up of cells that normally grow into skeletal muscles. Unfortunately in addition to her cancer diagnosis, due to the multiple areas her cancer had spread, she could not be cured of her disease. Her poor prognosis was understandably difficult for her mom and dad to accept. Her disease was responsive to chemotherapy and radiotherapy though never completely disappearing.

Jero and I had a love-hate relationship in the beginning. As the person designing her treatment, which was a week or two in the hospital, very frequently she did not look upon me very favourably. I was ignored as much as possible. However, her relationships with the other staff members were more favourable.

Gradually, Jero adjusted to the routine of being hospitalised and was less bothered by it. I was greeted with a smile and we would talk. Jerodene loved princesses and would dress up as one whenever she could.

As Jerodene grew older and matured she became more attuned to other people's suffering, especially the children on the ward. She would always have an encouraging word or offer to pray with any family who were going through a difficult time. She was conscious of her own suffering as gradually the cancer spread throughout her body causing her much pain but remarkably this spurred her on to take away suffering from other individuals. She would encourage others to smile and not complain, explaining to them that if she can smile despite having stage 4 muscle cancer they could too. Jero was a natural born preacher and would have uplifting words for her congregation at church. She would be very distressed at the death of another child as she was very empathetic. It was difficult to see how her journey had become so painful at the end but her impact was very far reaching for her tender years.

Jero you will always be loved. Your kindness and spark will never be forgotten. Rest in peace warrior princess.

*Dr. Michelle Reece-Mills (University Hospital of the West Indies, Jamaica)*

∞∞∞

Jerodene, you were the true epitome of purpose. At only seven years old, you fulfilled your God given mission. Your love for the Lord and the faith you demonstrated were extraordinary. You have impacted our lives tremendously and with great esteem we will forever cherish your precious memories.

*Uncle Randal and Aunty Veneica Thomas (Jamaica).*

∞∞∞

Jerodene was an angel sent from God to touch the lives of many not just family and friends – but the world. When she spoke and you listened to her, your mouth would fall open. The knowledge she had of God was an extraordinary one that I have never seen in a seven year old child.

What I loved about Jerodene was her FAITH in God, it heals, it mends the broken heart. It changes lives. When I listened to her praying, tears filled my eyes and my heart. She was a powerful warrior for God.

I believe that her seven years spent on earth was a mission accomplished by God. Her soul is resting in the bosom of Jesus.

*Nickecia Robinson (Jamaica)*

∞∞∞

There are not enough words to describe the immeasurable flood of joy that filled my heart when Jerodene was born.

As I proudly cradled her in my arms for the first time, I smiled as I cuddled and admired her beautiful little face. I was drawn to her mysterious big brown eyes which twinkled and seemed to say, "Hi aunty, I love you!" Jerodene was a child of love. She received love from all who knew her. She gave love unselfishly to everyone even the little creatures. Her love for Jesus was evident from a very early age. We were supposed to shape her life but somehow, she shaped our lives with her empathy and knowledge which was way beyond her age and never short in supply. It never entered my mind that seven years later I would be reflecting on her life. The mystery of her life and purpose on earth had unfolded.

Her favourite colours: pink and purple are the colours of the rainbow. It is said that at the end of a rainbow is a pot of gold, but at the end of this specific rainbow we will find Jerodene.

Pink is a delicate colour that means sweet, nice, playful, cute, charming, feminine and tenderness. The colour pink is the colour of universal love of oneself and of others. The colour purple is often associated with royalty, nobility, luxury, power, ambition and wisdom.

Jerodene epitomises all the qualities and more. My beautiful niece was sent from God. The little girl with the mysterious twinkling brown eyes and unending love in her heart had a million lives. That was her mission.

Upon completion she went back to her creator. Even though she is no longer here Jerodene is still touching lives. Her work on earth may be done but her mission lives on.

When I look upon the night sky with millions of stars, I am still drawn to a twinkling star which seems to say, "Aunty I love you!"

*Aunty Sandra Pusey (Jamaica)*

∞∞∞

Jerodene Jaiyana Bailey was the life in her class in K1. From the day she set her feet at the Hope Demonstration Basic School she was well loved. She was always early and was never absent while in K1. Jerodene was a vibrant and energetic student who was always encouraging her classmates to do their work. She was a very positive and God-fearing little girl.

With me being her K1 teacher, I can clearly remember one morning while she was in K1 as she stepped into the classroom, she said, **"Good Morning teacher, my father says that I can do all things through Christ who strengthens me."** I was totally surprised to have heard that from a child of three years old.

Jerodene was always participating especially when it came to devotion time. She would clap, sing and dance during devotion.

Another incident with Jerodene was one day while she was at school she was in pain and she was crying. A friend of hers fell and was also crying Jerodene went over to her and consoled her even though she (Jerodene) was in pain. That was the spirit of our little princess. In times of sorrow, in times of joy Jerodene never stopped loving and praising God.

*Mrs. Venice Allison (Jamaica)*

∞∞∞

It gives me great pleasure to offer a tribute to a little angel who could be described as: courageous, gracious, precious, loving, energetic, favourable, brilliant, happy, wonderful, kind and those are few adjectives that can be used to describe this little angel called Jerodene.

She was such a child that any human being could emulate. As a seven year old she portrayed a life of Godliness. She allowed children and adults alike to really pull up their sleeves and take a new step in serving God. When one listened to Jerodene pray, testified and sing songs of Zion one would wonder if she was seven years old.

However, I believe that she has finished her task and fulfilled her God given purpose on this earth and is now resting in the arms of Jesus Christ. Rest well my little angel, Jero.

*Aunty Nora Thomas (Jamaica)*

∞∞∞

This angel came one day and my life has never been the same. She touched my life in so many ways. She was kind, sharing and never asked for too much. She was happy in the midst of her pain and she always revered her Lord and Saviour Jesus Christ. Jerodene was different from all the children I knew and it was my pleasure to sit with her or watch her trying to take care of everyone even in the midst of her pain.

She was no ordinary girl. She was intelligent, fashionable and stylish. She was so beautiful and was so grateful for anything given to her. I loved this child to the point that there was nothing I wouldn't do for her. She inspired me to go looking for other children like her who needed help. She inspired me to live, she inspired me to continue giving my best.

Now that the angel has taken flight, every now and then she flies down and touches my shoulder and reminds me to continue giving my best. She stops and watches me and leaves a smile on my face. Every now and then she reminds me that every little thing is going to be alright. May she continue to fly so others can be touched on the shoulder with her wings. Love you always my little angel.

*Love, Melionie Hanson (Jamaica)*

∞∞∞

Jerodene will always be remembered for her bravery, strength, intelligence, love for others especially her parents and brother. I remember on one occasion as I accompanied her to have her radiation treatment, while we were in the ambulance, she was talking about her family. She was actually expressing her love for them and how she appreciated them for working so hard taking care of her and her little brother, Rasheed. She was also asking God to keep them safe because she doesn't want anything bad to happen to them.

I remember the first day I went with her to her radiation treatment, I had accompanied her to the room. I was amazed as to the amount of courage she showed.

Jerodene was loved and she has touched everyone that she came across. She was a special rose, an angel who was called home early. May her precious soul continue to rest in peace.

Love, Myrtel Humes (P.C.A., University Hospital of the West Indies. Jamaica)

Jerodene was an amazing child, she has touched our lives in such an awesome way. James and I went to see her in March of 2016 and she was just so bubbly and she had a lot to say.

She will always be in our hearts, we will never forget such a light that shone so brightly. She made sure that we never and will never forget her with her beautiful personality. Her love for God was just so strong. We love you Jero and we miss you so much. Sleep well princess.

*James and Novalyn Thomas (England)*

∞∞∞

My sister, Jerodene, and I watched cartoons and Mommy and Daddy would give us jokes and we would laugh. Jerodene and I rode on the bicycle, we also played with the ball and she would give me a jockey ride.

I loved Jerodene and I cared about her. Mommy would have played some music and Jerodene and I would have danced. We both played with our toys.

*Rasheed Bailey (Jamaica)*

∞∞∞

I met an angel once. She was a true light on this earth. Not just beautiful but kind and generous of spirit always. Grace personified. She became my friend, a friend I loved and still love dearly. Her name was Jerodene Bailey. She has inspired me to change my life in a significant way that made me healthier, happier and more fulfilled. She was a genuine soul, a prayer warrior and a motivational speaker. She had a big heart, she cared for just about anyone. It didn't matter what age group you fell under. She touched many lives but I will speak for me.

She had a strength that I couldn't fathom. I kept asking myself, *"How dis fine bone pickney suh strong?"* Giving up was not an option for her. When I heard prayers, recorded videos of her speaking and having personal conversations with her, I noticed that she always mentioned God, praying for other persons, always encouraging others and showing others how God has been good to her. She wasn't selfish. She went through a rough time but she made it look easy. All of that made me look at life differently. I remember my last visit with her and she told me to take out a few piercings. I had because I am beautiful without them, so said, so done.

After her passing, I decided to take that big step and that was to accept Christ as my Lord and Saviour. I promised her that I would see her again and that was the only thing that I could do for me not to break that promise. Jerodene Bailey was exceptional. She had a heart of gold. She was and still is my angel. I think of her everyday and I know that she is with me always. Continue to rest well in the arms of our creator. I miss you my dear friend.

*Kimoy May (USA)*

∞∞∞

Jerodene, you fought the great fight and you won. God was ready because He prepared a special little place in Heaven just for you. You had the biggest personality and the best spirit, you made me laugh and cry all in one. My child, you were blessed.

You had faith even when you were in the worst situations and that faith moved mountains. The pain that you were in was just too overbearing. God took you because He knew you would make a great little angel.

Sleep in perfect peace my dear angel. I loved you even though I never knew you personally. But your faith in God made my faith in him stronger. Thank you Jerodene.

*Shamoya S. Gayle (USA)*

∞∞∞

My beautiful little lioness, Jerodene Bailey. I met Jerodene in 2017 at the Relay for Life function in Kingston, Jamaica. Right away she blew our team away with her beautiful personality. I didn't even realise that children had cancer. She was so bubbly, and realistic about life and about living. When I had a down time, I would say, *"wow look at that children, she's dying,"* but that children didn't think that she was dying. Her mom told me once that she was at church testifying and Jerodene told the congregation that she didn't believe what the doctors said about her having cancer, and that she thought that the doctors diagnosed her wrongfully. I said to myself, *"wow, that's the spirit."* Because many adults don't have that spirit, that was actually how I looked at it as an adult saying if Jerodene was going through so much pain and remained positive, especially being just seven years old.

Her personality was off the hook and Jerodene was strength, she was a motivator, she was a crown one would want to wear on their head. I barely can express Jerodene. She made me laugh, and after a time she got into a business mood. To sum up Jerodene, wow, she was just an awesome child. Jerodene was down to earth and would have told you just as is. We both are Leos and we share the same birth month and I was just blown away by how realistic she was about life and many adults are nowhere in her league in terms of being positive and being realistic.

During her bad experience she didn't think that the world was coming to an end or why God did that to her. I think she thought that it was a way of connecting people for people to actually bond and for us to believe in ourselves.

I could go on and on about Jerodene but on a day to day basis I would look at her photo and say, "this is my strength, this is my motivator." And she's somebody when you want to laugh or remember something funny about her, you'd just crack up.

*Shauna Fung Yee (Jamaica)*

∞∞∞

Words will never explain how much Jerodene has touched the lives of the Magnificent Troopers Drum and Bugle Corp in Spanish Town, Jamaica. We were so touched just by listening to her speaking about her mom, dad and baby brother. Listening to her brought tears to almost every member of the marching band. She had leaders in tears for days and nights just by watching the clippings before her untimely death.

One of the most special thing about Jerodene, was that even though she was very ill she still found time to pray for others and thankful for life herself. To us she was just more than a person, she was like a reality check in each and every one of us. She also gave us more reason to appreciate life in the best and worst times.

Meeting her parents was another blessing to the Magnificent Troopers Drum and Bugle Corp. We felt the love, honesty and determination that was displayed by Jerodene Bailey from both parents in her will power to live and to spread her love in each and everyone she comes in contact with. Jerodene was not just a blessing to her family, but to us all.

*Magnificent Troopers (Jamaica)*

∞∞∞

I met Jerodene Bailey at the University Hospital of the West Indies in Jamaica when I was hospitalised there in July 2017. This is how it began:

One night while I was admitted on one of the Paediatric ward, my bed was moved and was placed beside Jerodene's bed she immediately spoke to me and asked if I was okay and I told her yes. In the morning when I woke up she was sitting on a chair beside her bed. We greeted each other and that was when I knew that we were going to be good friends. Our friendship grew as the days went by.

Whenever we became sad we would cheer each other up. We played games, we talked, we laughed, we read together, we watched television together, and we played on our tablets together. I was so happy that I had someone to keep my company. Every night before we went to bed Jerodene would encourage me to read my bible, then we would pray together. Her mom was always there to read with us. We were having so much fun it was as if we weren't sick.

We were best friends and I always felt sad whenever she was in pain and I couldn't do anything to help her. But she was strong and courageous. She had faith in God and believed that He would take care of her. She understood how sick she was but she wasn't afraid. She was the one who would cheer up those around her who were sick. She was the ray of sunshine that came to brighten my life only for a time. I know that she's gone to a better place where there is no pain and no more suffering but I miss her a lot and I will always keep the memories of the good times we had together in my heart.

## Nayoka Ennis (Jamaica)

∞∞∞

I first heard of Jerodene on Facebook. I was going through my Facebook page when I came across a video with a young lady in the hospital, so I decided to watch the video. As I listened to what she had to say she was actually sending a message to the world fastest man, Usain Bolt. What really touched me was when she used these words, *"I am sick,"* those words sank deeply into me. I was shaken up, I felt very sad, my heart was broken. I watched that video over and over again. I even played it to my friends.

I wanted God to heal her instantly. So I began to pray for her, I asked myself why does this have to happen to such a beautiful little girl. I questioned myself over and over but could not find an answer. Ever since that day I had been trying to keep a very close watch of any other photos or videos relating to her. I browsed through many of her photos that were on Facebook and constantly watched her videos whenever anything new came out. Each time I watched her videos they had a great impact upon my life, tears would fill my eyes. All I wanted was for her to get well soon.

I didn't know her in person but my spirit was connected to her as though she was a part of me. There were moments when I would be about my own business and the thought of her entered into my mind. I would stop everything I was doing just to meditate and focus purely on her and prayed for her healing. Jerodene really meant a lot to me, so easily she won my heart over. I talked about her many times to my friends and family. I would always tell them how special she has touched the hearts of many people even though she was going through her problems.

She touched me through her singing, her testimonies and her smile, she was brave and courageous. Each time I listened to her the tears just bubbled up inside of me filled my eyes. I was amazed by how brave she was throughout her illness. She was a real fighter, strong and dynamic throughout everything that was going on around her. Even though she was so young, she was very strong and powerful, she was not shy. I believe she was sent as a special person to win the hearts of many and has done a great job in the short time that she was with us.

She was a gift sent from Heaven to touch not only my life but I am sure that she has touched many others around the world. I am honoured just to be an associate with her parents. I wish that I could have met Jerodene in person but it was not meant to be. One thing for sure, she will always be in my thoughts and mind even though she's not around anymore. She has firmly bonded in my heart. She's in my heart to stay. Jerodene you are sadly missed by me. Sadly you've left but you have left your mark upon my life, which I will gladly hold onto. You've left something in my heart that will always be forever. Jerodene, you, I will never ever forget. You are my angel, you are my princess, you are my forever friend. I love you from the bottom of my heart. Rest in peace my little angel, Jerodene.

## Thomas Brown (England)

∞∞∞

Gone were the days I had a cousin who I love and miss dearly. On August 15, 2010, a baby girl was born by the name of Jerodene Jaiyana Bailey. When she was about one year old, I was her nanny on Saturdays. I was her favourite cousin. On Saturdays, her parents would have called and asked me if Jerodene could have stayed with me for the day because both parents had to go to work. I immediately told them yes. I was always excited to have her at home with me as my baby cousin. When we were at home we always enjoyed playing hide and seek with my brother, Everton and I. Whenever she was hungry she would always tell my mom that she wanted her favourite cornmeal porridge.

Jerodene was a people person as young as she was. Her favourite song at the time was, "Nobody greater" by Vashawn Mitchell. In May 2015, I was at home when I got an unexpected call from Rasheda that Jerodene was sick and that she was admitted in the hospital. My eyes were filled with tears as I heard. During that time I had just started my new job at KFC. So by the following day I got the call that she was transferred to the University Hospital of the West Indies. Right there and then I told her that I hoped that everything would work out fine. During that admission, I didn't get the chance to go visit her. But we always talked over the phone and Jerodene would often ask me when I was going to come and look for her. I always told her not to worry herself and that I would come to see her soon.

On November 13, 2017, I was at work on the morning shift, then a coworker came to tell me that there was someone there to see me. I had told the coworker to stop the lying because I wasn't expecting anyone. Nonetheless, I stopped what I was doing then went to see who it was. To my surprise there was my little cousin, Jerodene. When she saw me she shouted my name three times, we both ran to each other laughing and filled with excitement. We both hugged because we were excited to see each other.

On the 29th of January 2018, I called her mom to find out how Jerodene was doing but Rasheda didn't sound too happy. And that was when she told me that Jerodene wasn't doing too well. Immediately, tears fell from my eyes and I told her that my mommy and I were planning to come see her with a few of the church members on the 4th of February 2018.

On the third of February 2018, whilst I was in a particular supermarket, I received a call from my mother and she asked me several times if I was okay. Then she inquired about my whereabouts, I told her that I was in the supermarket. She kept asking if I was okay so by then I sensed that something was wrong I got angry and asked her what was wrong. And her response was, *"Rashelle, we won't be going to visit Jerodene again."* When I asked her the reason, that was when she told me that Jerodene was no longer with us. I was in total disbelief, I started crying and screaming as loud as possible. My phone then fell from my hand because it was hard for me to believe that Jerodene had really died, and I didn't get the chance to go see her.

It never occurred to me how much I could lose someone that I love so dearly. I found myself wishing that all this wasn't true, every time that I think of Jerodene, pain is all I can feel, tears uncontrollable. I could barely see, but my heart tells me that she's always with me. I am happy that she is no longer in any pain, now she lives in a perfect land. I can still feel the soft touch of her loving hands on my shoulder. I will love and miss her forever, until the day we are together again, together in that perfect place filled with caring, sharing and love. But until that day comes I will wipe my tears away and hope to see her again someday. Rest in peace Jero.

*Love, Rashelle Jackson (Jamaica)*

∞∞∞

Jerodene Bailey was a beautiful soul I met whilst on my commencement of night duty on Ward 16 in the year of 2015. At that time I was going through my own bereavement from the loss of my mom. I remember comforting her mother, Rasheda with the song, "Remember Heaven" by Garmel Grant and she asked me to get the words of the song and that began our staff, parent/ patient relationship.

Jerodene who the staff referred to as Jero was a proper child as the Word of God states in Hebrews 11:23 for she was more mature than her years. She knew her God and she acknowledged Him. She prayed for fellow patients and parents alike.

She was bright, intelligent, outspoken, assertive, kind, well mannered and a prodigy in her own right. This loving lady was not afraid to speak her mind nor show her emotions. Jerodene had friends from all around and close. Those dreaded days they came and kept watch with her mother. I spent evenings after my morning shift ended with Jero and her mom just to be at her bedside. We had lively conversations on everyday stuff but mostly on things of God.

Jerodene had two setbacks for which God gave her a comeback: that of no longer needing a catheter for voiding her urine and the wearing of diapers. When she realised that she was able to do these things on her own again she'd have a praise party. I can just imagine the Almighty God must be enjoying the spectacular reception she was giving Him in thanks and praise.

Whenever my duty ended especially my 7:30 shift we had this farewell parting competition and she always has the last say but on that fateful Saturday afternoon of February 3rd, she was in no mood to compete with me because she bowed out of this side of mortality through the portal into the peaceful rest awaiting her bliss of eternity.

Looking forward to seeing her at play on Heaven's Playground and her greeting me with I love you more… my love.

*Sincerely, Ms. S. Bartley - P.C.A, UHWI (Jamaica)*

∞∞∞

Jerodene, yesterday you were here with us, every memory of which we will never forget. Our hearts ache since the day you left us. Don't know why it hurts even though we know God takes none but the best, you will always be missed. Every day without you, life has not been the same.

I have never met Jerodene nor her parents, but their story have touched so many lives including my own. Jerodene, God saw you getting tired, when a cure was not to be. A golden heart stopped beating, hard working hands at rest. So He wrapped his arms around you and whispered, "come to me." God's garden must be beautiful he only takes the best. And when we saw you sleeping so peacefully and free from pain, we could not wish you back to suffer that again. Although we loved you dearly, we could not make you stay. God broke our hearts to prove to us, your time on earth was not in vain. As it reads in Romans 14:8 "if we live, we live for the Lord and if we die, we die for the Lord. So whether we live or die we belong to the Lord." 1 Thessalonians 4:13-14 reads "Brothers and sisters, we do not want you to be uninformed about those who sleep in death, so that you do not grieve like the rest of mankind who have no hope. For we believe that Jesus died and rose again, and so we believe that God will bring with Jesus those who have fallen asleep in Him."

Jerodene, I am grateful to have been a part of your life's journey and to be able to continue your legacy. May you continue to rest in peace in the arms of our beloved Father. Rest in peace little angel until we meet again.

*Simone Mitchell- Smart (USA)*

∞∞∞

THE SEED OF THE RIGHTEOUS.

On Ash Wednesday, February 14, 2018, I was scheduled to speak at the Annual Convention of the Byways and Hedges Youth for Christ Ministries in Clarendon led by Pastor Rose Thomas, the grandmother of Jerodene. I wondered what I could possibly say to comfort a grieving grandmother and a church in mourning. Seated before me would have been several congregants who had prayed for the recovery of their Pastor's beloved "Jero'" and had to cope with what seemed like her untimely passing.

Whilst doing some reading for my sermon that morning I came across a quote from Dr. Martin Luther King Jr. that said, "it's not how long you live, it's how well you live." I knew instantly that this was a timely word that undoubtedly summed up Jerodene's life. Though it is hard to grapple with how young she was when she returned to her maker, none of us who encountered her would argue whether she used the time God gave her well. She truly lived well even though she didn't get to live long.

During her ordeal and battle with sickness, Proverbs 11:21 gave me hope… it says the seed (offspring) of the righteous shall be delivered. Jerodene was a seed of the righteous lineage. To many, her funeral was the day she was buried but I also believed she was PLANTED. The corpse goes under the earth and remains, but the seed goes there and resurfaces bringing forth fruit. Even in death, the life she lived continues to bear fruit (John 12:24). Her life is a reminder to maximise the time our creator has given us here on earth and to leave a Godly legacy that will make a lasting impact when we are gone.

*Prophet Alexis Brown (Jamaica)*

∞∞∞

The day you came into this world, God knew that it would have been for a special reason. Your existence changed the world and made a huge difference where you touched, created, impacted and influenced the life of every single man, woman, boy and girl that knew about you. Jerodene, you were our little hero who embraced what you believed in. You were a caregiver, a prophetess, a healer, a worshipper, a singer and the list goes on. You were very tender hearted, loving and passionate in every single way that I had no other choice but to fall deeply in love with you and without a shadow of a doubt I know others can confirm what I said. Jerodene captured our hearts and lives in an unforgettable way.

Talking about a real warrior, that was Jerodene Bailey. Jero, hero, you showed us who a real warrior is, what a real warrior is made of and furthermore, how a real warrior should behave, and this was very helpful and effective to me personally as it brought out the warrior in me. You were fearless, and very bold as you did not hold back in doing what you enjoyed doing and the things that you did best. One of the ways in which I am touched by your generosity when it comes to God is the fact that you did not allow anything to deter your faith, belief or relationship with God, not even the very dreaded illness you did not allow to shake your faith.

I am truly inspired by you and give God thanks for the time He gave you to us and for the great knowledge that you filled us with. Your legacy will live on and I promise you that I will cherish and embrace the values and principles that you left behind as this is creating wonders for me as I seek to go higher and deeper in Christ Jesus daily.

It pains our hearts to see you go but God saw that the pain was getting a little bit too heavy for you so He chose what was best for you and that was to give you peace and sweet rest. I miss you dearly my Jero, hero but we rest assured that you are well secured where you are now. It was the Thursday night before your burial when I saw you in my dream. It was the funeral ceremony and we were viewing your body and crying, and you got up and said to me, *"please tell the people not to cry because I am not dead, I am okay and I am just sleeping."* Jero we love you dearly and are waiting until that day when you are awake. Sleep on our little Hero, Jerodene Bailey.

*Mervina Burnett-Mitchell (Jamaica)*

∞∞∞

Jerodene came on this earth as an ordinary child. No one dreamt that this ordinary little girl was destined for a short but extraordinary life. Behind her beautiful smile and her captivating shiny brown eyes was a wealth of knowledge and wisdom far beyond that which was expected of a child. How she acquired her common sense, advanced vocabulary and understanding with only a basic school education, remains a mystery.

Jerodene touched our lives with her empathy and profound love for others. She was truly Christ-like in many ways: like Christ she came from humble beginnings. Like Christ she touched the lives of Christians and non-Christian people at an early age. Like Christ, she loved unconditionally. Like Christ, she was faithful during her pain and suffering. Like Christ, she completed her mission and then went home to be with her Heavenly Father.

Jerodene was an angel, lent not given, to bud on earth and bloom in Heaven. Lastly, to Jermaine and Rasheda, be comforted in knowing that like Mary and Joseph you were both chosen to be the earthly parents of one of God's special little angels. You are blessed.

## Claudette Oliver (Jamaica)

∞∞∞

I don't remember how I met Jerodene. A thread linked to a thread, linked to a thread, pulled me into the weave of people who loved Jerodene and who wanted to help with her care. Even Usain Bolt was beautiful. I watched her and felt her playful delicate loving presence in my life. I grieve for her and I felt that I was with so many others, everywhere at the same time, holding her in our hearts. And so many others who felt with her parents and wanted to give them our strength.

Often I hate Facebook and say I'm going to quit it, that the 'friends' we make there are not real friends and the 'friendships' are not real friendships. But my connection to Jerodene and to everyone who loved her felt real and still feels real today. Especially to the lovely Rasheda, I will always be grateful for the love that passes between strangers.

## Karen Bermann (USA)

∞∞∞

The death of a child is the saddest thing that many people can think of but if I could imagine something more heartbreaking, it would be the death of the memory of their lives. I would rather not remain in a field that sees so many of God's angels disguised as children, that they become a blur or fade. I may always remember the voice calling so enthusiastically through the Paediatrics Ward window, ***"Dr. ALLEN!!"*** I may cry when I hear that voice in my head bidding me to come hear a story about her day, but may that voice never stop echoing through my head when I pass that ward.

I met and cared for a beautiful seven year old girl who lit up my ward and made a rough time in my job bearable even when she was being a difficult patient. I enjoyed going to work but hated the need for it, truthfully I love my patients but had no desire for the life of a Paediatrician.

Ironically, it was a Paediatrician who helped to spark my desire for a career in medicine hence before I was seven my destiny was a known destination with unknown direction, yet one day, yet one day I would become Dr. Allen. Being sick was only a chance to see my doctor who would engage me, as if I was her only colleague, in speculating what was wrong with me and even other young patients.

CCs (millilitres) of blood, sweat and tears later I was in medical school, well on my way to accomplishing my life's goal when I had the wonderful chance to meet this Paediatrician again. She aged like wine and her aura was majestic with years of knowledge and experience; poise and mastery emanated from her presence.

I reintroduced myself in case she couldn't recognize her favourite patient with facial hair, "Doc, do you remember me? I am –."

She quickly cut me off as if to nip something in the bud, "I have cared for generations of children, some even grow up to have their own. You think I'm just gonna remember you so-." I was crushed but had to man up and even appreciate her honesty and direct pragmatism. I moved on from the failed reintroduction to my hero but it was then sealed that I would never be in a medical specialty that allows for such a strong bond, with a child whose destiny I may be affecting, that so easily withers.

To this day I am caught between the thought of relief for having Jerodene move on to a better place and feeling robbed of a wonderful soul who could infect those around her with her own joy and bravery. I remember on her braver days she spoke in a 'ching, chong' language that only her favourite doctors could interpret. I remembered her puzzled look when a new doctor who had not yet formed such a bond innocently attempted a "ching schwing wonkawelo cashahamana (unintelligible)" only to be greeted with either a blank or puzzled look. She could not be fooled or baited, she was full of spirit and it had to, 'take to you'. Jerodene's poise stood out amongst those in the ward including staff and even in her weakest moments she was precocious. Knowing that I could still get her veins whose calibre had degenerated from chronic illness and therapy she tried to cooperate as best as she could, however one day she had enough. Exhausted with the routine she twisted, turned and tackled away from the needle which would come close but not be allowed to land on her skin.

I pleaded with her, "but you have been doing so well being a very brave lady, the kind that can cooperate very well". She protested to tears, ***"But I am not a laaaa-aaaa-aaaady..."*** And mid-sentence she switched in the calmest most pitiful and sobering 'gone with the wind voice', ***"I am just a poor little girl."*** Mothers usually have a hard time hearing their children scream in fear of the needle but at that moment her mother and I looked up at each other both wondering if it was indeed a child that we brought to the treatment room. We then busted out laughing, still puzzled and somewhat impressed with her Oscar –worthy performance.

My mind is still oscillating trying to find who got strength from the other: the parent who had to watch her child go through this ordeal or the child herself. Jerodene was taught to pray being grateful and having hope and through her public reaching out to God she inspired many who not only looked at her situation to gain perspective but admired her outlook. 'Jero' as her mommy would call her, would hold on to God's joy as tightly as her mother would hold on to God's hope.

I eventually left the Paediatrics rotation yet when I passed the ward I would hear Jero holler my name causing me to spin around trying to source the voice through the window. I would listen to Jerodene regale me with something she found interesting in her liveliest fashion and I would listen with equal enthusiasm; she was truly engaging. On the other hand out of her earshot, with equal enthusiasm and always with hope, this child's mother would sometimes explain how her interesting stories almost never happened. Jero's mother would be glad for every milestone, every break her daughter got from the ward but on few occasions there was relief that our angel was still with us touching our hearts as if some health scare never happened. Guiltily, I was relieved to hear that 'some children' that had unfortunately passed was not my favourite patient and yet that bitter relief kept hammering home: if it is 'some children' then this is not the specialty my heart can manage.

I was helping a friend with an errand in their apartment when I saw it by text but I was in disbelief and called to confirm that this was idle chatter: I was wrong. Who told me? I am not certain; it is they who have faded but I remember having to sit down and steady myself as I was not prepared to be broken so late. I fought away tears and left abruptly, driving away as if the car was powered by sighs. For months I pushed the thoughts away trying to logically accept the loss without feeling the sting. I wanted to call Mrs. Bailey, her mother, but to say what? How could I offer any strength who was so many measures stronger than even when they had their child. To watch your own gift from God physically fade, fatigue and get frustrated with cycle after cycle of therapy; when would that cup pass from them? To know that I could never display such character and peace should it happen to my own child, what could I say? No. Saying something would make it real. Yet I bit the bullet and finally called.

Mrs. Bailey embodied the Serenity prayer having been prepared by Jerodene herself who lived the very lessons her family taught her about trust in God. When she told me of another near death experience where 'Jero' reported to have seen the Lord I stifled with sighs moments ago came flowing this time hampering my ability to drive while we spoke on the phone. Jerodene was finally claimed by the only one who could out-parent her parents, who could speak to her not just in a child-like 'ching, chong' jest but in a Heavenly language and who was no limited Paediatrician or oncologist but was the Great Physician. He would not have her tethered to a bed but free from sickness, not just a cure but a new body and would not just tell her 'hush' but wipe the tears from her eyes permanently.

I still struggle to accept that I will not see an adult that I could remember as once my favourite Paediatric patient. I try to accept that she is in a better place and that God knows best including the fact that is NOT my specialty. In Jero's voice: *"I don't work or study miracles… I'm just a pooooor little doctor."* I again fight off tears as I write this and pray for some of the poise and strength of character Jerodene's mother displayed and the joy Jero herself had and if I could see her again I would put the needle down and pick her up for the tightest hug.

God bless her life, her soul and her memory. God bless her family who went through so much trying to hold on to her. Goodbye Jerodene Bailey. Play in Peace.

*Dr. Dane Allen (Jamaica)*

∞∞∞

Jerodene was a beautiful little princess…my girl. She was loved by everyone who came in contact with her. She transmitted a joyful spirit which brightened many of the lives she touched. Jerodene was known for her intelligence, mischievous wit, beautiful smile, generous heart, and of course her deep and passionate love for Christ and humanity.

I remember Jerodene's selflessness when my husband and I went to visit her home when she was sick. We spent time with her and brought to her all the Build-a-bear students in Canada had gifted to her. She was so surprised and thankful as she received each bear and gave each a name. Too soon it was time for us to leave and Jerodene's mom, Rasheda asked her if she'd like to pray and she did so with conviction.

Tears came to our eyes as she thanked God for us and asked that he bestow his blessings and protection over us as we prepared for our return journey. But what moved me the most was when Jerodene cried out to God with deep sincerity as she asked him to help the children in the world without family or food and those who are sick. She didn't even mention her own needs. She thanked God with such enthusiasm and faith. She presented as if she simply knew He would come through. I was humbled as I witnessed first-hand the power of God to use this special child to prophecy about Him as a refuge and never ending love.

*Michelle J. Buckle (Canada)*

∞∞∞

Passionate, wellness, radiance, brilliant, loved, peaceful, harmonious, powerful, strong, vibrant, warrior are just a few words to describe my Jero. God's hand reached forth to touch you, Jero softly, gently they too will be quiet in the kingdom of God. Peace fills the air, happy and tranquil. I know my Jero is there.

God's hand reached forth to touch your heart softly and gently. You are no longer apart seeing fighting that monster inside you. Seems like nothing to you, and because of that I can face anything.

Whenever I meet upon hard times I will always hear your voice saying, **"satan yu lose again."** Sometimes courage is the little voice at the end of the day that says, **"God yu a di best yaa man."** Sadly missed.

*Mervalyn Osbourne (Jamaica)*

∞∞∞

Jerodene, Jerodene, Jerodene was a blessing in my life, she taught me a lot. I can remember when she was younger and her dad used to take her to my home. Jerodene used to cry out saying, **"Daddy don't go away leave me,"** As he would leave to go get a taxi she would still be crying as my mom would console her telling her to calm down and for her to remember that she was with aunty. On some occasions, my mom would be washing and I would still be sleeping. As soon as Jerodene would see me she would run to me with a big smile. And her arms opened wide shouting out my name and immediately she stopped crying.

If Jerodene should really sit and have a conversation with you, she would have sat and talked to you for the entire day without you doing anything because that was how intelligent she was. Jerodene was made wonderfully, she was made different. For a little child like that, being so smart and intelligent, I just loved her. My sister, Rashelle and I taught her a song entitled, "Nobody greater." And each and every Saturday that she would stay with us, she'd always be singing that song.

My little cousin, Jerodene was just a blessing. If I should happen to leave home while she was there, she would have cried the entire time even if I told her that I was not going far. I can't find enough words to describe my cousin, Jerodene. She was just one of a kind.

*Everton Jackson (Jamaica)*

Some people come into your life for a reason, some for a season and some for a lifetime. Through the CVM Inspire Jamaica Program that highlights children with health challenges I learnt of Jerodene and her family. I believe this little girl came into my life for a reason, a season and for a lifetime since ultimately she will never be forgotten.

I became aware of this giant of a girl whose dream was to become a nurse. The situation hit me hard, and worst I found out that she was from an adjoining community to the place of my employment – the Bellefield High School.

I was drawn to the passion with which her mother keenly explained Jerodene's health challenges. I jumped at the opportunity to make an impact. I tried getting Kerlyn Brown, CVM host for the Inspire Jamaica Program but without success. At a senior staff meeting at my school while I sought permission to raise funds inside for the cause, a teacher told me she can give me the number since they attend the same church. I was elated. More elated after the Principal after making a brief statement she gave in to my request.

I had a team of students mostly from my business department ready to roll. I started making containers from my creativity and immediately began the collection drive. By then I was able to make contact with Kerlyn who gave her blessings.

Our first presentation to the family was on December 15, 2016 at the school's Christmas Carol service. It created a stir when the CVM team arrived to supervise the handing over of the proceeds to the father who was present, and we met for the first time. Kerlyn was so pleased that it was the season of giving. She applauded the effort. The program was heart-warming. Jerodene was unable to attend since she was again in the hospital.

January 2017, after her discharge from the hospital, she joined the school family for the morning's devotion. A little weak, but courageous she sang and prayed. Her prayer was focused on children loving each other. This gesture brought many to tears. Our second contribution was handed over personally to Jerodene. Her mother expressed heartfelt gratitude to the Bellefield family for standing with them. I followed Jerodene's journey. I spoke with Rasheda, the mother on Thursday night the 1st of February 2018 for a good length of time. On Saturday night the 3rd of February 2018 her mom called to let me know that Jerodene's battle was over. It really took a toll on me. I felt like she was mine. My children were again impressed to make another contribution which was aligned with the final goodbye.

I can clearly remember the reaction of all the students, my teacher, Mrs. Mckenzie- Gordon and myself went and gave a tribute. For me it was so hard to console six crying children amidst my own tears. It was so sad, but when I reflected on the strength, fortitude, courage of this little girl I knew she came into my life for a reason, a season and a lifetime. Hats off to Mr. and Mrs. Bailey, her parents, for fighting valiantly with Jerodene until the very end. I love you all and always will.

*Janet O. Raynor- Williams on behalf of the Bellefield High School family and friends who contributed. (Jamaica)*

∞∞∞

The angel, who was Heaven sent was Jerodene Bailey. For some they would say she was not here long enough, but for her she knew she lived a purpose driven life. She was sent by God not to tell people to love, but to show them what love looks like and how to be humble and not to take his grace for granted. Her purpose was to make sure that you got to know God. She was sick as most people would say but for me she was blessed and was a blessing to anyone that she met, because she was a prayer warrior. She prayed for everyone she met and even for people that she had never met.

She was the example we needed, someone in this time who put God first no matter what she was going through. She stayed faithful to God and her mission. She has touched my life and many more. I never knew her personally but met her via my cell phone here in the Bahamas and the United States of America. Persons have said to me, "if Jerodene can do it, well so can you." It hurts to see her pass away but that was the beginning of her story because I know that her crown was well decorated in her home.

We have to remember that she was an ambassador for Christ and He has a place for her and she never lost sight of that. She lived among us just to show us the way so we could stop being selfish and learn, grow and change in Christ. Because of her love, many live and not just exist, so we will always miss her and follow her example so that one day we too can live with her in our Father's house. Just want to say thank you to Jerodene, you are my hero and the biggest person whom I came across, she went home empty. She taught all she knew that God wanted us to learn. Pray for one another and live in love.

Hero of mine you will be forever missed, but you left us with hope, love and most of all faith. My family and I can never say thanks enough and job well done, and as long as we are down here on earth we will remember that we are clay and He is the potter. No words can explain our loss, but Heaven gained you. So keep playing in that Heavenly playground until we meet again. Heaven sent we love you too.

*Jermaine Howe (Bahamas/ USA)*

∞∞∞

A famous writer once said, "There is no foot too small that it cannot leave an imprint on this world."

A beautiful angel called Jerodene Jaiyana Bailey flew from Heaven and landed perfectly in the heart of Hope Demonstration Basic School family; in September 2013. Her polite and confident persona drew everyone to her. She always said *"Good Morning"*.

It was evident that Jerodene's first school was the church because of her profound and overwhelming love for the Lord. Her K1 teacher recalls her repeating Phillipians chapter 4:13. *"I can do all things through Christ who strengthens me, my daddy taught me that,*" she would say. Jerodene had an inner strength that was way beyond that of any child of her age. Her bravery and extraordinary measure of faith left everyone with whom she made contact with in absolute awe. She had an adamant spirit, which drove her to participate wholeheartedly in most if not all school activities during her illness. She was fully engaged in devotional exercises every morning, once she was present for school. In fact, one teacher recalled one occasion when she was very weak and had to sit during the worship.

Jerodene participated competitively in sports and her academics. She even played her role well as a registered nurse on career day and she marched proudly with her graduating class on June 19, 2016. Jerodene's life touched many lives; the memories of her are forever etched in the hearts of many. We reminisced about a moment when she was admitted in the Mandeville Hospital and was singing the song, "I've been through the storm," this melted our hearts. Our former principal, Ms. Anderson who has predeceased Jerodene told us of the day she went to visit her at the University Hospital. She mentioned that when she saw Jerodene coming, she saw an angel.

Without a doubt we can say that this baby girl fought a good fight; she has finished her course and she has kept the faith.

The famous British Theologian Hooker once said, "Think of your child then, not as dead, but as living, not as a flower that has withered, but as one that is transplanted and touched by a Divine hand is blooming in richer colours and sweeter shades than those on earth."

While God now has Jerodene in His arms we will forever have her in our hearts. Sleep well sweet Jerodene.

*Hope Demonstration Basic School (Jamaica)*

∞∞∞

My daughter, Jerodene Jaiyana Bailey, whom I often called Jero B. Where do I begin? You were the first fruit of my womb and I give God thanks for that. He had truly blessed your dad and I with a princess. I remember your first movement in my belly and the exact place where I was. I was so excited and hurriedly called your dad on the phone to inform him. That was such a wonderful feeling, one I would never forget.

 Baby girl you have taught me so much, one of which was that I should be still and listen to the voice of God, and also to trust Him that everything will work out well. The faith you had in God was unexplainable. Jerodene, you taught and showed me how to forgive people whenever they hurt my feelings. Even through your heartache and pain I remember you telling me that you were not giving up after more than 10 needlesticks in the treatment room. And even though God has taken you to a better place, you still didn't give up. You showed me the true meaning of love and affection.

Only God knows how much I miss you, not one day goes by when I don't think of you. The good thing is that your dad and I have no sense of guilt whatsoever because we did all that we could to keep you here with us. But you were just loaned to us for a short while. You knew how much we loved you and God knows that we still do.

You will always be in my heart baby girl as we continue to honour your memories. Your laughter, your jokes, your acts of kindness, your prayers and your encouraging words will always be a part of me. God took an angel. He saw that this world was too corrupt for you to have stayed on earth. So He chose you to play on that Heavenly playground that you spoke so much about. Rest well Jero B, until we meet again.

*Love, Mommy (Jamaica)*

∞∞∞

Meeting this little angel was a life changing experience for me. I saw Jerodene on Facebook asking Usain Bolt to come pay her a visit, and I fell in love with this little girl. Her attitude was what drew me to her and her love for Christ. She was a soldier, and she kept her belief to the end, so young and the strong faith that she had in God was really amazing, so I became a follower of her journey. In her journey home to Christ, it was a sad and dark journey, and was sad but happy at the end because I knew she went home as one of God's angels.

Doctors told me that I have that sickness and Jerodene showed me how to be strong. On my sad days I remember Jerodene's strength, so I keep fighting and I won my battle with I never lose my way in You, Jesus, and I'll never lose my way in You, God. Rest In Peace princess Jerodene.

*Sonia Morrison (USA)*

∞∞∞

"How wonderful it is that those people that we meet by chance invite us to live again. The memory of them will keep hope alive forever." - Mimi Novic, Guidebook To Your Heart.

From the first day I met Jerodene Bailey, I can say with conviction that she was someone special. Her confidence and mannerism could not go unnoticed. We crossed paths when I went to volunteer at the University Hospital of the West Indies where she was admitted due to her illness. I still laugh about our first encounter to this day as she approached me saying, *"you have games in your bag?"* When I said no, she then went on to ask me how my bag was so big and I didn't have any games. I promised her that I would bring games the next time I went to visit and surely I was met at the door. *"So did you carry the games?"* She made note that I had a smaller bag this time around and said, *"That means you didn't carry the games,"* but surely I did.

She literally wanted to play card games all day long. She loved to play games in general, some of her favourites being 1 2 3 red light, rock paper scissors and minecraft. I sometimes had to use this to my advantage in getting her to eat her food as she was more focused on playing the games rather than eating her food. *"Eat some more"* I would say after beating her in a game of rock paper scissors.

There was never a visit where Jero did not put a smile on my face. Her mother and I then formed a bond and I was allowed to speak to her on whatsapp video call on the occasion I could not visit the hospital. Our first video call took me by surprise so I rushed to the mirror to ensure I was not looking too 'crazy.' Would you believe that Jerodene greeted me by saying, *"How you took so long to answer the phone?"* I could not help but laugh for a good five minutes.

Jerodene, though young, was a very intelligent and knowledgeable girl. I was often left amazed by how much she knew despite her age. She was so aware of what she was going through and life on a whole. Her positivity was so contagious that after each visit I left feeling uplifted.

I looked forward to seeing her all the time. She basically became a part of me. Whenever I went shopping I would always say, "Jero would like this" if it was just even a sweetie. I spoke about her so much that I had to bring a few of my friends to see who this infamous Jero was. Surely that visit left an impact on them and it was nothing but smiles and laughter as they saw how we interacted.

There is a quote by O. Henry that says, "No friendship is an accident" and I believe that it applies to Jero and I as I can honestly say that Jerodene became my true friend. I will surely miss our little talks, playing our little games and most of all her smile that I was always greeted with. We shared many moments that are forever etched in my mind and that I will cherish dearly for the rest of my life. Sleep in peace my sweet girl and you know that you are forever loved by me.

*Danique Williams (Jamaica)*

∞∞∞

### *The sun that never sets*

I have known Jerodene for all her life. My first encounter with her was as an infant, a small bundle of joy that I'd often babysit, and she easily became my 'favourite baby'. Some time had elapsed and I had moved away from our hometown of Mandeville, Jamaica to University and unfortunately we had reunited whilst I was in my clinical years in medical school when I was on my Paediatric rotation. After hearing that her diagnosis was stage IV rhabdomyosarcoma, I was very heartbroken and found it hard to try to re-introduce myself to Jerodene who would have forgotten me since her infant years.

It was a great surprise to me, the Jerodene I expected to see given that diagnosis was a far cry from what I actually saw. What I saw was a very positive and energetic six year old and it surprised me and during the next year and a half we formed a very close friendship. It always amazed me how someone so young could be so strong, not one ounce of negativity. Always speaking about her getting better, her family, her church, how she wanted to get better and become a nurse. All this taught me a very hard lesson about myself, about my perspective on life, taught me about all the things I should not worry about. It's amazing how much I could learn from someone almost 20 years younger than me.

During the ensuing months, even when I was no longer on my Paediatrics rotation, I would continue to have a very close relationship with Jerodene and her mother, frequent visits and all. Checking up on her progress and bonding sessions. I always remember the days when I would walk to the medical library which was right behind the Paediatric ward and I'd hear her shouting out my name through the window on the ward and telling everyone how I used to babysit her and that she was my 'favourite baby'. These and all my interactions with her would have always put a positive spin on my stressful day. Some days you could see that she was in pain and suffering but she never gave up or gave up on her faith in God even at such a tender age. I remember the early parts of January 2018 when I went to visit her and I was heartbroken as this wasn't the Jerodene I remembered. Even trying to be positive and upbeat I started to see a child that had a little bit too much on her plate. I started to question why was it for a child to suffer so much.

Visiting her from then on weighed very heavily from my heart, I can still remember the time and place on the 3rd of February 2018 when I received the call from her mother that Jerodene had passed and it still weighs heavily on my heart as I am writing this. I'm very thankful for being able to meet this young angel. Someone who did no wrong, someone who taught me so much about appreciation and life.

No matter what she never stopped smiling and that's why I think an appropriate name for this tribute for Jerodene Bailey is, "The sun that never sets".

*Dr. Michael Townsend (Jamaica)*

∞∞∞

Time would have passed and I wouldn't have seen my friend for years. I met Mrs. Rasheda Thomas-Bailey back when I was in high school, back then we were children. I have grown throughout the years to respect her because she has always had that look of a prayer warrior.

However, years would have gone by and people's lives change. I know that she got married and has a beautiful family, I respect and honour her for that. One day while I was navigating through Facebook my heart stopped beating for a while when I saw her on Inspire Jamaica with her daughter, little angel, Jerodene Bailey, my heart fell to the ground. I was more connected to the situation because I knew her mother.

But knowing her mother had nothing to do with the fact that Jerodene had touched my life in ways that I could not understand. I was going through a small problem compared to her life beating situation. But yet still I fail to give God thanks for the blessings that He has given to me. Throughout life stages, one would meet people who would have an impact on your life. Unfortunately, I wanted to meet her before tragedy struck.

While going through my struggles it was without a doubt she had the most impact on my life. I remember watching her on Facebook, she always had the most joyful spirit. She had a heart that was filled with gold. I remember listening to her talking about the love of God. Everyone is special but I believe that God's light shines on some more than others.

It is without a doubt that God's grace did exist in her life. I do appreciate meeting her in spirit. I do hope to meet her one day after this life is over to tell her well done for the little time she had spent on earth. A lot of people lived for a long time but never had that impact on anyone like she did.

I am truly blessed to have known her mother because it's through her mother that I have known her. You were truly a beautiful soul, rest in peace baby girl, Jerodene Bailey. Heaven does have a playground and you are resting well in the arms of the Lord. Thank you baby girl.

*Andrei Smith (Jamaica)*

∞∞∞

An inspiration like no other, my hero whom I've never met. That's how I feel about the life of one Jerodene Bailey that has touched the lives of everyone who had known her or heard of her story. She has given me a new perspective of life. Through all her pain and adversities she remained a tower of strength to not just to her family but to all those she has encountered.

Her optimism, encouragement and prayers also helps me to appreciate life more. Amidst all that, when it really came to me that Jero was special was the fact that she was only six years old going seven and spoke like a centurion with a wealth of experience. That was when it really gripped me that she was a woman of purpose and she had done her part among the human family. Rest well princess Jerodene until we meet again.

*Tevin Jones (Jamaica)*

∞∞∞

Jerodene has been an inspiration to everyone whom she came in contact with. She has always been a bright spark, she knew how to express herself and always demanded one's attention. She had always been very outspoken. She just loved unconditionally. We would rather have nothing more than to have you here with us baby girl but Heaven needed another princess. The angels needed another choir member and God loves humour so He needed your comfort just for laughs.

God gave Jerodene a mandate which she fully accomplished, she touched the lives of more people than she could ever imagined. I think I can hear God saying, "well done my child, this is my child with whom I am well pleased." Uncle Neville and Aunty Kemarie love you endlessly little angel, you will always be in our hearts. You just make the angels laugh until we meet again.

*Uncle Neville and Aunty Kemarie (Jamaica)*

∞∞∞

My name is Trudiann and this is my testimony. From the time I was nine until the age of 17 years old I was molested by my uncle and grandfather. It was a very traumatic time for me so much that I tried committing suicide on three separate occasions.

    I then migrated to the United States at the age of 18, where I tried to seek help, which was not a huge success for me. That was until the age of 43 I came across videos of little seven year old Jerodene Bailey whom throughout her sickness was more looking out and praying for others who was going through their struggles. It just amazed me to no end.

It was at that moment after going through so much pain, trials and tribulations that I knew that this brilliant, bright and intelligent young lady Jerodene Bailey literally saved my life. I finally felt free from all the pain I was feeling.

I have and will always be forever grateful to her for allowing me to know that I can smile and to know that there is a reason for life and to live it serving the Lord.

In signing off I just want to say many many thanks to my forever angel in Heaven, Jerodene Bailey for again saving my life and I can truly smile again.

*Trudiann Ross (USA)*

∞∞∞

# Afterword

From the Bailey's family to yours, we say a big thank you to one and all who took the time out in reading our first book. We hope that after reading this book your lives will be positively impacted.

Please tell a family member, a friend and even a stranger about this book and let their lives be touched too. Our journey was indeed a rough one, but nonetheless God carried us through and we are now smiling through it all.
Jerodene has impacted thousands of lives across this universe and it is therefore with this in mind we are in the process of starting a foundation in her memory hence the name, **"The Jerodene Bailey Foundation"**. We would love to get as much assistance as possible for sick children, who are basically going through what she went through or similar circumstances.

We also created a page and channel in her memory "In Memory of our late Daughter, Jerodene Bailey" and "Jerodene Bailey, Our Warrior Princess", on Facebook and YouTube respectively. Feel free to watch her videos and be encouraged.

After reading this book we anticipate your feedback, please email us at rashthombailey@gmail.com or send us a Whatsapp message on 876-336-6974.

May God continue to bless, provide for and protect you all.

# Acknowledgement

Many people have blessed our daughter and our family financially and otherwise. We give thanks first and foremost to Almighty God for giving us the added strength that we needed at the time. We say thanks to the following:

1. Our family and friends near and far who stood with us throughout it all
2. The Optimist Club of Mandeville, Jamaica.
3. The Bombay New Testament Church Of God.
4. The Johnnies Hill Development Youth Club.
5. Jodian Pantry and friends.
6. Bishop W. A. Blair and wife, Yvonne Blair from The New Testament Church of God, Head Office.
7. Kerlyn Brown and the Inspire Jamaica team.
8. Usain Bolt
9. The Radiation Office in Kingston.
10. The Byways and Hedges Youth for Christ Ministry, Kellits, Clarendon.
11. The Johnnies Hill New Testament Church of God.
12. The staff members that worked on Ward 16 (UHWI) during 2015-2018.
13. The Bellefield High School. (Mrs. Janet Jaynor Williams)
14. The Hope Demonstration Basic School.
15. The Staff at the Mandeville Regional Hospital, Jamaica.
16. Natasha Thomas- Francis
17. Neiko Brown
18. Cherriel Passley
19. Portia Davis
20. Patrice Watt-Beckord
21. Andrea Robinson
22. Magnificent Troopers Drum Corp

If you played a role throughout our journey and your name was not listed here, hats off to you as well. You all did well and we say thanks.

For people who just turned up at the hospital to visit Jerodene or even sent money via Western Union or to my account to assist with her medical expenses or to help with her Homegoing Service, we say a big thanks to you all. My cell phone was a little phone company, the little notes, your encouraging words on her birthday party for her big seven. We say a very big thank you.

For the people who sent messages and comments on Facebook, your kindness has not gone unnoticed. Her Oncologist was special to her. Jerodene always replayed what was said to her and even mimicked some people. All of you had made her comfortable, and helped us to make her happy. To our relatives who supported us from the beginning to the end - you all still do - you have had our backs through thick and thin, we are grateful for your support. Jerodene loved you all, and she knew that you all loved her too.

A BIG BIG THANK YOU!

      As the saying goes, we save the best for last. A huge thank you to the dedicated staff of the Paediatric Ward (Ward 16) of the University Hospital of the West Indies from 2015-2018 in our beautiful Island of Jamaica. Our doctors, nurses, Patient Care Assistants (PCAs), the janitors, the grounds staff, the security guards, and just about everyone, but especially the doctors and nurses who worked tirelessly and endlessly to make sure that our little princess was comfortable, especially during Jerodene's last days. You knew how much she loved you all. It was a pleasure meeting you all in such an unfortunate situation. May God continue to bless you all as you continue to save lives.

Blessings to one and all, as we continue to honour and cherish the memories and legacy left by our daughter, Jerodene Jaiyana Bailey.

~ Rasheda

# About The Author

## Rasheda Thomas-Bailey

Rasheda Thomas-Bailey is the loving and caring mother of the beloved Jerodene Bailey, who was diagnosed with stage 4 rhabdomyosarcoma cancer in May 2015. As one of the primary caretakers of Jerodene, Rasheda went through the experiences of the healthcare system with her firstborn child learning about the disease and the treatment from year to year. In this account, Rasheda documents the entire life journey of Jerodene and the former years when she met her beloved husband, Jermaine. After Jerodene's transition, Rasheda saw this book as an authentic way to pay tribute to her darling princess. Rasheda has appeared on Inspire Jamaica with Kerlyn Brown to discuss Jerodene's diagnosis and treatment at the time, along with other interviews on other platforms. Rasheda is the mother of three with Jerodene being her only princess, and her princes: Rasheed and Jhari Bailey. Rasheda has always been a great storyteller and poet from high school and used to journal her thoughts from time to time. She is a woman of great faith and loves her family and extended family. Her husband, Jermaine is a devoted husband, father and man of God who stands by and protects his family at all costs. This work of art is a reflection of the dedication and united effort of both Rasheda and Jermaine, even though Rasheda held the pen.

Made in the USA
Columbia, SC
12 December 2022